Timberland Regional Library
Service Center
415 Airdustrial Way S.W.
Olympia, WA 98501

FEB 2 7 2002

S0-AXJ-572

MASTER THE GED LANGUAGE ARTS, READING

2 0 0 2

TEACHER-TESTED STRATEGIES AND

TECHNIQUES FOR SCORING HIGH

ARCO
™
THOMSON LEARNING

Australia • Canada • Mexico • Singapore • Spain • United Kingdom • United States

An ARCO Book

ARCO is a registered trademark of Thomson Learning, Inc., and is used herein under license by Peterson's.

About Peterson's

Founded in 1966, Peterson's, a division of Thomson Learning, is the nation's largest and most respected provider of lifelong learning resources, both in print and online. The Education Supersite^{SM} at www.petersons.com—the Internet's most heavily traveled education resource—has searchable databases and interactive tools for contacting U.S.-accredited institutions and programs. In addition, Peterson's delivers unmatched financial aid resources and test-preparation tools. Peterson's serves more than 100 million education consumers annually.

Peterson's is a division of Thomson Learning, one of the world's largest providers of lifelong learning. Thomson Learning serves the needs of individuals, learning institutions, and corporations with products and services for both traditional and distributed learning. Headquartered in Stamford, Connecticut, with offices worldwide, Thomson Learning is a division of The Thomson Corporation (www.thomson.com), one of the world's leading e-information and solutions companies in the business, professional, and education marketplaces. For more information, visit www.thomsonlearning.com.

An American Bookworks Corporation Project

For more information, contact Peterson's, 2000 Lenox Drive, Lawrenceville, NJ 08648; 800-338-3282; or find us on the World Wide Web at: www.petersons.com/about

COPYRIGHT © 2002 Peterson' a division of Thomson Learning, Inc.
Thomson Learning™ is a trademark used herein under license.

ALL RIGHTS RESERVED. No part of this work covered by the copyright herein may be reproduced or used in any form or by any means—graphic, electronic, or mechanical, including photocopying, recording, taping, Web distribution, or information storage and retrieval systems—without the prior written permission of the publisher.

For permission to use material from this text or product, contact us by
Phone: 800-730-2214
Fax: 800-730-2215
Web: www.thomsonrights.com

ISBN 0-7689-0794-2

Printed in the United States of America

10 9 8 7 6 5 4 3 2 1   04 03 02

Contents

Acknowledgments

Excerpt from HARPER COLLINS AUTHOR'S GUIDE. Copyright © 1992 by Harper-Collins Publishers, Inc. All rights reserved.

Excerpt from Henry D. Thoreau's FAITH IN A SEED: THE DISPERSION OF SEEDS and OTHER LATE NATURAL HISTORY WRITINGS by Bradley P. Dean, ed. Copyright © 1993 by Island Press.

Excerpt from THE CHASM by John Keeble. Reprinted by permission of International Creative Management, Inc. Copyright © 1993 by John Keeble.

From WORLD OF ART/ 2E by Henry M. Sayre, ©. Reprinted by permission of Pearson Education, Inc., Upper Saddle River, New Jersey.

Reprinted by permission of the publishers and the Trustees of Amherst College from THE POEMS OF EMILY DICKINSON, Thomas H. Johnson, ed., Cambridge, Mass.: The Belknap Press of Harvard University Press, Copyright © 1951, 1955, 1979 by the President and Fellows of Harvard College.

From LOSING BATTLES by Eudora Welty, copyright © Eudora Welty. Used by permission of Random House, Inc.

From ORDINARY LOVE AND GOOD WILL by Jane Smiley, copyright © 1989 by Jane Smiley. Used by permission of Alfred A. Knopf, a division of Random House, Inc.

Reprinted with the permission of Que Publishing, as represented by Pearson Computer Publishing, a division of Pearson Education, from "Special Edition Using Microsoft Office 2000, 1/e" by Ed Bott, Woody Leonhard, Brady Merkel, Kate Chase, David Karlins. Copyright © 2001 by Que Publishing.

Excerpt from DEATH OF A SALESMAN by Arthur Miller. Copyright © 1949 by Arthur Miller. Reprinted by permission of the Viking Press, Inc.

From LUCY by Jamaica Kincaid. Copyright © 1990 by Jamaica Kincaid. Published by Farrar, Straus and Giroux, LLC and Jonathan Cape. Reprinted by permission of Farrar, Straus and Giroux, LLC and the Random House Group Limited.

"Do Not Boast of Your Speed" by Hwang Chin-I from ANTHOLOGY OF KOREAN LITERATURE: FROM EARLY TIMES TO THE NINETEENTH CENTURY, edited by Peter H. Lee. Reprinted by permission of University of Hawaii Press.

From THE GUITARRON by Lynne Alvarez. Copyright © 1983 by Lynne Alvarez. CAUTION NOTE: All inquiries concerning production or other rights to THE GUITARRON should be addressed in writing to the author's agent. No amateur performance or reading of the play may be given without obtaining, in advance, written permission.

From FENCES by August Wilson. Copyright © 1986 by August Wilson. Used by permission of Dutton Signet, a division of Penguin Books USA Inc.

From COME BACK, LITTLE SHEBA by William Inge. Copyright © by William Inge. CAUTION: Professionals and amateurs are hereby warned that COME Back, LITTLE

SHEBA is subject to a royalty. It is fully protected under the copyright laws of the United States of America, the British Commonwealth, including Canada, and all other countries of the Copyright Union. All rights are strictly reserved.

By William Carlos Williams, from COLLECTED POEMS: 1909–1939, Volume I, © 1938 by New Directions Publishing Corp. Reprinted by permission of New Directions Publishing Corp.

Other credits were pending at time of publication

Introduction

WHAT WILL I FIND ON THE LANGUAGE ARTS, READING TEST?

The GED Language Arts, Reading test—Test 4 on the GED—measures your ability to understand, analyze, and respond to ideas found in works of literature as well as in business and how-to documents. In other words, you will interpret thoughts, feelings, and ideas expressed in writing by other people. The following information will help you understand what you will find on the Language Arts, Reading test.

The GED Language Arts, Reading test is *not* a measure of how much you know about literary history, techniques, or writers. It does *not* ask you to identify writers or to remember when a work of literature was written. The visual component passages do *not* test your knowledge of art history. Finally, the test does *not* include trick questions designed to make you doubt your impressions and opinions about a literature passage. Most questions on the test ask you to think logically and carefully about what a written passage is communicating to you.

The Language Arts, Reading Test includes two major content areas, literature and nonfiction. These are further broken down into the following categories:

- **Literature** includes fiction, poetry, and plays. Literature, which makes up 75 percent of the test, is broken down into three time periods:

  - *Pre-1920*

  - *1920 to 1960*

  - *1960 to the Present*

All time periods are included on the test.

- **Nonfiction** makes up 25 percent of the test and includes two major types of passages:

  - *Viewing component*, which consists of detailed descriptive prose. Questions test your understanding of the descriptions in the passage.

  - *Business-related document*, such as an employee handbook or instructions for using hardware or software. Questions test your ability to understand and follow directions.

The test includes both types of documents, viewing and business-related.

The test you will take consists of 40 multiple-choice questions. Each set of questions relates to a literature passage that is 300–400 words long or a poem that is 8–25 lines long. To give you an idea of what each passage is about, each passage begins with a *purpose question*. For example, a passage about applying for a job might begin with the question, "How Do You Submit Your Application?" This question helps you to focus on the central idea of the passage even before you begin to read it.

Each of the 40 questions on the test is multiple choice and has five answer choices. These questions are based on four different learning objectives: *Comprehension*, or understanding; *Application*, or using information learned from the passage; *Analysis*, or understanding literary language; and *Synthesis*, or grasping overall or underlying meanings. You may be asked to identify the passage's main idea, to determine a character's motives or feelings, or to define a term.

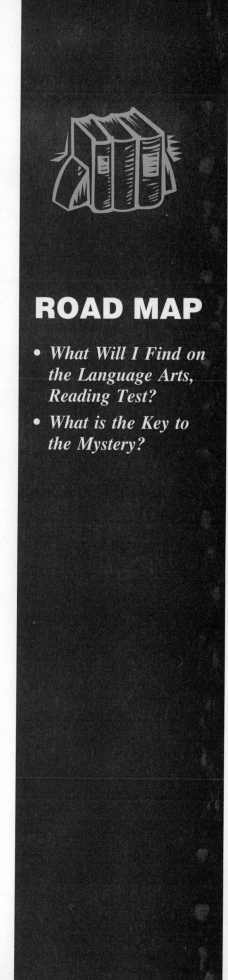

ROAD MAP

- *What Will I Find on the Language Arts, Reading Test?*
- *What is the Key to the Mystery?*

Comprehension questions comprise approximately 20 percent of the test. *Application* questions account for approximately 15 percent. *Analysis* and *Synthesis* questions each comprise 30 to 35 percent of the test. Therefore, more than half the test is designed to measure these higher-order thinking skills.

Read the following passage, an excerpt from a novel. Then take a look at the questions that follow. One question of each type is given here, along with the correct answers and detailed explanations.

WHAT IS THE KEY TO THE MYSTERY?

Line   Although it was midafternoon it was nearly as dark as a summer night. The ship swayed uneasily at her anchor as the wind howled around her, the rigging giving out musical tones, from the deep bass of the shrouds to the high treble of the running rigging. Already the snow was thick enough to blur the outlines of the objects on deck.

5   . . . The officer of the watch stood shivering in the little shelter offered by the mizzenmast bitts, and forward across the snow-covered deck a few unhappy hands crouched vainly seeking shelter under the high bulwarks.

The two officers who emerged upon the quarter-deck held their hats onto their heads against the shrieking wind. The shorter, slighter one turned up the collar of his

10   heavy coat and attempted instinctively to pull the front of it tighter across his chest to keep out the penetrating air. As he spoke in the grey darkness he had to raise his voice to make himself heard, despite the confidential nature of what he was saying.

"It's your best chance, Peabody."

The other turned about and stood to windward with the snow driving into his

15   face before he answered with a single word.

"Aye," he said.

—from *The Captain from Connecticut*, by C.S. Forester

1. Based on the information in this passage, when and where does this scene take place?

    (1) On a ship on a summer night
    (2) On a ship on a winter afternoon
    (3) On a ship on a winter night
    (4) On a ship on a summer afternoon
    (5) In an inn on a winter afternoon

    The correct answer is (2). The first paragraph reveals the answer to this *Comprehension* question. The passage states that "although it was midafternoon it was nearly as dark as a summer night," so we know it is afternoon. Later we learn that snow is falling, so we know it is winter. In the second sentence we learn that "the ship swayed uneasily," and many other nautical details are given as well. Careful attention to these details reveals that the correct answer choice is (2).

2. Based on what we learn about Peabody at the end of the passage, we can tell that, in a dangerous situation, he would be likely to

    (1) run away.
    (2) try to talk his way out.
    (3) act decisively.
    (4) ask for help.
    (5) pray for guidance.

The correct answer is (3). This *Application* question directs your attention to the end of the passage, lines 14–16. Note that when his companion hints at danger, Peabody faces directly into the storm and answers with a single word, "Aye." These are not the actions of a man who is likely to run away, to use his verbal abilities, or to rely on others for assistance. The best choice is (3)—Peabody would be likely to act decisively to face the danger directly.

3. Which phrase from the passage is an example of personification?

   (1) It was nearly as dark as a summer night
   (2) The deep bass of the shrouds
   (3) The shrieking wind
   (4) Stood shivering in the little shelter
   (5) The ship swayed uneasily

   The correct answer is (5). Later in this book (see Chapter 1, "Fiction," and Chapter 2, "Poetry") we will discuss various figures of speech in detail. Personification means describing something that is not human in human terms. In this case, choice (5) describes the ship as swaying "uneasily," a feeling that applies only to human, so it is the correct choice.

4. What is likely to happen next in this novel?

   (1) Peabody will attempt a daring and reckless exploit.
   (2) Peabody will report his friend for spying.
   (3) The two officers will seek shelter from the storm.
   (4) The two officers will tell the sailors to go inside.
   (5) The sailors will turn against the officers.

   The correct answer is (1). This *Synthesis* question asks you to consider the overall feeling of the passage as well as details of character and plot. To *synthesize* means to mix things together to create something new, so synthesis questions ask you to create a new understanding of a reading passage by brining together all the clues at your disposal. In this case, details of the setting—the ship is "swaying uneasily"—and of the characters' actions point to a daring and reckless exploit, so choice (1) is the correct answer. The first speaker's words, "It's your best chance," hint that it isn't much of a chance, so something dangerous is afoot. Peabody's stance, with the snow driving into his face, indicates that he will face danger. The other choices are not indicated by the details of the passage.

Pretest

Directions: Read each passage; then answer the questions that follow. Choose the *one best answer* to each question.

Items 1–9 refer to the following excerpt from a novel.

Who Are the Observers at This Trial?

Line   Inside Amity Harbor's courthouse, opposite the courtroom's four tall windows, a table had been set up to accommodate the influx of newspapermen to the island. The out-of-town reporters—one each from Bellingham, Anacortes, and Victoria, and three from the Seattle papers—exhibited no trace of the solemnity

5   evident among the respectful citizens in the gallery. They slumped in their chairs, rested their chins in their hands, and whispered together conspiratorially. With their backs only a foot from a steam radiator, the out-of-town reporters were sweating.

  Ishmael Chambers, the local reporter, found that he was sweating, too. He

10   was a man of thirty-one with a hardened face, a tall man with the eyes of a war veteran. He had only one arm, the left having been amputated ten inches below the shoulder joint, so that he wore the sleeve of his coat pinned up with the cuff fastened to the elbow. Ishmael understood that an air of disdain, of contempt for the island and its inhabitants, blew from the knot of out-of-town reporters

15   toward the citizens in the gallery. Their discourse went forward in a miasma of sweat and heat that suggested a kind of indolence. Three of them had loosened their ties just slightly; two others had removed their jackets. They were reporters, professionally jaded and professionally immune, a little too well traveled in the last analysis to exert themselves toward the formalities San

20   Piedro demanded silently of mainlanders. Ishmael, a native, did not want to be like them. The accused man, Kabuo, was somebody he knew, somebody he'd gone to high school with, and he couldn't bring himself, like the other reporters, to remove his coat at Kabuo's murder trial. At ten minutes before nine that morning, Ishmael had spoken with the accused man's wife on the second floor

25   of the Island County Courthouse. She was seated on a hall bench with her back to the arched window . . . "Are you all right?" he'd said to her, but she'd responded by turning away from him. "Please," he'd said. "please, Hatsue."

—From *Snow Falling on Cedars* by David Guterson

1. The trial is taking place in

  (1) Seattle.
  (2) Amity Harbor.
  (3) Bellingham.
  (4) Anacortes.
  (5) Victoria.

2. From the content of the passage, it is most likely that Ishmael lost his arm

  (1) as a result of an accident.
  (2) when he was a child.
  (3) during a war.
  (4) in a knife fight.
  (5) in a duel.

3. The passage presents a contrast between

    (1)   San Piedro and Seattle.
    (2)   reporters and jurors.
    (3)   veterans and civilians.
    (4)   islanders and mainlanders.
    (5)   the jury and the spectators.

4. That reporters from the mainland attend the trial suggests that

    (1)   there was something important about it.
    (2)   they conferred with each other.
    (3)   the reporters traveled frequently.
    (4)   they looked down on the islanders.
    (5)   their behavior was informal.

5. Ishmael's unwillingness to remove his coat emphasizes

    (1)   that he is cold in spite of the courtroom's warmth.
    (2)   his respect for the seriousness of the proceedings.
    (3)   his embarrassment about his missing arm.
    (4)   that he had spoken to the defendant's wife.
    (5)   he is a native of San Piedro Island.

6. When Ishmael says "Please" to Hatsue, a reader can conclude that he

    (1)   is a polite person.
    (2)   is about to ask her to do him a favor.
    (3)   wants her to respond to him.
    (4)   cares about her feelings.
    (5)   dislikes having to question her.

7. Based on the dialogue, it is likely that

    (1)   Ishmael and Hatsue have never met before.
    (2)   Ishmael is in love with Hatsue.
    (3)   Hatsue is afraid of Ishmael.
    (4)   Ishmael has known Hatsue for some time.
    (5)   Hatsue and Kabuo were high school classmates.

8. Kabuo and Hatsue are Japanese-Americans. His trial for murder takes place in 1954. Thus, one factor affecting the trial's outcome could logically be

    (1)   opinions about the origin of World War II.
    (2)   the mainlander's disdain for the islanders.
    (3)   racial prejudice.
    (4)   age discrimination.
    (5)   laws preventing Asians from owning property in the United States.

9. The structure of this passage is best described as

    (1)   a narrative of events in sequence.
    (2)   a description of the courthouse.
    (3)   an explanation of the causes of Ishmael's feelings.
    (4)   a contrast of mainland reporters and Ishmael.
    (5)   an analysis of Ishmael's character.

Items 10–12 refer to the following excerpt from a magazine article.

Why Do People Choose to Get Married in Las Vegas?

Line Las Vegas seems to exist only in the eye of the beholder . . . which makes it an
extraordinarily stimulating and interesting place, but an odd one in which to want to
wear a candlelight satin Priscilla of Boston wedding dress with Chantilly lace inset,
tapered sleeves, and a detachable modified train.

5   And yet the Las Vegas wedding business seems to appeal to precisely that
impulse.

           Las Vegas seems to offer something other than "convenience." It is
merchandising "niceness," the facsimile of proper ritual to children who do not know
how else to find it, how to make the arrangements, how to do it "right." All day and
10 evening along on the Strip, one sees actual wedding parties waiting under the harsh
light at a crosswalk, standing uneasily in the parking lot of the Frontier while the
photographer hired by the Little Church of the West ("Wedding Place of the Stars")
certifies the occasion, makes the picture: the bride in a veil and white satin pumps, the
bridegroom usually in a white dinner jacket, and even an attendant or two, a sister or
15 best friend in hot pink *peau de soie*, a flirtation veil, a carnation nosegay. "When I Fall
in Love It Will Be Forever," the organist plays, then a few bars of Lohengrin. The
mother cries; the stepfather, awkward in his role, invites the chapel hostess to join
them for a drink at the Sands. The hostess declines with a professional smile; she has
already transferred her interest to the group waiting outside. One bride out, another in,
20 and again the sign goes up on the chapel door: "One moment please—Wedding."

           I sat next to one such wedding party in a strip restaurant the last time I was in
Las Vegas. The marriage had just taken place; the bride still wore her dress, the
mother her corsage. A bored waiter poured a few swallows of pink champagne ("on
the house") for everyone but the bride who was too young to be served.

—From "Marrying Absurd" by Joan Didion

10. The wedding described in paragraph 3 is

  (1)   the author's own wedding.
  (2)   the wedding of people the author sat next to in a restaurant.
  (3)   a traditional wedding created by a traditional family.
  (4)   a typical Las Vegas wedding.
  (5)   a wedding which is merely convenient

11. The tone of paragraphs 1 and 2 could best be described as

  (1)   admiring.
  (2)   amused.
  (3)   respectful.
  (4)   surprised.
  (5)   disgusted.

12. The description of the wedding includes all of these EXCEPT

  (1)   wedding photos.
  (2)   a bridal gown.
  (3)   a flower girl.
  (4)   flowers.
  (5)   music.

Items 13–18 refer to the following poem.

What Is the Speaker Saying to Death?

Line Death, be not proud, though some have called thee
      Mighty and dreadful, for thou art not so;
      For those whom thou think'st thou dost overthrow
      Die not, poor Death, nor yet canst thou kill me.
5   From rest and sleep, which but thy pictures be
      Much pleasure; then from thee much more must flow,
      And soonest our best men with thee do go,
      Rest of their bones, and soul's delivery.
      Thou art slave to fate, chance, kings, and desperate men,
10   And dost with poison, war, and sickness dwell,
      And poppy or charms can make us sleep as well
      And better than thy stroke; why swell'st thou then?
      One short sleep past, we wake eternally
      And death shall be no more; Death, thou shalt die.

—Sonnet 10 by John Donne

13. Which of the following best summarizes the speaker's message to death?

    (1) "I fear that you will vanquish me."
    (2) "You are a monstrous devil."
    (3) "Nothing can ever stop you."
    (4) "You have no real power over me."
    (5) "You have every reason to be arrogant."

14. The word closest to the meaning of "but" in line 5 is

    (1) only.
    (2) not.
    (3) also.
    (4) consequently.
    (5) thus.

15. "Thou art slave to fate, chance, kings and desperate men, And dost with poison, war, and sickness dwell . . ." (lines 9 and 10)

    In these lines, the speaker portrays Death as

    (1) unyieldingly strong.
    (2) peaceful and attractive.
    (3) weak and unappealing.
    (4) exaggerated and laughable.
    (5) threatening but unbelievable

16. To "wake eternally" (line 13) means to

    (1) survive illness.
    (2) enter Heaven.
    (3) embrace Death.
    (4) understand life.
    (5) regain one's faith.

17. In line 6, the speaker personifies Death as

    (1)   an evil leader who chases people.
    (2)   a teacher who instructs learned men.
    (3)   a guide who takes people away.
    (4)   a sea captain.
    (5)   a kind and gentle savior.

18. Who would be most likely to appreciate the main idea of this poem?

    (1)   A doctor
    (2)   A pastor or rabbi
    (3)   New parents
    (4)   A woman about to be married
    (5)   A person with AIDS

Items 19 and 20 refer to the following excerpt from a contract.

What Are the Rights and Responsibilities of a Faculty Member Called for Jury Duty?

Line   A Faculty Member may be absent from duty without loss of pay as the result of having been called for and appearing for jury duty.

In order to be eligible to be paid while on jury duty, the Faculty Member must notify the Dean of the Division as soon as the Faculty Member receives the first
5   notification and any subsequent notifications that the Faculty Member may be called for jury service.

The School District reserves the right to require that a Faculty Member seek exemption from jury duty or apply for postponement of jury service to a later period outside the Faculty Member's contract of employment.
10   The Faculty Member serving on jury duty who receives pay from the School District while on jury duty shall be required to collect jury duty fees from the court and remit such fees to the School District.

A Faculty Member shall be required to perform the assigned services to the District during the remainder of the work day if the Faculty Member is released at or
15 before 2:00 p.m. from jury service, provided that a reasonable period of time shall be allowed for necessary travel. Assigned services include but are not limited to teaching scheduled classes, maintaining office hours, and shared governance duties such as departmental, divisional or schoolwide committee service and Faculty Senate meetings. A Faculty Member who serves a full day of jury duty shall not be required
20 to perform assigned services for that day. A Faculty Member serving on jury duty shall be required to return to assigned duties unless due to the assignment of a substitute or in the best interest of the instructional program, the Dean of the Division approves otherwise.

—From Contract between Community College District and
Community College District Federation of Teachers

19. Which of the following is the best restatement of paragraph 3 of this passage?

   (1) A Faculty Member must ask that jury service be postponed if it conflicts with teaching duties.

   (2) The District requires the Faculty Member to ask for an exemption from jury duty.

   (3) The District may ask the Faculty Member to request exemption from or postponement of jury service.

   (4) A Faculty Member is permitted to ask that the court exempt him/her from jury service.

   (5) The Faculty Member's contract of employment may be terminated if the Faculty Member does not seek an exemption from or postponement of jury duty.

20. A Faculty Member is serving on a jury. The jury is released at 11:30 a.m. The Faculty Member has no classes scheduled that afternoon. The Faculty Member should

   (1) notify the Dean of the Division jury service is completed.

   (2) go home, eat lunch, and take the afternoon off.

   (3) continue with normal teaching duties.

   (4) return to school if any office hours are scheduled that day.

   (5) call members of the Faculty Senate to see when the next meeting will be.

Items 21–26 refer to the following excerpt from a play.

What Issues Are Walter Struggling with?

Walter: Yeah, you see this little liquor store we got in mind cost seventy-five thousand and we figured the initial investment on the place be 'bout thirty thousand, see. That be ten thousand each. Course, there's a couple of hundred you got to pay so's you don't spend your life just waiting for them clowns to let your license get approved—

Ruth: You mean graft?

Walter: *(frowning impatiently)* Don't call it that. See there, just goes to show you what women don't understand about the world. Baby, don't nothing happen for you in this world 'less you pay somebody off!

Ruth: Walter, leave me alone! *(She raises her head and stares at him vigorously—then says, more quietly)* Eat your eggs, they gonna be cold.

Walter: *(straightening up from her and looking off)* That's it. There you are. Man say to his woman: "I got me a dream." His woman say: "Eat your eggs." *(Sadly but gaining in power.)* Man say: "I got to take hold of this here world, baby!" And a woman will say: "Eat your eggs and go to work." *(Passionately now,)* Man say: "I got to change my life, I'm choking to death, baby!" And his woman say—*(In utter anguish as he brings his fists down on this thighs—*"Your eggs is getting cold!"

Ruth: *(softly)* Walter, that ain't none of our money.

Walter: *(not listening at all or even looking at her)* This morning I was lookin' in the mirror and thinking about it . . . I'm thirty-five years old; I been married eleven years and I got a boy who sleeps in the living room—*(very, very quietly)*— and all I got to give him is stories about how rich white people live . . .

Ruth: Eat your eggs, Walter.

Walter: Damn my eggs . . .damn all the eggs that ever was!

Ruth: Then go to work.

Walter: *(looking up at her)* See—I'm trying to talk to you 'bout myself—*(Shaking his head with the repetition)*—and all you can say is eat them eggs and go to work.

—From *A Raisin in the Sun* by Lorraine Hansberry

21. Walter will need a couple of hundred dollars more than the cost of the business because

    (1)   he needs to split this money with his partners.
    (2)   he has to pay an application fee for a license.
    (3)   he plans to pay a bribe to speed approval of the license.
    (4)   he will need to buy merchandise to stock the store.
    (5)   he wants to give a present to Ruth.

22. Walter becomes frustrated with Ruth because he believes that she

    (1)   is not listening to him.
    (2)   wants him to do something illegal.
    (3)   loves their son more than him.
    (4)   won't let him have his dreams.
    (5)   wants to leave him.

23. Which of the following actions is most similar to the plan Walter proposes in his first speech?

    (1)   Going to City Hall to request permission to purchase a liquor license
    (2)   Arguing with a family member about right and wrong
    (3)   Purposely leaving a car in an illegal parking spot
    (4)   Buying a used car with money earned at a weekend job
    (5)   Giving someone with connections money to get good basketball seats

24. Which of the following best describes Ruth's reason for disliking Walter's plan?

    (1)   It will interfere with his job.
    (2)   He will have to spend more time away from home.
    (3)   She is a non-drinker and doesn't want him to sell liquor.
    (4)   Her son will be upset by it.
    (5)   Her sense of integrity makes her think it's wrong.

25. The stage directions in Walter's third speech enhance it by revealing his

    (1)   financial security.
    (2)   growing frustration.
    (3)   emotional stability.
    (4)   physical strength.
    (5)   increasing happiness.

26. From the information in this dialogue, we can assume that Walter

    (1)   dislikes his job.
    (2)   doesn't like eggs the way his wife cooked them.
    (3)   is a hard worker.
    (4)   doesn't love his wife.
    (5)   thinks women lack business sense.

Items 27–31 refer to the following excerpt.

What Makes This Architect's Work Special?

Line In this age of high technology when construction projects seem invariably to carry multimillion-dollar price tags, it is refreshing to encounter the work of Eladio Dieste. Working quietly for nearly a half century, often in remote corners of his native Uruguay, this structural engineer has designed large buildings for communities and

5 industries that are at once inexpensive and of high aesthetic quality. Avoiding costly steel or reinforced concrete structural systems characteristic of so many twentieth century buildings, Dieste has favored fired brick, a material both attractive and easily produced locally . . .

Rooted in tradition yet futuristic in feeling, Dieste's buildings are sturdy, easily

10 maintained, and possessed of genuinely beautiful lines. His human structures are so light and airy they almost seem to flap in the wind.

It is no accident that two of Dieste's best-known buildings are churches. He brings to all of his work (even industrial projects) a serious kind of devotion that borders on the spiritual. As he has said, "Besides its obvious functions, architecture

15 has in common with other arts the ability to help us contemplate the universe. All the spiritual activity of man is a conscious or unconscious search for such contemplation. A building cannot be as profound as art, without serious and subtle fidelity to the law of the materials; only reverence to this fidelity can make our works serious, lasting, worthy companions for our daily contemplative discourse."

—From "Making Bricks Soar" by Caleb Bach

27. Which of the following best summarizes Dieste's opinions on architecture as expressed in the third paragraph?

(1) Architecture is not a true art form.
(2) The most important element of a building is its materials.
(3) Architecture and spirituality are not related.
(4) Good architecture helps us to contemplate the universe.
(5) The universe is unfathomable to humans.

28. Which of the following best describes why the reviewer admires Dieste's buildings?

(1) They are beautiful and inexpensive.
(2) Dieste has built beautiful churches.
(3) Dieste often uses steel and concrete.
(4) They seem a part of the natural environment.
(5) They have many windows.

29. Comparing Dieste's buildings to flags being lifted by the wind

(1) shows how flimsy and thin the walls are.
(2) reveals Dieste's love of nature.
(3) suggest the buildings' open, inspirational feel.
(4) emphasizes that they have many doors.
(5) illustrates how costly Dieste's work is.

30. If Dieste were a jewelry maker, which material would he most likely use?

   (1)   Diamonds
   (2)   Emeralds
   (3)   Copper
   (4)   Gold
   (5)   Rubies

31. In the first paragraph, why does the reviewer emphasize the high cost of architecture today?

   (1)   To highlight the low-cost simplicity of ancient building
   (2)   To provide a contrast with Dieste's elegant low-cost works
   (3)   To praise Dieste's policy of working free of charge
   (4)   To criticize the high cost of home insurance
   (5)   To prove that, decades ago, materials were less expensive

Items 32–40 refer to the following excerpt from a short story.

What Is the Nature of this Couple's Conflict?

Line   Early that day the weather turned and the snow was melting into dirty water. Streaks of it ran down from the little shoulder-high window that faced the backyard. Cars slushed by on the street outside, where it was getting dark. But it was getting dark inside too.

5   He was in the bedroom pushing clothes into a suitcase when she came to the door.

         "I'm glad you're leaving! I'm glad you're leaving," she said. "Do you hear?" He kept on putting his things into the suitcase. "Son of a bitch! I'm so glad you're leaving." She began to cry. "You can't even look me in the face, can you?"

10   Then she noticed the baby's picture on the bed and picked it up. He looked at her and she wiped her eyes and stared at him before turning and going back to the living room.

         "Bring that back," he said.

         "Just get your things and get out," she said.

15   He did not answer. He fastened the suitcase, put on his coat, looked around the bedroom before turning off the light. Then he went out to the living room.

         She stood in the doorway of the little kitchen, holding the baby.

         "I want the baby," he said.

         "Are you crazy?"

20   "No, but I want the baby. I'll get someone to come by for his things."

         "You're not touching this baby," she said. The baby had begun to cry and she uncovered the blanket from around his head. "Oh, oh," she said, looking at the baby.

         He moved toward her.

         "For god's sake!" she said. She took a step back into the kitchen.

25   "I want the baby."

         "Get out of here!" She turned and tried to hold the baby over in a corner behind the stove. But he came up. He reached across the stove and tightened his hands on the baby.

         "Let go of him," he said.

         "Get away, get away!" she cried.

30   The baby was red-faced and screaming. In the scuffle, they knocked down a flowerpot that hung behind the stove.

—From "Popular Mechanics" by Raymond Carver

32. The best explanation of why the author includes the sentence, "But it was getting dark inside too" is that it

    (1) shows that night is approaching.
    (2) shows the setting is dimly lit.
    (3) anticipates that something evil will enter the room.
    (4) indicates the characters are entering a troubled situation.
    (5) lets the reader know the baby is asleep.

33. When the wife picks up the picture of the baby in paragraph 6, this anticipates that

    (1) the husband will leave.
    (2) they will argue about the baby.
    (3) later, someone will come for the baby's things.
    (4) the husband will retrieve the picture of the baby.
    (5) the wife will shout at the husband.

34. The situation most similar to the one in this passage would be

    (1) a divorcing couple arguing about which spouse will keep the family pet.
    (2) a brother and sister fighting about who will play with a favorite toy.
    (3) two cousins discussing which one will inherit their uncle's estate.
    (4) a husband and wife trying to decide with whose family they will spend Christmas.
    (5) an engaged couple deciding in what month they will get married.

35. From the wife's words and actions, a reader can conclude that she

    (1) hates her husband.
    (2) continues to love her husband in spite of their quarrels.
    (3) is unhappy about the failure of the marriage.
    (4) wishes he had decided to leave sooner.
    (5) hopes that they will reconcile.

36. The story most likely takes place in

    (1) a rural area.
    (2) a high-rise apartment building.
    (3) a house in a suburb.
    (4) a house with an ocean view.
    (5) a very large city.

37. From the passage, a reader may infer the true cause of the argument is

    (1) which parent loves the baby more.
    (2) each person wanting to hurt the other emotionally.
    (3) the couple's loss of love for one another.
    (4) that they enjoy fighting.
    (5) to see which person will dominate.

38. If the quarrel continues, the husband is most likely to

    (1) scream at the wife.
    (2) hit the wife.
    (3) give up and leave without the baby.
    (4) struggle until he holds the baby.
    (5) try not to injure the baby.

39. The point of view from which this story is told is that of

    (1) the husband.
    (2) the wife.
    (3) the baby.
    (4) an unnamed narrator.
    (5) a sympathetic observer.

40. In another story by Raymond Carver, "What We Talk About When We Talk About Love," one of the characters says, "There was a time when I thought I loved my first wife more than life itself. But now I hate her guts. I do. How do you explain that? What happened to that love? What happened to it, is what I'd like to know." How does this quotation relate to the passage from "Popular Mechanics"?

    (1) It shows that Carver liked to write about unhappy people.
    (2) It explains why the couple is quarreling.
    (3) This character's first wife is like the wife in "Popular Mechanics."
    (4) The question is one the husband or wife might ask.
    (5) The husband is always the one who leaves the relationship.

ANSWERS AND EXPLANATIONS

Who Are the Observers at This Trial? *(page 5)*

1. **The correct answer is (2). (Comprehension)** The passage indicates that all the reporters from the other places are out-of-towners, so Amity Harbor is the only possible correct choice.

2. **The correct answer is (3). (Synthesis)** The previous sentence tells the reader he was a veteran, so a war injury is the best choice. While the other choices are ways in which one could lose an arm, nothing in the passage suggests they apply to Ishmael.

3. **The correct answer is (4). (Analysis)** Choice (1) is incorrect because the passage is about the difference between people, not places. In choices (2), (3), and (5), one part of the contrast is mentioned in the passage; reporters in choice (2), veterans in choice (3), spectators in choice (5); the other, civilians in choice (3), the jury in choices (2) and (5), is not.

4. **The correct answer is (1). Synthesis** While all the other statements are true according to the passage, none of them are reasons for attending this trial.

5. **The correct answer is (2). (Analysis)** Nothing in the passage indicates that Ishmael is cold as stated in choice (1). Choice (3) is incorrect because the fact that his arm is missing would be apparent even with his coat on, according to the description of its pinned-up sleeve. Choices (4) and (5) are true statements, but they are not related to why he keeps his coat on.

6. **The correct answer is (3). (Analysis)** Choice (1) does not explain why he says "Please" to her in the circumstances described in the passage. There is nothing to indicate that he wants her to do him a favor or that he dislikes questioning her, (choices (2) and (5)). While choice (4) is a possibility, it is not a direct explanation of why he responds to her silence by saying "Please."

7. **The correct answer is (4). (Synthesis)** Choice (1) is incorrect because he addresses her by her first name. Nothing in the dialogue indicates he loves her, choice (2), or that she is afraid of him, choice (3), or that Hatsue and Kabuo went to school together, choice (5).

8. **The correct answer is (3). (Synthesis)** Because Kabuo is the defendant, and he is Japanese-American, jurors' prejudices about Japanese-Americans may shape their opinions. While the Japanese fought America in World War II, choice (1) is not correct because a disagreement about the causes of the war (its origin) is not likely related to a specific person's acts. Choice (5) describes laws that existed at one time, but there is nothing to indicate the trial is related to these laws. There is nothing in the information given that could lead to a conclusion about the mainlander's feelings about islanders, choice (2), or the defendant's age, choice (4), are issues.

9. **The correct answer is (4). (Analysis)** Choice (1) is incorrect because the passage goes backward in time, from the courtroom to Ishmael's conversation with Hatsue, which occurred before the courtroom was open. While there is some description of the courtroom's heat, the passage is not primarily a description of the courthouse, as choice (2) states. The end of the passage explains why Ishmael will not remove his coat, but this is not the passage's main subject, so choice (3) is incorrect, as is choice (5), because the passage gives some information about Ishmael but it is not a complete analysis of his character.

Why Do People Choose to Get Married in Las Vegas? *(page 7)*

10. **The correct answer is (4). (Comprehension)** The context of the paragraph is general; therefore, the description is of a typical Vegas wedding. Choice (2) is incorrect because the people the author sat next to are described as "one such" party in paragraph 4, showing that they are an example of what is described in paragraph 3. Choice (3) contradicts the passage's idea that there is something unusual about a Las Vegas wedding. The description is not in the first person, so the author is not describing her own wedding, choice (1). Choice (5) is contradicted by the first sentence of paragraph 3.

11. **The correct answer is (4). (Synthesis)** The words "odd," "and yet," and "seems to appeal to" imply the author thinks the choice to marry in Las Vegas is an unlikely one. Choices (1), (3), and (5) indicate a strong emotional reaction that is not present in these paragraphs. While Didion may find the idea of marriage in Las Vegas amusing in choice (2), nothing in the first two paragraphs has a tone of humor.

12. **The correct answer is (3). (Comprehension)** Although the description states there may be an "attendant or two," the following description is of adult women; flower girls are customarily children. All of the other choices are included in the description of the wedding.

What Is This Speaker Saying to Death? *(page 8)*

13. **The correct answer is (4). (Synthesis)** In line 1, the speaker states, "Death be not proud. . ." The rest of the poem describes why Death can be conquered and is not as mighty as many believe. Choices (1), (3), and (5) contradict this message. Though the speaker might agree with choice (2), this is not the point of his message to Death.

14. **The correct answer is (1). (Comprehension)** The speaker compares rest and sleep to death. Choice (1) makes this comparison explicit. Choice (2) contradicts the comparison; choice (3) suggests the comparison is in addition to something else, and choices (4) and (5) set up cause/effect relationships that are not logical.

15. **The correct answer is (3). (Analysis)** Describing death as a "slave to fate" (line 9) and a friend of poison and sickness creates a weak and unattractive image of Death. Choice (1) and (2) can be eliminated because they are positive characterizations. Since the speaker's tone is sincere, he does not exaggerate or distort his description of Death; thus, choice (4) is incorrect. Choice (5) can be eliminated, for while Donne is not afraid, he does believe that Death is real.

16. **The correct answer is (2). (Comprehension)** The speaker describes entering a place where Death cannot reach people any longer; only an afterlife could be described in that way. Of the other options, only choice (5) comes close to that meaning; it can be eliminated, however, because the expression is meant literally rather than figuratively.

17. **The correct answer is (3). (Analysis)** This description of people going somewhere with Death creates an image of Death as a guide who leads people away. Choice (1) can be eliminated because the people do not seem to be running from Death. Choices (2), (4), and (5) are incorrect because there is no reference to teaching, the sea, or being saved in this personification.

18. **The correct answer is (5). (Application)** The message of this poem—that one need not fear Death—probably would be most appreciated by someone who is facing Death. Choices (3) and (4) can be eliminated because they refer to people who could generally be described as looking to a bright future, in a time of new beginning. The people named in choices (1) and (2) might have more reason to appreciate Donne's message, but that message would be more immediate to a person with a deadly illness.

What Are the Rights and Responsibilities of a Faculty Member Called for Jury Duty? *(page 9)*

19. **The correct answer is (3). (Comprehension)** "Reserves the right" means the District may or may not ask a Faculty Member to postpone service. Choices (1) and (2) state positive requirements. Choice (4) is about the Faculty Member's action, not the District's. Nothing in the passage indicates any instance of termination of the contract, so choice (5) is incorrect.

20. **The correct answer is (4). (Application)** The contract states the Faculty Member is required to perform assigned services for the rest of the day, including office hours. Choice (3) is incorrect because the question states the Faculty Member has no teaching duties that day. There is no requirement to notify the dean or check on future meetings, so choices (1) and (5) are incorrect. Choice (2) specifically contradicts the requirements of the contract.

What Issues Are Walter Struggling With? *(page 10)*

21. **The correct answer is (3). (Application)** While choice (2) is a logical possibility, Ruth's comment that this would be "graft" indicates he plans to bribe someone. None of the other choices are suggested by the passage.

22. **The correct answer is (4). (Synthesis)** Walter complains to Ruth, "See—I'm trying to talk to you 'bout myself . . . and all you can say is eat them eggs and go to work." He believes that she won't let him dream about a better future. Choice (1) is incorrect because Walter knows that Ruth is listening—she just doesn't want to talk about his plans. It is Walter, not Ruth, who is considering doing something illegal; thus, choice (2) can be eliminated. There is no support in the passage for choices (3) and (5).

23. **The correct answer is (5). (Analysis)** Walter is proposing to bribe someone to get his liquor license approved quickly, much as a person might pay someone off to get tickets for excellent seats. Choice (2) describes what Walter and Ruth are doing but does not apply to Walter's plan. Choice (3) is not as similar as choice (5), since this action does not provide as clear an advantage. Choices (1) and (4) can be eliminated because they are legal and respectable.

24. **The correct answer is (5). (Analysis)** Ruth's use of the word "graft," and her later comment that the money is not theirs demonstrate her sense of integrity. Nothing in the passage suggests the other choices.

25. **The correct answer is (2). (Analysis)** The stage directions in this speech indicate that Walter goes from sadness to passion to anguish—a range of emotions best summarized as "growing frustration." Choice (1) is incorrect because the friction in the conversation arises from Walter's need to feel financially secure; he does not feel that way yet. In this speech, Walter becomes angrier and less stable; thus choices (3) and (5) can be eliminated. The stage directions suggest that his emotions trigger physical response; however, physical strength, choice (4), is not mentioned.

26. **The correct answer is (5). (Synthesis)** Walter's negative reaction to his wife's telling him to go to work and eat his eggs is a result of his frustration in this scene, so choices (1) and (2) are not correct. That he wants to open his own business, choice (3), doesn't let us know if he works hard or not. His frustration with her doesn't mean he does not love her, choice (4). He explicitly states, "Women don't understand about the world," so choice (5) is the only possible answer.

What Makes This Architect's Work Special? *(page 12)*

27. **The correct answer is (4). (Comprehension)** Dieste states that "architecture has in common with other arts the ability to help us contemplate the universe." Dieste considers architecture both as an art and something spiritual; thus, choices (1) and (3) can be eliminated. Although Dieste might agree with choices (2) and (5), the ideas in those choices are not related to this quotation.

28. **The correct answer is (1). (Synthesis)** This choice paraphrases the main idea of the first paragraph, and the building's beauty is referred to again in the second paragraph. Choice (3) is contradicted in paragraph 1. While choice (2) is a true statement, it does not answer the general question of why Dieste's buildings are admired. Choice (5) is incorrect because the passage does not say if the buildings have many windows. While one might infer choice (4) as a possibility, the reviewer does not give it as a reason for his admiration of the buildings.

29. **The correct answer is (3). (Analysis)** Choice (5) is contradicted by the passage. Although the buildings are described as light, choice (1) uses words with negative connotations, "flimsy" and "thin," while the author clearly admires the buildings. Nothing in the passage indicates how many doors are in the buildings (choice (4)). While the passage shows Dieste's concern for the spiritual, it does not discuss his feelings about nature, so choice (5) is not a possible answer.

30. **The correct answer is (3). (Application)** Since Dieste uses inexpensive materials, this is the appropriate answer. Choices (1), (2), and (5) are expensive gems, and choice (4), gold, is more expensive than copper.

31. **The correct answer is (2). (Analysis)** Choices (1) and (5) are incorrect because the subject of the passage is not ancient architecture but Dieste's work. Choices (3) and (4) present statements of facts not presented in the passage.

What Is the Nature of This Couple's Conflict? *(page 13)*

32. **The correct answer is (4). (Analysis)** The word "too" indicates the author is interested in more than the physical setting. Thus, choices (1), (2), and (5) are not appropriate answers. While choice (3) is a possibility, the word "dark" does not necessarily suggest evil. Choice (4), a "troubled" situation, indicates the darkness of the actions and the characters' emotions.

33. **The correct answer is (2). (Synthesis)** Just as the wife later does not want her husband to take the baby, here she does not want him to pack the baby's picture, and he says, "Bring that back," indicating he does want to take it. While choices (3) and (5) are events that happen in the story, they are not anticipated by the picking up of the picture. Choice (4) is contradicted by the passage, and we do not know whether choice (1) occurs.

34. **The correct answer is (1). (Application)** Choices (2) and (3) represent disagreements about material possessions. Choices (4) and (5) are disagreements about a personal situation, but as presented they do not represent a serious argument. Ownership of a beloved living being, a pet, is closest to the situation in this story.

35. **The correct answer is (3). (Synthesis)** Although she claims to be happy he is leaving, she cries. Since she does not seem to love him, her tears must be for their relationship. There is not enough evidence to conclude she hates him (choice (1)), or that she continues to love him (choice (2)). While choice (4) may be possible, there is no evidence for it in the passage. Choice (5) contradicts what she says.

36. **The correct answer is (3). (Synthesis)** Because cars are going by on the street outside, this is not likely to be a rural area, choice (1). Because of the mention of the backyard, it is not a high-rise apartment building, choice (2), and more than likely not in a very large city, where few houses have backyards, choice (5). Because of the proximity of the yard and the street, this is not likely to be a home with a view of the ocean, choice (4).

37. **The correct answer is (5). (Synthesis)** The baby seems almost incidental to their fight, which could have occurred over the picture of the baby. Neither claims to be a better parent or to love it more, choice (1). Neither seems to want to hurt the other (choice (2), and, by implication, choice (3)), and there is no indication they enjoy this argument choice (4).

38. **The correct answer is (4). (Application)** The husband has spoken very little and has not raised his voice, nor has he struck her. Thus, choices (1) and (2) are not correct. Because his determination is reflected by his repetition of "I want the baby," it is unlikely he would leave without the baby, choice (3). Since he is treating the baby as an object, he is not thinking of whether or not the baby will be hurt, choice (5). Thus, choice (4) is the best answer.

39. **The correct answer is (4). (Analysis)** The characters' dialogue is reported to the reader, but the narrator makes no comment about it; nor does the narrator take a side in the quarrel. Thus choice (5) is incorrect. Since the dialogue is reported, choices (1), (2), and (3) cannot be correct.

40. **The correct answer is (4). (Synthesis)** The reader cannot determine from only two examples what Carver liked to write about, and there is no indication that the character in "What We Talk About When We Talk about Love" is unhappy when he makes this statement (choice (1)). Choice (2) is incorrect because the quotation indicates couples lose their love for each other, but it does not explain why that occurs. Choice (3) is wrong because we don't know anything about the character's first wife. Choice (5) may be true about the husband in "Popular Mechanics," but we don't know if it is true of this character.

Fiction

In this chapter, you will practice reading and interpreting **fiction**, or made-up stories about imaginary people and events. The examples of fiction you read may be contemporary or classic, old or new, Western or from other parts of the world, but all are works of imagination. In fiction, writers use imaginative language, choosing words carefully to create atmospheric and meaningful effects, as we saw in the passage in the introduction.

This chapter is divided into several units, each of which describes a different aspect of fiction: topic and main idea; diction, tone, and figurative language; conclusions; setting and characters; and plot. Learning about each of these topics will help you to read and understand works of fiction. The exercises in each unit will help you further extend your knowledge of the elements of fiction. They will also help you understand how these elements fit together into a complete work of fiction. And of course, working through the exercises and studying the answers and explanations will help you determine your strengths as well as areas in which you may need more practice before you take the GED exam.

ROAD MAP

- *Finding a Topic and Main Idea*
- *Diction, Tone, and Figurative Language*
- *Drawing Conclusions*
- *Setting and Characters*
- *Plot and Genre*

UNIT 1: FINDING A TOPIC AND MAIN IDEA

No matter what you are reading—a story, a memo from your boss, a letter from a friend, or a passage on the GED test—the first thing you should ask yourself is 'What is this about?' In other words, what is the topic? The topic of a story is simply its subject. Identifying the topic will lead you to the writer's main idea. The **main idea** is the central point or idea that the writer wants to communicate. A main idea may be stated directly, or it may be unstated but strongly suggested. In works of fiction, the main idea is usually unstated.

Like a *stated* main idea, an *unstated* or *implied* main idea also conveys the writer's most important point. To identify an unstated main idea, ask yourself these questions:

- What is the topic? How can I tell?

- What do the supporting details say about that topic?

- What central idea or point do the details make clear?

If a main idea is stated directly, it often appears in the first or last sentence of a passage. The rest of the sentences in the passage contain **supporting details** that give more information about the main idea.

If the main idea is unstated, use all the details in the passage to determine the main idea. For example, if the passage tells you what a character is thinking, the main idea or purpose may be to allow you to know more about that character. If the passage is descriptive, the purpose may be to provide a setting or to suggest a mood.

Work through Exercise 1 to find out how much you know about determining an author's main idea.

EXERCISE 1

Directions: Items 1 and 2 refer to the following passage from a novel. As you read the passage, ask yourself, 'What is the author's topic?' Then answer the questions.

How Are Guido and Vincent Related?

Line   Guido Morris and Vincent Cardworthy were third cousins. No one remembered which Morris had married which Cardworthy, and no one cared except at large family gatherings when this topic was introduced and subject to the benign opinions of all. Vincent and Guido had been friends since babyhood. They had been strolled together
5   in the same pram and as boys were often brought together, either at the Cardworthy house in Petrie, Connecticut, or at the Morris's in Boston to play marbles, climb trees, and set off cherry bombs in trash cans and mailboxes. As teenagers, they drank beer in hiding and practiced smoking Guido's father's cigars, which did not make them sick, but happy. As adults, they both loved a good cigar.
10   At college they fooled around, spent money, and wondered what would become of them when they grew up. Guido intended to write poetry in heroic couplets and Vincent thought he might eventually win the Nobel Prize for physics.

     In their late twenties they found themselves together again in Cambridge . . .

—from *Happy All the Time* by Laurie Colwin

1. What is this passage mostly about?

   (1) The Cardworthy house in Petrie, Connecticut
   (2) The Cardworthy and Morris families
   (3) The friendship between Guido and Vincent
   (4) Guido's and Vincent's childhood mischief
   (5) Guido's and Vincent's college life

2. Based on this passage, this entire novel is going to be about Guido's and Vincent's

   (1) childhood.
   (2) quarrels.
   (3) families.
   (4) adult lives.
   (5) wives.

Check your answers on page 46.

Notice that in Exercise 1, what the passage was mostly about was not any of the details that were directly stated. Rather, the passage was mostly about the overall idea that all those details related to the friendship between the two main characters. This is an example of an unstated main idea.

EXERCISE 2

Directions: Read the passages and think about the main ideas—in each excerpt, what is the most important point the author is making? Then answer the questions that follow.

What Kind of Day Is This?

Line   It had been one of the warm and almost sultry days which sometimes come in
November; a maligned month, which is really an epitome of the other eleven, or a sort
of index to the whole year's changes of storm and sunshine. The afternoon was like
spring, the air was soft and damp, and the buds of the willows had been beguiled into
5   swelling a little, so that there was a bloom over them, and the grass looked as if it had
been growing green of late instead of fading steadily. It seemed like a reprieve from
the doom of winter, or even from November itself.

The dense and early darkness which usually follows such unseasonable mildness
had already begun to cut short the pleasures of this springlike day, when a young
10   woman, who carried a child in her arms, turned from the main road of Oldfields into
a foot-path which led southward across the fields and pastures.

—from *A Country Doctor* by Sarah Orne Jewett

1. The main idea of this passage is that

   (1)   the young woman's child is a burden to her.
   (2)   the long November day was very enjoyable.
   (3)   spring is about to begin.
   (4)   the springlike weather is deceptive and fickle.
   (5)   November is much the same as the other months.

2. The first sentence of the second paragraph suggests that

   (1)   the weather is sure to turn cold again.
   (2)   the young woman will lose her way.
   (3)   the young woman has enjoyed the day.
   (4)   the willow will bloom again.
   (5)   the young woman hates November.

What Made Charles Strickland Great?

Line   I confess that when I first made acquaintance with Charles Strickland I never for a
moment discerned that there was in him anything out of the ordinary. Yet now few
will be found to deny his greatness. I do not speak of that greatness which is achieved
by the fortunate politician or the successful soldier; that is a quality which belongs to
5   the place he occupies rather than to the man; and a change of circumstances reduces it
to very discreet proportions. The Prime Minister out of office is seen, too often, to
have been but a pompous rhetorician, and the General without an army is but the tame
hero of a market town. The greatness of Charles Strickland was authentic. It may be
that you do not like his art, but at all events you can hardly refuse it the tribute of your
10   interest. He disturbs and arrests. The time has passed when he was an object of
ridicule, and it is no longer a mark of eccentricity to defend or of perversity to extol
him.

—from *The Moon and Sixpence* by W. Somerset Maugham

3. According to the passage, Charles Strickland was

   (1)   a politician.
   (2)   a general.
   (3)   a prime minister.
   (4)   a writer.
   (5)   an artist.

4. The main idea of the passage is that Charles Strickland is great because his work

   (1)   disturbs and arrests people.
   (2)   helps people's lives.
   (3)   is easy to understand.
   (4)   is admired by politicians.
   (5)   inspires generals to victory.

5. Strickland's greatness is more authentic than that of a politician or general because Strickland's

   (1)   was apparent at an earlier age.
   (2)   does not depend on his office.
   (3)   soothes and calms people.
   (4)   affects more people.
   (5)   is universally admired.

Check your answers on page 46.

THEME

The **theme** of a work of fiction is the belief about life that the author is expressing through the work. Themes in literature are often related to universal issues such as love, death, or the passage of time.

The theme of a work is always closely related to its main idea. For example, if the theme of a work is 'growing up,' the main idea might be 'Young people are too eager to become adults.' If the theme is 'the dignity of old age,' the main idea might be 'A lifetime of overcoming hardship can make a person dignified and wise.' To identify a writer's theme, ask yourself, 'What does this passage say about life and about how people live?'

On the GED Language Arts, Reading Test certain questions ask you to apply information from the passage to new situations. These are frequently theme-related questions that ask you to use what you know about the theme to answer a question about a new situation. Keep in mind that the answers to questions are never directly stated in the text of a passage—only the clues are stated. To find the correct answer, search for details in the passage that can be related to the situation in the question, and then draw a logical conclusion. (In Unit 3, below, we will discuss several different types of items on the Language Arts, Reading Test that require you to draw conclusions about passages.)

The following exercise will allow you to practice finding the main idea and theme of a passage as well as applying that information to a new situation.

EXERCISE 3

Directions: Read the passage carefully, searching for the main idea, related details, and theme. Then answer questions 1–3.

Does the Passage of Time Bring Improvements?

Line   In that place, where they tore the nightshade and blackberry patches from their roots to make room for the Medallion City Golf Course, there was once a neighborhood. It stood in the hills above the valley town of Medallion and spread all the way to the river. It is called the suburbs now, but when black people lived there it was called the
5   Bottom. One road, shaded by beeches, oaks, maples, and chestnuts, connected it to the valley. The beeches are gone now, and so are the pear trees where children sat and yelled down through the blossoms to passersby. Generous funds have been allotted to level the stripped and faded buildings that clutter the road from the Medallion up to the golf course. They are going to raze the Time and a Half Pool Hall, where feet in
10   long tan shoes once pointed down from chair rungs . . . Men in khaki work clothes will pry loose the slats of Reba's Grill, where the owner cooked in her hat because she couldn't remember the ingredients without it.

There will be nothing left of the Bottom (the footbridge that crossed the river is already gone), but perhaps it is just as well, since it wasn't a town anyway: just a
15   neighborhood where on quiet days people in valley houses could hear singing sometimes, banjos sometimes, and, if a valley man happened to have business up in those hills—collecting rent or insurance payments—he might see a dark woman in a flowered dress doing a bit of cakewalk, a bit of black bottom, a bit of 'messing around' to the lively notes of mouth organ . . .

—from *Sula* by Toni Morrison

1. The main idea of this passage is that

    (1) the Bottom is being replaced by a golf course.
    (2) the Bottom was a place where poor people lived.
    (3) music was heard all the time in the Bottom.
    (4) the Bottom was not a real town.
    (5) children in the bottom liked to climb trees.

2. What is the theme of this passage?

    (1) The importance of sports
    (2) The joy of music
    (3) The passage of time
    (4) Seize the day
    (5) Have no regrets

3. Which situation is most closely related to the main idea of the passage?

    (1) The state buys and preserves a wide expanse of beech and maple forest.
    (2) A farmer opens his pear orchard to people who want to pick their own fruit.
    (3) An anthropologist seeks out elderly people who perform folk music.
    (4) A golf course owner sets aside part of his land to preserve native wetland.
    (5) A developer tears down an almost deserted village to build a shopping mall.

Check your answers on page 47.

UNIT 2: DICTION, TONE, AND FIGURATIVE LANGUAGE

The term **diction** refers to word choice. Just as you change your spoken words to make them appropriate for different situations, writers change their words to clarify and strengthen their ideas. Diction can be casual, formal, informal, conversational, or even full of slang.

As writers make decisions about their diction, they are developing the tone of their writing. **Tone** is the attitude, or feeling, that a passage conveys. The tone of a passage can be funny, scary, impersonal, passionate—anything the writer wants it to be.

The following two sentences show how different word choices can change the tone of a passage:

Sentence 1: Chandra listened with quiet surprise to her supervisor's words; then she put down the phone and walked into the hall.

Sentence 2: Chandra listened with astonishment to her supervisor's lecture; then she slammed down the phone and stormed into the hall.

Another tone that you will find in literature is **irony**. Irony in literature—and in life—happens when there is a startling difference between what you expect to happen and what actually happens.

Diction and, especially, tone go a long way toward conveying the author's main idea because they hint at the narrator's feelings toward the characters in the story. An ironic tone, for example, may indicate that the narrator disapproves of the characters' actions. Understanding diction and tone can therefore help you grasp the underlying meaning of a passage.

EXERCISE 1

Directions: Read the following passage and answer questions 1–4. As you read, consider the author's main idea, choice of diction, and tone.

What Are the Characters Waiting For?

Line   General Sash was a hundred and four years old. He lived with his granddaughter, Sally
Poker Sash, who was sixty-two years old and who prayed every night on her knees
that he would live until her graduation from college. The General didn't give two slaps
for her graduation but he never doubted he would live for it. Living had got to be such
5   a habit with him that he couldn't conceive of any other condition. A graduation
exercise was not exactly his idea of a good time, even if, as she said, he would be
expected to sit on the stage in his uniform. She said there would be a long procession
of teachers and students in their robes but that there wouldn't be anything to equal *him*
in his uniform. He knew this well enough without her telling him, and as for the damn
10   procession, it could march to hell and back and not cause him a quiver. He liked
parades and floats full of Miss Americas and Miss Daytona Beaches and Miss Queen
Cotton Products. He didn't have any use for processions and a procession full of
schoolteachers was about as deadly as the River Styx to his way of thinking. However,
he was willing to sit on the stage in his uniform so that they could see him.
15   Sally Poker was not as sure as he was that he would live until her graduation.
There had not been any perceptible change in him for the last five years, but she had
the sense that she might be cheated out of her triumph because she so often was.

                          —from 'A Late Encounter with the Enemy,' by Flannery O'Connor

1. The diction in this passage could best be described as

    (1) informal.
    (2) literary.
    (3) formal.
    (4) archaic.
    (5) comical.

2. Which statement best describes the tone of this passage?

    (1) The tone is extremely melodramatic.
    (2) The author obviously strives to create a tone of suspense.
    (3) The tone is highly ironic.
    (4) The tone is droll and deliberately flat.
    (5) No particular tone comes across from this passage.

3. What is the source of the irony in this passage?

    (1) Sally Poker's desire to triumph at her graduation
    (2) The General's desire to sit on the stage at the graduation
    (3) The hints that the General will die before the graduation
    (4) Sally Poker and the General's agreement about the importance of the graduation
    (5) Sally Poker and the General's different feelings about the graduation

4. Based on the passage, the General can best be described as

    (1) kind and generous.
    (2) angry and mean.
    (3) selfish and vain.
    (4) good-hearted but silly.
    (5) well-meaning but awkward.

Check your answers on page 47.

Notice that identifying tone requires you to read the whole of the passage and to synthesize all the hints the language provides. In the preceding passage, you must read both the General's and Sally Poker's points of view and compare them to understand the ironic tone. As this passage illustrates, irony is often based on the *different* points of view of various characters.

The next exercise demonstrates a different kind of irony—the narrator's ironic view of all of his characters and the society they represent. This ironic view includes even the reader of the novel.

EXERCISE 2

Directions: Read the passage, and choose the *one best answer* to each item. Carefully consider the passage's tone and main idea.

What Does the Narrator Think?

Line I know that the tale I am piping is a very mild one (although there are some terrific chapters coming presently), and must beg the good-natured reader to remember that we are only discoursing about a stock-broker's family in Russell Square, who are taking walks, or luncheon, or dinner, or talking and making love as people do in
5 common life, and without a single passionate or wonderful incident to mark the progress of their lives. The argument stands thus—Osborne, in love with Amelia, has asked an old friend to dinner and to Vauxhall—Jos Sedley is in love with Rebecca. Will he marry her? That is the great subject now in hand.

    We might have treated this subject in the genteel, or in the romantic, or in the
10 facetious manner. Suppose we had laid the scene in Grosvenor Square, with the very same adventures—would not some people have listened? Suppose we had shown how Lord Joseph Smedley fell in love, and the Marquis of Osborne became attached to Lady Amelia, with the full consent of the Duke, her noble father: . . .

                —from *Vanity Fair* by William Makepeace Thackeray

1. The tone of this passage can best be described as

    (1) sad.
    (2) frenzied.
    (3) lyrical.
    (4) ironic.
    (5) comic.

2. The main idea of this passage is that

    (1)   the lives of ordinary people are important.
    (2)   Rebecca will marry Jos Smedley.
    (3)   the characters are going to dinner at Vauxhall.
    (4)   people read novels to find out about dukes and duchesses.
    (5)   novels should not describe love affairs and marriages.

3. Of the following choices, the author of this passage would probably prefer to read

    (1)   a fantasy novel.
    (2)   science fiction.
    (3)   realistic fiction.
    (4)   an epic poem.
    (5)   a gossip column about rich people.

Check your answers on page 48.

Diction can show many moods besides irony. Formal, elevated language can heighten a story by making the action seem important or dramatic, and simple, everyday language can make the action seem ordinary. Whatever the type of language used, an author's choice of language is always deliberate, and it provides an important clue to the tone and meaning of a work of fiction.

EXERCISE 3

Directions: Read the passage. Carefully consider the tone and choice of language. Choose the *one best answer* to each item.

What Effect Is the Author Aiming At?

Line But it was not fated that I should sleep that night. A dream had scarcely approached my ear, when it fled affrighted, scared by a marrow-freezing incident enough.

This was a demoniac laugh—low, suppressed, and deep—uttered, it seemed, at the very key-hole of my chamber door. The head of my bed was near the door, and I
5 thought at first the goblin-laugher stood at my bedside—or rather, crouched at my pillow: but I rose, looked round, and could see nothing; while, as I still gazed, the unnatural sound was reiterated: and I knew it came from behind the panels. My first impulse was to rise and fasten the bolt; my next, again to cry out, 'Who is there?'

Something gurgled and moaned. Ere long, steps retreated up the gallery towards
10 the third story staircase: a door had lately been made to shut in that staircase; I heard it open and close, and all was still.

1. The tone of this passage can best be described as

    (1)   ironic.
    (2)   dramatic.
    (3)   merry.
    (4)   humorous.
    (5)   droll.

2. What happens in the second paragraph of the passage?

    (1) The narrator has a dream.
    (2) The narrator hears steps retreating up the gallery.
    (3) The narrator chases an intruder.
    (4) The narrator laughs demoniacally.
    (5) The narrator hears a frightening laugh.

Check your answers on page 48.

Recognizing Figurative Language

In the description of Ignatius J. Reilly on page 36, the author describes Ignatius's head as a "fleshy balloon." Of course, the author doesn't mean that Ignatius's head is actually a balloon. Instead, he uses **figurative language** to create a humorous, vivid **image**, or mental picture, of the size and shape of Ignatius's head.

When you read figurative language, remember that the words aren't supposed to be taken literally. They're meant to capture your imagination and help you see new relationships between things. Compare these types of figurative language:

Sentence 1: Juanita's sparkling eyes are like gemstones. (simile)

Sentence 2: Juanita's smile is dynamite. (metaphor)

A **simile** is a comparison. You can always recognize a simile because it contains the words *like* or *as*. A **metaphor** takes a comparison one step further: two things are described as if they are one and the same. The words *like* or *as* do not appear. For example, to make a stronger point about Juanita's powerful smile, the writer of sentence 2 says that her smile actually *is* dynamite.

Another type of figurative language is the symbol. A **symbol** is something that is used to *represent* another thing. For example, a flag is a symbol of a country. The dove symbolizes peace.

EXERCISE 4

Directions: Item 1 refers to the following passage. Read the passage and answer the question.

What Happens to Deerslayer?

Line   When about a hundred yards from the shore, Deerslayer rose in the canoe . . . then quickly laying aside the instrument of labor, he seized that of war. He was in the very act of raising the rifle, when a sharp report was followed by the buzz of a bullet that passed so near his body, as to cause him involuntarily to start.

5   The next instant Deerslayer staggered, and fell his whole length of the bottom of the canoe. A yell—it came from a single voice—followed, and an Indian leaped from the bushes upon the open area of the point, bounding towards the canoe. This was the moment the young man desired. He rose on the instant, and leveled his own rifle at his uncovered foe; but his finger hesitated about pulling the trigger on one whom he held

10   at such a disadvantage. This little delay, probably, saved the life of the Indian, who bounded back into the cover as swiftly as he had broken out of it.

In the meantime Deerslayer had been swiftly approaching the land, and his own canoe reached the point just as his enemy disappeared. . . . [He] did not pause an instant, but dashed into the woods and sought cover.

—From *The Deerslayer* by James Fenimore Cooper

1. The climax, or most dramatic point, of this passage is when

   (1) Deerslayer paddles toward land
   (2) the Indian takes cover in the woods
   (3) Deerslayer takes cover in the woods
   (4) Deerslayer's canoe touches ground
   (5) Deerslayer raises his rifle and takes aim

Directions: Items 2 and 3 refer to the following passage. Read it and consider the kind of language the author uses before answering the questions.

What Kind of Winter Is This?

Line It was a deluge of a winter in the Salinas Valley, wet and wonderful. The rains fell gently and soaked in and did not freshet. The feed was deep in January, and in February the hills were fat with grass and the coats of the cattle looked tight and sleek. In March the soft rains continued, and each storm waited courteously until its
5 predecessor sank beneath the ground. Then warmth flooded the valley and the earth burst into bloom—yellow and blue and gold.

　　Tom was alone on the ranch, and even that dust heap was rich and lovely and the flints were hidden in grass and the Hamilton cows were fat and the Hamilton sheep sprouted grass from their damp backs.

　　　　　　　　　　—from *East of Eden* by John Steinbeck

2. 'Each storm waited courteously until its predecessor sank beneath the ground.' This is an example of

   (1) personification.
   (2) metaphor.
   (3) alliteration.
   (4) simile.
   (5) symbolism.

3. In this passage, the rains most likely symbolize

   (1) birth.
   (2) punishment.
   (3) food.
   (4) danger.
   (5) renewal.

Check your answers on page 48.

UNIT 3: DRAWING CONCLUSIONS

In fiction, authors often give you clues about actions or characters but want you to figure out for yourself what those clues mean. In other words, they want you to become actively engaged with the text and to draw conclusions from it. When you draw a **conclusion** about something, you use analysis or synthesis skills to make a judgment. When you read, you use information about people, places, and events to arrive at ideas not directly stated in the passage. For example, in the passage about the General and Sally Poker in Unit 2, the author never states that the General is vain and selfish; you draw this conclusion based on what you know of his thoughts.

CONSIDERING NEW SITUATIONS

On the GED test, you will be asked to apply information and ideas from a fiction or other passage to new situations. This is like drawing a conclusion, because you must use knowledge, skills, or information in new ways. One of the best ways to practice for questions like this is to consider how you might apply an author's ideas, experiences, or characters to your own life. For example, have you ever thought or acted like General Sash? Have you ever been in a frightening situation like the character in the last passage in Unit 2?

RECOGNIZING TIME PERIOD

Recognizing the time period in which a story takes place is another kind of conclusion you can draw about works of fiction. The fiction passages on the GED are divided into three time periods: before 1920, 1920–1960, and 1960 to the present. Some questions ask you to identify the time period in which a story takes place. You can do this based on details about the characters' dress, about means of transportation and other technology mentioned in the passage, and about manners and modes of speech. For example, if characters speak in formal language and mention riding in a stagecoach, the passage probably comes from a novel set in the time period before 1920. On the other hand, if they mention time travel, it is probably from a novel set in the future.

MAKING COMPARISONS BETWEEN TEXTS

Some synthesis questions on the GED Language Arts, Reading test ask you to make comparisons between a given passage and a brief excerpt from another work of literature. You can do this by looking for clues about the main passage's overall meaning or tone and contrasting with it features of the brief excerpt. For example, is the tone of the two passages similar or different? Do they appear to be set in the same or different time periods? Do they express the same or a different central idea?

The exercises in this Unit will allow you to practice drawing all these types of conclusions about works of fiction. Read the passages carefully and consider all the elements we have discussed so far—tone, diction, time period, and recognizing the main idea—before answering the questions.

EXERCISE 1

Directions: Read the passage and choose the *one best answer* to each item.

What Is This Man Feeling?

Line Noise fills Andras Melish's house. Andras's daughter, Renee, is practicing piano, banging away. His son, Alex, clatters up and down the stairs with an old fish tank he's converted into a terrarium. Outside, the Curtis boy is mowing the lawn. Andras hides upstairs in the bedroom, reading about the Syrian invasion of Lebanon in the
5   *Economist*, and hoping Nina won't call him.

Often he avoids her. It makes him feel guilty, but he can't help it. She is beautiful, his young wife. Her red hair, her Spanish accent—even her sharp temper—seem to him exotic, a remnant of her childhood in Buenos Aires. Andras still carries with him his first seventeen years in Budapest and the corresponding mystique
10   of the tropical, the sun, the flaming colors, on the other side of the world. Nina is all that to his cool grey eyes.

—from *Kaaterskill Falls* by Allegra Goodman

1. Andras's feelings about his wife and family can best be described as

    (1)   angry.
    (2)   distant.
    (3)   adoring.
    (4)   ambivalent.
    (5)   passionate.

2. 'All this light was pouring in on me, and I started to open my eyes. I didn't know where in the world I was, and I reached over, but no one was there.' In what way does this excerpt contrast strongly with the passage above?

    (1)   The central character of this excerpt is a woman, whereas Andras is a man.
    (2)   The central character of this excerpt is alone, but Andras is at home with his family.
    (3)   The central character of this excerpt tells us her thoughts, however Andras does not.
    (4)   The excerpt mainly concerns the sense of hearing, whereas the passage concerns the sense of sight.
    (5)   The central character of the excerpt is described vividly, and Andras is not.

3. What is the main idea of the first paragraph?

    (1)   Noise fills Andras Melish's house.
    (2)   Andras is reading the *Economist*.
    (3)   Lebanon has been invaded.
    (4)   Renee is banging on the piano.
    (5)   Alex clatters up the stairs.

4. When does this story take place?

    (1)   In ancient times
    (2)   Between 1600 and 1700
    (3)   Between 1700 and 1800
    (4)   Between 1800 and 1900
    (5)   In the present

Check your answers on page 49.

In the preceding exercise, you drew various types of conclusion about an excerpt from a modern work of fiction. You learned to look for clues about characters' feelings and about time periods. You also learned to draw comparisons between different literary works. Use these same skills as you complete Exercise 2.

EXERCISE 2

Directions: Read the passage carefully, consider the main idea, and draw conclusions about the main character and her situation. Choose the *one best answer* to each item.

What Does Carol Want?

Line Carol was not unhappy and she was not exhilarated, in the St. Paul Library. She slowly confessed that she was not visibly affecting lives. She did, at first, put into her contact with the patrons a willingness which should have moved worlds. But so few of these stolid worlds wanted to be moved. When she was in charge of the magazine
5   room the readers did not ask for suggestions about elevated essays. They grunted, 'Wanta find the *Leather Goods Gazette* for last February. . .'

She was fond of the other librarians; proud of their aspirations. And by the chance of propinquity she read scores of books . . . : volumes of anthropology with ditches of foot-notes filled with heaps of small dusty type, Parisian imagistes, Hindu
10   recipes for curry, voyages to the Solomon Islands . . . She took walks, and was sensible about shoes and diet. And never did she feel that she was living.

She went to dances and suppers at the houses of college acquaintances. . . During her three years of library work several men showed diligent interest in her—the treasurer of a fur-manufacturing firm, a teacher, a newspaper reporter, and a
15   petty railroad official. None of them made her more than pause in thought. For months no male emerged from the mass. Then, at the Marburys', she met Dr. Will Kennicott.

—from *Main Street* by Sinclair Lewis

1. Based on the passage, you can conclude that Carol will

    (1)   marry Dr. Kennicott.
    (2)   become head of the Library.
    (3)   marry the newspaper reporter.
    (4)   visit the Solomon Islands.
    (5)   go to more parties.

2. The first paragraph of this passage suggests that Carol wants to

    (1)   get married.
    (2)   have fun.
    (3)   read a lot of books.
    (4)   help people.
    (5)   stay healthy.

3. You could best describe Carol as someone who is

   (1)   fun-loving but timid.
   (2)   searching for a purpose in life.
   (3)   intelligent but lacking in common sense.
   (4)   anxious to be popular.
   (5)   extremely bold and brave.

4. 'For months no male emerged from the mass.' This sentence is an example of

   (1)   simile.
   (2)   metaphor.
   (3)   exaggeration.
   (4)   pun.
   (5)   alliteration.

Check your answers on page 49.

UNIT 4: SETTING AND CHARACTERS

Recognizing Setting and Mood

When you begin to read a passage of fiction, you're entering a new world that an author has imagined. You'll want to discover the place you're reading about . . . what it looks like . . . how it makes you feel.

Often the first thing you learn about is the *setting*, the place and time of the story. Knowing the setting helps you analyze the characters' words and actions and understand what's happening.

The setting also helps you recognize the **mood**, or atmosphere, the author creates. Atmosphere is the way a place *feels*. It is the emotional effect created by the setting. For example, think about the feeling each of these settings creates:

- a sunrise in the mountains (hope; expectation)

- a bleak, crumbling castle during a thunderstorm (mystery; horror)

- a cozy fireside in a cabin in the woods (relaxation; romance)

Setting is important to what characters do and say. When you identify a setting, think about how it might influence the events of the story. For example, if the setting is a funeral, the action and events may reflect people's feelings about the person who died and how that death will affect them. Whatever the setting, you can be sure that the writer chose it for a reason.

Understanding Characterization

Sometimes you may hear a comment like, "Oh, my Uncle Frank is such a character!" By this, the person speaking probably means that Uncle Frank is a particularly interesting person with many memorable qualities and habits. In much the same way, **characters** in fiction writing are distinct people with specific qualities of personality and physical appearance. The characters' appearance or basic traits may be based on those of real people, but the characters never actually existed. They come to life through the written word.

Writers describe characters in two ways: by telling us *what the person looks like* and *by showing how the person behaves, or acts*. Both kinds of description help to create a picture of the character in the reader's mind.

Identifying Narrator and Point of View

Perspective is a way of looking at people, events, or issues. In nonfiction, the perspective is usually that of the writer. In fiction, however, the person who tells the story is called the **narrator**. The narrator's perspective is called **point of view**.

For example, if a character named Lee is telling his own story, he might say "I went on a date last Friday" or "I felt lost and worried." In this story, Lee is the narrator, and the story is told from his point of view. We say the story is told in the *first person*. If someone else (an outside observer) is telling the story, however, that person might say "*Lee* went on a date last Friday" or "*He* felt lost and worried." Then the author is telling the story in the *third person*. First person and third person are the two main narrative *voices* in fiction.

EXERCISE 1

Directions: Items 1 and 2 refer to the following passage. As you read the description of this prairie setting, think about how it could affect the characters' lives as the story develops. Then answer the questions.

How Might This Place Affect This Couple's Life?

Line   Although it was only four o'clock, the winter day was fading. The road led southwest, toward the streak of pale, watery light that glimmered in the leaden sky. The light fell upon the two sad young faces that were turned mutely toward it: upon the eyes of the girl, who seemed to be looking with such anguished perplexity into the future; upon
5   the sombre eyes of the boy, who seemed already to be looking into the past.

The little town behind them had vanished as if it had never been, had fallen behind the swell of the prairie, and the stern frozen country received them into its bosom. The homesteads were few and far apart; here and there a windmill gaunt against the sky, a sod house crouching in a hollow. But the great fact was the land
10   itself, which seemed to overwhelm the little beginnings of human society that struggled in its sombre wastes. It was from facing this vast hardness that the boy's mouth had become so bitter; because he felt that men were too weak to make any mark here, that the land wanted to be let alone, to preserve its own fierce strength, its peculiar, savage kind of beauty, its uninterrupted mournfulness.

—From *O Pioneers!* by Willa Cather

1. Which of the following best describes this landscape?

    (1) Wealthy and luxurious
    (2) Sunny and bright
    (3) Barren and powerful
    (4) Green and flowering
    (5) Warm and nurturing

2. Based on this description, which of the following would be most likely to happen?

    (1) The pioneers will be able to cultivate this land easily.
    (2) A tornado will destroy everything the pioneers have worked for.
    (3) The pioneers will nearly starve during a fierce winter storm.
    (4) The land will challenge the pioneers as they try to build their town.
    (5) The young couple will die before completing their prairie home.

Directions: Items 3–5 refer to the following passage. In this passage, the face and cap of a character named Ignatius J. Reilly are described in detail. As you read, think about this character. Then answer the questions.

What Does Ignatius Look Like?

Line   A green hunting cap squeezed the top of the fleshy balloon of a head. The green earflaps, full of large ears and uncut hair . . . stuck out on either side like turn signals indicating two directions at once. Full, pursed lips protruded beneath the bushy black moustache and, at their corners, sank into little folds filled with disapproval and potato
5   chip crumbs. In the shadow under the green visor of the cap Ignatius J. Reilly's blue and yellow eyes looked down upon the other people waiting under the clock at the Holmes department store.

—From *A Confederacy of Dunces* by John Kennedy Toole

3. Comparing the green earflaps to turn signals effectively creates a vivid image of

    (1) ears that lie flat to the head.
    (2) a handsome man.
    (3) ears that stick straight out.
    (4) Ignatius's good driving skills.
    (5) Ignatius's warm personality.

4. In this description, Ignatius seems to be

    (1) part of the crowd around him.
    (2) hiding under his cap while observing people.
    (3) dressed to go somewhere formal.
    (4) aware that he looks somewhat out of place.
    (5) angry at the shoppers in the store.

5. Which of the following best describes the narrator's tone?

    (1) Humble
    (2) Suspenseful
    (3) Uncertain
    (4) Comical
    (5) Angry

Check your answers on page 50.

In one very common type of novel, the *coming-of-age novel*, it may almost be said that the main character and the plot are one and the same. This kind of novel focuses on a single central character, detailing that character's experiences as he or she reaches adulthood. Usually the central character faces an important crisis that tests his or her maturity. Passing through the crisis and solving an important problem successfully signals that the character has reached maturity.

EXERCISE 2

Directions: Following is an excerpt from a famous coming-of-age novel that focuses on a young woman named Emma Woodhouse. Read the passage, paying particular attention to the hints given about Emma's future life. Then choose the *one best answer* to each item.

What Will the Future Hold for Emma?

Line Emma Woodhouse, handsome, clever, and rich, with a comfortable home and happy disposition, seemed to unite some of the best blessings of existence; and had lived nearly twenty-one years in the world with very little to distress or vex her.

She was the youngest of the two daughters of a most affectionate, indulgent
5   father, and had, in consequence of her sister's marriage, been mistress of his house from a very early period. Her mother had died too long ago for her to have more than an indistinct remembrance of her caresses, and her place had been supplied by an excellent woman as governess, who had fallen little short of a mother in affection . . .

The real evils indeed of Emma's situation were the power of having rather too
10   much her own way, and a disposition to think a little too well of herself; these were the disadvantages which threatened alloy to her many enjoyments. The danger, however, was at present so unperceived, that they did not by any means rank as misfortunes with her.

—from *Emma* by Jane Austen

1. You can conclude from the passage that if Emma encounters a crisis in the novel, it will result from

    (1) poverty.
    (2) sickness.
    (3) death of her father.
    (4) vanity and bossiness.
    (5) loss of friends.

2. What aspect of the passage most clearly suggests that this novel was written before 1920?

    (1) Emma has an older sister.
    (2) Emma's mother is dead.
    (3) Emma has a governess.
    (4) Emma is rich.
    (5) Emma is handsome and clever.

3. This story is being told from the point of view of

    (1) Emma.
    (2) the governess.
    (3) Emma's father.
    (4) Emma's sister.
    (5) a nameless narrator.

Check your answers on page 50.

Fiction writers use all the elements we have discussed so far—main idea, language, setting, characters, and point of view—to weave together a seamless whole. As you read the final excerpt in this section, think about how all the different pieces fit together to create a complex scene.

EXERCISE 3

Directions: Read the following excerpt from a novel, and choose the *one best answer* to each question. Attend carefully to details of character, setting, and mood.

Do These Characters Understand Each Other?

Line   Amid a medley of laughter, old shoes, and elderwine, Dick and his bride took their departure side by side in the excellent new spring-cart which the young tranter [cart-driver] now possessed. The moon was just over the full, rendering any lights from lamps or their own beauties quite unnecessary to the pair. They drove slowly
5   along Yalbury Common, where the road passed between two copses [small woodlands]. Dick was talking to his companion.

'Fancy,' he said, 'why we are so happy is because there is such full confidence between us. Ever since that time you confessed to that little flirtation with Shiner by the river (which was really no flirtation at all), I have thought how artless and good
10   you must be to tell me o' such a trifling thing, and to be so frightened about it as you were. It has won me to tell you my every deed and word since then. We'll have no secrets from each other, darling, will we ever?—no secret at all.'

'None from today,' said Fancy. 'Hark! what's that?'

From a neighbouring thicket was suddenly heard to issue in a loud, musical, and
15   liquid voice—

'Tippiwit! swe-e-et! ki-ki-ki! Come hither, come hither, come hither!'

'Oh, 'tis the nightingale,' murmured she, and thought of a secret she would never tell.

—from *Under the Greenwood Tree* by Thomas Hardy

1. Dick and Fancy have just

    (1)   gotten married.
    (2)   left home.
    (3)   walked by the river.
    (4)   come home from a drive.
    (5)   confessed their secrets.

2. Fancy most likely says, 'Hark, what's that?' because she

    (1)   has never heard a nightingale before.
    (2)   is frightened.
    (3)   wants to change the subject.
    (4)   is angry at Dick.
    (5)   wants to tell her secret.

3. Dick can best be described as

    (1)   suspicious.
    (2)   devious.
    (3)   stupid.
    (4)   open and honest.
    (5)   carefree and playful.

4. The best description of the tone of this entire passage is

    (1)   somber.
    (2)   merry.
    (3)   frightened.
    (4)   tender.
    (5)   carefree.

5. What is the source of the irony in this scene?

    (1)   Dick knows Fancy's secret, but Fancy does not know whether he knows it.
    (2)   Fancy has a secret that Dick does not know.
    (3)   Fancy has decided to tell Dick her secret.
    (4)   Fancy knows a secret about Dick.
    (5)   Dick is keeping a secret from Fancy.

Check your answers on page 51.

UNIT 5: PLOT AND GENRE

PLOT

Every work of fiction has a plot. The plot is simply the sequence of events in the story—the answer to the question, *What happened?*

    Usually, the plot follows a simple pattern of rising action, crisis, and falling action. The meaning of these terms is explained in Figure 1.

FIGURE 1

A plot usually follows the sequence of rising action,
crisis, and falling action

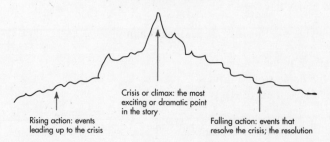

Crisis or climax: the most
exciting or dramatic point
in the story

Rising action: events
leading up to the crisis

Falling action: events that
resolve the crisis; the resolution

EXERCISE 1

Directions: Item 1 refers to the following passage. Read the passage and answer the question.

What Happens to Deerslayer?

Line When about a hundred yards from the shore, Deerslayer rose in the canoe . . . then quickly laying aside the instrument of labor, he seized that of war. He was in the very act of raising the rifle, when a sharp report was followed by the buzz of a bullet that passed so near his body, as to cause him involuntarily to start.

5   The next instant Deerslayer staggered, and fell his whole length of the bottom of the canoe. A yell—it came from a single voice—followed, and an Indian leaped from the bushes upon the open area of the point, bounding towards the canoe. This was the moment the young man desired. He rose on the instant, and leveled his own rifle at his uncovered foe; but his finger hesitated about pulling the trigger on one whom he held

10   at such a disadvantage. This little delay, probably, saved the life of the Indian, who bounded back into the cover as swiftly as he had broken out of it.

In the meantime Deerslayer had been swiftly approaching the land, and his own canoe reached the point just as his enemy disappeared. . . . [He] did not pause an instant, but dashed into the woods and sought cover.

—From *The Deerslayer* by James Fenimore Cooper

1. The climax, or most dramatic point, of this passage is when

    (1)   Deerslayer paddles toward land
    (2)   the Indian takes cover in the woods
    (3)   Deerslayer takes cover in the woods
    (4)   Deerslayer's canoe touches ground
    (5)   Deerslayer raises his rifle and takes aim

Check your answer on page 51.

UNDERSTANDING GENRE

Genre is a French word that means 'kind' or 'type.' Therefore, the genre of a work of fiction is the kind of work it is. Identifying the genre of a work will help you know what to expect when you read it. For example, in a nineteenth century novel, you would expect to find more figurative language and more character description than in a modern novel. In a mystery novel, you would expect to find important details of the plot throughout the story. In an adventure story (for example, *The Deerslayer*, in Exercise 1 of this Unit), you would expect to find fast-paced action.

Here are some examples of literary genres you may encounter on the Language Arts, Reading Test:

- *Modern realistic fiction.* This type of fiction focuses on everyday details. The writing is often plain and straightforward, with little use of figurative language. The characters are ordinary people.

- *Eighteenth- and nineteenth-century realistic fiction.* As in modern fiction, this type of novel focuses on the details of everyday life, but the characters are more likely to be rich and important people (like Emma Woodhouse, whom you read about in Unit 4). There is likely to be more figurative language than in modern fiction.

- *Adventure stories.* The emphasis in adventure stories is on action rather than on character or theme. The action is likely to be fast-paced. The language may be plain or ornate, depending on when the story was written.

- *Mystery stories.* The emphasis in mystery stories is on the unraveling of the plot. The author usually focuses on a central character who is often a detective with almost superhuman powers of observation and logic.

- *Science fiction stories.* The emphasis here is on the marvels of technology and on how humans use it. There is often detailed description of technological inventions that are expected to amaze the reader.

Of these, the one you will most frequently see on the test is modern realistic fiction. Several of the examples in this chapter belong to that genre: *Happy All the Time* and *Sula*, both in Unit 1; *East of Eden*, in Unit 2; and *Kaaterskill Falls* and *Main Street*, both in Unit 3, are some examples. What they all have in common is a focus on ordinary people and attention to the details of everyday life.

In the remainder of this Unit, you will read and answer questions about excerpts from novels that belong to three other important genres: an early nineteenth-century novel, a mystery novel, and a science fiction novel. As you read each one, think about how being able to identify the genre helps you put the excerpt in perspective and decide what aspects of the writing to focus on.

EXERCISE 2

Directions: Choose the *one best answer* to each item.

What Is Mrs. Bennet Hoping?

Line   It is a truth universally acknowledged, that a single man in possession of a good fortune, must be in want of a wife.

However little known the feelings or views of such a man may be on his first entering a neighbourhood, this truth is so well fixed in the minds of the surrounding families, that

5   he is considered as the rightful property of some one or other of their daughters.

"My dear Mr. Bennet," said his lady to him one day, "have you heard that Netherfield Park is let at last?"

Mr. Bennet replied that he had not.

"But it is," returned she, "for Mrs. Long has just been here, and she told me all

10   about it."

Mr. Bennet made no answer.

"Do you not want to know who has taken it?" cried his wife impatiently.

"*You* want to tell me, and I have no objection to hearing it."

This was invitation enough.

15   "Why, my dear, you must know, Mrs. Long says that Netherfield is taken by a young man of large fortune from the north of England; that he came down on Monday in a chaise and four to see the place, and was so much delighted with it that he agreed with Mr. Morris immediately; that he is to take possession before Michaelmas, and some of his servants are to be in the house by the end of next week."

20   "What is his name?"

"Bingley."

"Is he married or single."

"Oh! Single, my dear, to be sure! A single man of large fortune; four or five thousand a year. What a fine thing for our girls!"

—From *Pride and Prejudice* by Jane Austen

1. Where is the main idea of this passage stated?

    (1)   In the middle of the excerpt
    (2)   In the first sentence
    (3)   Nowhere, except indirectly
    (4)   In the last sentence
    (5)   Nowhere, because there is none

2. In this conversation, Mrs. Bennet assumes that

    (1)   Netherfield Park has been rented.
    (2)   her husband is interested in her story.
    (3)   her oldest daughter will fall in love with Bingley.
    (4)   Mr. Bingley is looking for a wife.
    (5)   her husband is an interfering man.

3. Based on this passage, if Mrs. Bennet worked in an office instead of keeping a home, she could be expected to

    (1)   fight for employees' rights.
    (2)   quickly become the office manager.
    (3)   be the most industrious worker in the office.
    (4)   consistently arrive late for work, without an excuse.
    (5)   pry into the personal lives of her coworkers.

4. Why is Mrs. Bennet interested in Mr. Bingley?

    (1)   He is a wealthy man.
    (2)   His goal is to get married.
    (3)   He is the son of a politician.
    (4)   He is a poor man.
    (5)   He has a promising career.

Check your answers on page 51.

The novel excerpted in this example is one of the most famous works of English literature, a comic work written in the early nineteenth century that focuses on marriage. Comic novels focusing on love and marriage are an important group of works you will frequently encounter on the GED. Another example is *Vanity Fair,* which was presented in Unit 2. Note that irony is an important element of works of this type, as authors make fun of the manners they describe.

The next exercise in this Unit is based on another important genre, detective fiction. As you read it, decide who the detective is and what puzzle he is trying to solve. That will allow you to see how the details in the passage support the main idea.

EXERCISE 3

Directions: Items 1–3 refer to the following excerpt from a detective novel. Choose the *one best answer* to each item.

What Piece of the Puzzle Is the Detective Working On?

Line The moment Wimsey's eyes fell upon the visitor in his sitting-room he felt an interior conviction that his hopes were in a far way to be realized. Whatever the results, he had, at any rate, been upon the right track in the matter of the razor. Here were the sandy hair, the small stature, the indefinite crookedness of shoulder so graphically

5 described . . . The man was dressed in a shabby . . . suit . . . and held in his hands a limp felt hat . . . Wimsey noticed the soft skin and well-kept fingernails, and the general air of poverty-stricken gentility.

'Well, Mr. Bright,' said Hardy, as Wimsey entered, 'here is the gentleman you want to see. Mr. Bright won't come across with his story to anybody but you, Wimsey,

10 though, as I have explained to him, if he's thinking of claiming the *Morning Star* reward, he'll have to let me in on it.'

Mr. Bright glanced nervously from one man to the other, and passed the tip of his tongue once or twice over his pallid lips.

'I suppose that's only fair,' he said, in a subdued tone, 'and I can assure you that

15 the money is a consideration. But I am in a painful position, though I haven't done any willful harm. I'm sure that if I had ever thought what the poor gentleman was going to do with the razor—'

'Suppose we begin from the beginning,' said Wimsey, throwing his hat upon a table and himself into a chair. . . 'It is very good of you, Mr. Bright, to have put

20 yourself to so much inconvenience in the interests of justice.'

'Justice?'

'I mean, in order to help us in this inquiry. . . Now, about this razor. By the way, your full name is—?'

—from *Whose Body?* by Dorothy L. Sayers

1. Wimsey's overall purpose in this scene is to

    (1) give Bright a reward.
    (2) find out about a razor.
    (3) prevent Hardy from getting information.
    (4) arrest Bright.
    (5) interview Hardy.

2. The main purpose of the first paragraph of the passage is to

    (1) show off Wimsey's detective abilities.
    (2) describe Wimsey.
    (3) confuse the reader with insignificant details.
    (4) give the reader important clues.
    (5) describe Hardy.

3. Bright can best be described as

    (1) unimportant.
    (2) rich.
    (3) a major suspect in the murder.
    (4) nervous.
    (5) evil.

Check your answers on page 52.

The final excerpt in this chapter comes from a science fiction novel. As you read it, note the ways in which it is similar to a work of modern realistic fiction as well as ways in which it differs. In science fiction, authors deliberately use realistic situations as jumping-off points for the more fantastic plot elements they introduce. This blending of the real and the imaginary helps make the fiction seem more scientific.

EXERCISE 4

Directions: Items 1–3 refer to the following excerpt from a science fiction novel. Choose the *one best answer* to each item.

What Are They Looking For?

Line A handful of other scientists and technicians, alerted on their buzzers by the Argus computer, had gathered around the command console. There were half smiles on their faces. None of them were thinking seriously of a message from another world quite yet, but there was a sense of no-school-today, a break in the tedious routine to which
5   they had become accustomed, and perhaps a faint air of expectation.

'If any of you can think of any other explanation besides extraterrestrial intelligence, I want to hear about it,' she said, acknowledging their presence.

'There's no way it could be Vega, Dr. Arroway. The system's only a few hundred million years old. Its planets are still in the process of forming. There isn't time for
10   intelligent life to have developed there. It has to be some background star. Or galaxy.'

'But then the transmitter power has to be ridiculously large,' responded a member of the quasar group who had returned to see what was happening. 'We need to get going right away on a sensitive proper motion study, so we can see if the radio source moves with Vega.'

15   'Of course, you're right about the proper motion, Jack,' she said. 'But there's another possibility. Maybe they didn't grow up in the Vega system. Maybe they're just visiting.'

—From *Contact* by Carl Sagan

1. The scientists and technicians believe that they might have discovered

    (1) the Vega system.
    (2) proper motion.
    (3) the Argus computer.
    (4) aliens who have landed on Earth.
    (5) extraterrestrial intelligence.

2. If this were an excerpt from a mystery novel, Dr. Arroway would represent the

    (1) suspect.
    (2) victim.
    (3) detective.
    (4) newspaper reporter.
    (5) police officer.

3. In line 4, the phrase 'no-school-today' means that

    (1) Dr. Arroway is not teaching any classes.
    (2) the computers are closed down.
    (3) it feels like a holiday.
    (4) the scientists are going on a trip.
    (5) the signal is moving.

Check your answers on page 52.

ANSWERS AND EXPLANATIONS

UNIT 1: FINDING A TOPIC AND MAIN IDEA

Exercise 1 *(page 22)*

How Are Guido and Vincent Related?

1. **The correct answer is (3). (Analysis)** Although the main idea is never directly stated in this passage, every sentence is about the relationship between Guido and Vincent, leading to the conclusion that that is the topic of the passage. The other choices given are all details that support the main idea.

2. **The correct answer is (4). (Synthesis)** This question really asks you to speculate about the main idea of the entire work the passage comes from. The key to this question appears in the last full paragraph, where Guido and Vincent begin to think about their future careers. Finally, we learn that they find themselves together again in their late twenties. This implies that the novel will focus on this time period and the key events that determine the characters' adult lives. The remaining choices are details from the passage.

Exercise 2 *(page 23)*

What Kind of Day Is This?

1. **The correct answer is (4). (Synthesis)** The passage is mostly about the weather—all the details add up to that. All those details suggest that the springlike November weather is changeable and will not last. Choices (1) and (2) are unsupported by the passage. Choice (3) is incorrect because we know that November comes right before winter. Choice (5) is incorrect because the passage states that November is the 'index' to the other months' changes—it is therefore not like the other months but rather exemplifies all of their changes.

2. **The correct answer is (1). (Analysis)** Even though the day has been warm, it is short and therefore will turn cold. Choices (2), (3), and (5) are unsupported by the passages—we cannot tell if they are correct or not. Choice (4) is incorrect because we know that the buds have merely been 'beguiled'—fooled into swelling—and winter will come and stop them from blooming.

What Made Charles Strickland Great?

3. **The correct answer is (5). (Comprehension)** The passage states that Strickland is an artist. Choices (1), (2), and (3) are mentioned in the passage as contrasts. Choice (4) is unsupported by the passage.

4. **The correct answer is (1). (Comprehension)** This main idea is stated directly in the passage. Choices (2) and (5) are unsupported in the passage. Choices (3) and (4) are based on details in the passage, but they are not the stated reason for Strickland's greatness.

5. **The correct answer is (2). (Analysis)** The passage states that when the politician or general is out of office, he is no longer great, implying that Strickland's greatness, by contrast, depends only on his work, not his official position. Choices (1) and (4) are unsupported by the passage. Choices (3) and (5) are contradicted by the passage.

Exercise 3 *(page 25)*

Does the Passage of Time Bring Improvements?

1. **The correct answer is (1). (Synthesis)** This item requires you to find the main idea of the passage. Choice (1) restates the main idea, which is stated early in the the passage (lines 1–5). Choices (2), (3), (4), and (5) are all details from the passage.

2. **The correct answer is (3). (Synthesis)** The passage compares the present day, when the golf course is being built, to the past, in which a rich and full life was lived in the Bottom. Therefore, the theme concerns the passage of time. Choices (1) and (2) are based on details from the passage, but they are not universal enough to be the theme. Choices (4) and (5) are unrelated to the passage.

3. **The correct answer is (5). (Application)** The situation described in choice (5) is exactly parallel to that in the passage: an old settlement is being destroyed to provide room for a modern convenience. The situations described in choices (1), (3), and (4) are the opposite of this; in each, part of our cultural or natural heritage is being preserved or opened to the public. Choice (2) mentions a detail from the passage (pear trees), but it is unrelated in meaning.

UNIT 2: TONE AND DICTION

Exercise 1 *(page 27)*

What Are the Characters Waiting For?

1. **The correct answer is (1). (Analysis)** The diction is best described as informal, conversational, or everyday. No formal or archaic (old-fashioned) words are used, as in choices (2), (3), and (4). Although the passage is slyly comic, this term applies to tone more than to diction.

2. **The correct answer is (4). (Synthesis)** The author uses very simple, undramatic language in an effort to keep the tone flat. The drollness and sly comedy comes out in the choice of language, such as 'the General didn't give two slaps.' Because the language used is so simple, choices (1), (2), and (3) are incorrect. Choice (5) is incorrect because the flat tone obviously results from careful choice of language rather than from lack of artistry.

3. **The correct answer is (5). (Analysis)** The passage makes it clear that the General is bored by the idea of the graduation but will consent to sitting on stage and being admired, while Sally is sure that he will die before her 'triumph.' To him, the graduation is a bore; to her, it is a triumph. This difference is a source of great irony. Choices (1) and (2) are incorrect because each provides only half of the right answer. Choices (4) and (5) are not supported by the passage.

4. **The correct answer is (3). (Analysis)** The General is vain because he thinks only of people admiring him in his uniform. He is selfish because he thinks only of himself and his own likes and dislikes.

Exercise 2 *(page 28)*

What Does the Narrator Think?

1. **The correct answer is (4). (Synthesis)** The tone is ironic because the narrator is making fun of the reader's tendency to be more interested in dukes than in ordinary people. Throughout the passage, the narrator pokes gentle fun at the reader for his or her supposed lack of interest in ordinary life.

2. **The correct answer is (1). (Synthesis)** This unstated main idea is implicit in the entire passage. The author ironically plays down the importance of the incidents he describes and makes fun of the reader for preferring to read about a duke's family.

3. **The correct answer is (3). (Application)** The passage implies that the author thinks the lives of ordinary people are important and worth writing and reading about. Therefore, he would probably prefer a realistic novel to the other choices, which all contain strong elements of fantasy.

Exercise 3 *(page 29)*

What Effect Is the Author Aiming At?

1. **The correct answer is (2). (Analysis)** By analyzing the language of the passage, you can eliminate all but choice (2). All the language used is elevated, and the pace is deliberately leisurely, adding to the dramatic effect.

2. **The correct answer is (5). (Comprehension)** Although the language is formal and somewhat old-fashioned, the author does state clearly in this paragraph that the narrator hears a frightening laugh: 'This was a demoniac laugh—low, suppressed, and deep—uttered, it seemed, at the very key-hole of my chamber door.'

Exercise 4 *(page 30)*

How Does the Boy Interpret His Surroundings?

1. **The correct answer is (2). (Analysis)** Everything that the boy sees reminds him that he has stolen something. Choices (1), (3), and (4) are incorrect because he does not state his fear of being lost, his love of nature, or his fear of the outside world. He probably is happy to have some food, as choice (5) states; in this passage, however, what he thinks about is his guilt.

What Kind of Winter Is This?

2. **The correct answer is (1). (Analysis)** Personification means attributing human actions or feelings to an inanimate object, in this case, the rainstorms. Choices (2) and (4) are incorrect because both similes and metaphors are types of comparisons, and no comparison is made. Choice (3) is incorrect because alliteration, or repetition of the sounds at the beginning of words, is not used. Choice (5), symbolism, is applicable to the passage as a whole, but not to this particular clause.

3. **The correct answer is (5). (Synthesis)** The key to this item is given in the second paragraph: 'even that dust heap was made lovely'—was renewed—by the winter rains.

UNIT 3: DRAWING CONCLUSIONS
Exercise 1 (page 33

What Is This Man Feeling?

1. **The correct answer is (4). (Synthesis)** Andras is engaged throughout the passage in thinking deeply about his wife and family, so he is not distant—choice (2)—but rather ambivalent. Ambivalent implies that his feelings are both positive and negative, a statement borne out by the passage. Although angry feelings, choice (1), are mentioned, they refer to Nina, not to Andras. And while Andras seems to love Nina, his feelings cannot be described as adoring or passionate, so choices (3) and (5) are incorrect.

2. **The correct answer is (2). (Synthesis)** This question asks you to compare two passages, one of which is a brief excerpt. The major point of contrast is that the central character in the novel is alone, whereas Andras is at home and surrounded by his family. Choice (1) can be eliminated because we do not know if the central character in the excerpt is a woman or not. Choice (3) is incorrect because we hear the thoughts of both characters. Choice (4) is incorrect because the opposite is true—the excerpt uses images of light, while the passage describes sounds. Choice (5) is incorrect because neither character is described vividly.

3. **The correct answer is (1). (Analysis)** The main idea of the paragraph is stated in the first sentence. The remaining choices are details from the paragraph.

4. **The correct answer is (5). (Synthesis)** Many clues point to this: the reference to the Israeli invasion of Lebanon; the references to the movement of people across the globe, from Argentina and Budapest; the reference to the *Economist* newsmagazine. In addition, the language is quite modern.

Exercise 2 (page 34)

What Does Carol Want?

1. **The correct answer is (1). (Synthesis)** Dr. Kennicott is introduced as a kind of culmination of a list of other men, of which he is the only one mentioned by name. This makes his introduction a sort of climax and hints that he will be very important to Carol. The other choices are details from the passage but are not supported by the narrative as a whole.

2. **The correct answer is (4). (Synthesis)** This correct answer is strongly hinted at by the sentence, 'She slowly confessed that she was not visibly affecting lives.' The other choices are based on details from the second and third paragraphs of the passage, not the first paragraph.

3. **The correct answer is (2). (Synthesis)** The beginning of the passage suggests this answer when it states that Carol is neither unhappy nor exhilarated and hints at dissatisfaction. The other choices are unsupported by the passage.

4. **The correct answer is (5). (Analysis)** The repetition of *m* sounds at the beginning of several words is an example of alliteration. Choices (1) and (2) are incorrect because both similes and metaphors are types of comparisons, and no comparison is made here.

UNIT 4: SETTING AND CHARACTER

Exercise 1 *(page 36)*

How Might This Place Affect This Couple's Life?

1. **The correct answer is (3). (Literal comprehension)** Lines 7 and 9–10 describe the landscape as frozen and overwhelming, respectively. It is a place of "vast hardness" (line 11) and of a "savage kind of beauty" (line 14). All of the other choices present positive descriptions.

2. **The correct answer is (4). (Inferential comprehension)** According to lines 9–11, "the great fact was the land itself, which seemed to overwhelm the little beginnings of human society that struggled in its sombre wastes." Thus, it is likely that the pioneers will face many challenges as they try to tame this land. Choice (1) contradicts this likelihood. There is no evidence for the other choices, although such events could take place.

What Does Ignatius Look Like?

3. **The correct answer is (3). (Analysis)** Ignatius's ears stick out from his head, much like turn signals. Choice (1) suggests the opposite. Choices (2), (4), and (5) all suggest a positive impression of Ignatius's appearance or behavior, which the passage does not support.

4. **The correct answer is (2). (Inferential comprehension)** Ignatius seems to be hiding under his cap and observing the other people from a distance. Choice (1) suggests the opposite, that he is part of the crowd. Ignatius is casually dressed, so choice (3) is incorrect. There is no evidence to support choices (4) and (5).

5. **The correct answer is (4). (Inferential comprehension)** The best choice is comical. The author's images suggest that there may be morbid or absurd elements to the story. That is a literary genre known as *black humor*.

Exercise 2 *(page 38)*

What Will the Future Hold for Emma?

1. **The correct answer is (4). (Synthesis)** The passage states that 'the real evils indeed of Emma's situation were the power of having rather too much her own way, and a disposition to think a little too well of herself'—in other words, she is vain and bossy. The other choices are tangentially related to details mentioned in the passage, but they are not suggested as potential problems.

2. **The correct answer is (3). (Synthesis)** The fact that Emma has a governess, or private teacher, suggests that the novel was written some time ago (it was, in fact, first published in 1816). The other choices could still be true today, although choice (5) uses somewhat old-fashioned language.

3. **The correct answer is (5). (Analysis)** The narrator is nameless and omniscient, or all-knowing. We can tell that the point of view is not Emma's, choice (5), since the narrator knows things about Emma that Emma herself does not know.

Exercise 3 *(page 39)*

Do These Characters Understand Each Other?

1. **The correct answer is (1). (Comprehension)** The first paragraph of the passage speaks of old shoes being thrown at Dick and his bride, so they have just gotten married. Choices (2) and (4) are incorrect because the characters are now going home. Choice (3) is incorrect because the walk by the river took place some time ago, according to the passage. Choice (5) is incorrect because we know that Fancy will never confess her secret.

2. **The correct answer is (3). (Analysis)** We learn at the end of the passage that the nightingale's song reminds Fancy of a secret she will never tell—presumably, what really happened with Shiner down by the river. She quickly changes the subject because she is forced to answer Dick's appeal for truth only partially: 'None from today.' Then she quickly changes the subject.

3. **The correct answer is (4). (Synthesis)** Dick's speech is remarkably open, honest, and trusting, making choices (1) and (2) incorrect. Choice (3) is incorrect because Dick's trust seems based on innocence and faith rather than on stupidity. Choice (5) is incorrect because the tone of the passage as a whole is calmly happy, not carefree and playful.

4. **The correct answer is (5). (Synthesis)** Choice (1) is incorrect because the tone is not somber or sad. Choices (2) and (5) are incorrect because the tone, while light, is not without shadow. Choice (3) is incorrect because there is no hint of fear in the passage. That leaves choice (5) as the best answer.

5. **The correct answer is (2). (Synthesis)** Irony exists when there is a difference between what different characters know or between what the characters and the reader know. In this case, Fancy has a secret she will never tell, while Dick believes that they are being completely honest with one another: 'why we are so happy is because there is such full confidence between us.'

UNIT 5: PLOT AND GENRE

Exercise 1 *(page 41)*

What Happens to Deerslayer?

1. **The correct answer is (5). (Analysis)** The most exciting, dramatic moment is when Deerslayer takes aim at the Indian. This moment of tension is followed by events that result from his decision not to fire. The other choices are all events that either lead up to or follow this climax.

Exercise 2 *(page 42)*

What Is Mrs. Bennet Hoping?

1. **The correct answer is (2). (Literal comprehension)** The main idea of this passage, that ". . . a single man in possession of a good fortune, must be in want of a wife," is stated directly in the first sentence. The rest of the conversation serves to illustrate this belief.

2. **The correct answer is (4). (Inferential comprehension)** Mrs. Bennet is assuming that Bingley actually does want a wife. Choice (1) is incorrect because the reader knows for a fact that Netherfield Park has been rented. There is no mention of Mrs. Bennet's older daughter in particular, as choice (3) indicates. Lines 15–19 suggest that Mrs. Bennet does not care whether her husband is interested, so choice (2) can be eliminated. There is no evidence for choice (5).

3. **The correct answer is (5). (Application)** Mrs. Bennet's main characteristic in this passage is her nosiness into the lives of those around her. Choices (3) and (4) can be eliminated because the passage does not indicate how hardworking or lazy she might be. Ambition, which is suggested in choices (1) and (2), is hinted at, but it is not nearly as strong a characteristic in Mrs. Bennet as are curiosity and love for gossip.

4. **The correct answer is (1). (Inferential comprehension)** Mrs. Bennet's references to Mr. Bingley's yearly salary and his having rented Netherfield Park indicate that she is impressed by his wealth. Choice (4) states the opposite, that he is poor. She does not know for certain who his father is or that he wants to marry, so choices (3) and (2) are incorrect. There is no discussion of his career, so choice (5) can be eliminated.

Exercise 3 *(page 44)*

1. **The correct answer is (2). (Synthesis)** This is actually a question about the main idea of the passage. You can tell that Wimsey is trying to find out about a razor because he keeps mentioning it whenever one of the other characters strays from the topic.

2. **The correct answer is (1). (Analysis)** In this paragraph, Wimsey congratulates himself on a correct hunch and makes observations that confirm his suspicions. Choices (2) and (5) are incorrect because it is Bright who is described. Choices (3) and (4) are both incorrect because we do not yet know if these details are important.

3. **The correct answer is (4). (Synthesis)** From this excerpt, all we can tell about Bright is that he is nervous, which is stated in line 12. Although every character introduced in a mystery novel is a potential suspect, we do not have enough information about Bright to tell if he is important, evil, or suspicious, choices (1), (3), and (5). Because he is claiming a reward, it is unlikely that he is rich, choice (2).

Exercise 4 *(page 45)*

What Are They Looking For?

1. **The correct answer is (5). (Comprehension)** This is another main idea question in disguise. Dr. Arroway states in lines 6–7 her belief that there is no other explanation besides extraterrestrial intelligence. Choices (1), (2), and (3) are incorrect because they are details from the passage. Choice (4) is incorrect because the scientists are discussing something in the Vega system, not something found on Earth.

2. **The correct answer is (3). (Application)** Just like the detective in a mystery story, Dr. Arroway is in the center of the action, looking for clues, listening to and ruling out her sidekicks' explanations. The other choices given are all standard characters present in many mystery novels. Choice (5) is incorrect because in mystery novels police officers usually rely on the hero or heroine to solve the crime for them.

3. **The correct answer is (3). (Analysis)** The expression means that it feels like a holiday, a day when there is no school.

GLOSSARY

characters: the imaginary people portrayed in a piece of fiction

conclusion: a judgment or opinion based on information an author provides

diction: word choice; the types of words a writer uses in different situations

fiction: writing about imaginary people and events

figurative language: imaginative words and phrases that create a vivid image

image: a mental picture created for the reader by a skillful choice of words

irony: a situation in which there is a startling difference between what is expected to happen and what actually does happen

main idea: the point or idea that the writer wants to communicate

metaphor: a comparison in which two things are described as the same—without the use of the words *like* or *as*

mood: the feeling or atmosphere that a piece of writing conveys

narrator: the person or character who tells the story

plot: the sequence of events in the story

point of view: the perspective of the narrator

simile: a figure of speech in which two things are compared through the use of the words *like* or *as*

supporting detail: a fact that provides more information about a main idea

symbol: something used to represent something else

theme: a statement or belief about life

tone: the attitude or feeling that a piece of writing conveys

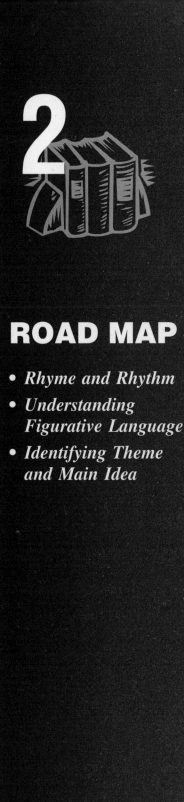

Poetry

A **poem** is a piece of writing that communicates an intense and often emotional message. In general, poems are different from other literary forms in two ways: (1) Poems are often shorter pieces of writing, and (2) they have a different structure. A poet usually divides the lines of a poem into stanzas, which are like the verses of a song.

Poets often express ideas indirectly through rhyme, rhythm, and figurative language. The rhyme and rhythm help set the mood of a poem. They stem from a time when poems were sung out loud before they were written down.

UNIT 1: RHYME AND RHYTHM

A writer of prose uses paragraphs to break up a passage, making it easier to understand. Similarly, a poet breaks a poem into **stanzas**, or sections. Stanzas can do more than make a poem simpler to read, however. With each new stanza, the poet may introduce a new setting or speaker, a plot element, or a change in mood or tone.

Think about the song you have heard on the radio most recently. In popular songs, rhyme and rhythm make the words and the message more powerful. Poets use rhyme and rhythm in much the same way.

For this reason, it often helps to read the poem aloud, sometimes more than once, in order to better understand what the poet is trying to convey. As you say the words, try to feel the emotions that the words express. These emotions contribute to the setting, or the atmosphere, of the poem. Knowing the setting for the poem can often guide you toward understanding its overall meaning.

Rhyme is the sound likeness of two words. Rhyming words are effective in poetry because their sounds complement each other. Sometimes those sounds are exactly alike (as in *cat/hat* and *alive/survive*); at other times (as in *pound/pond*), the sounds are not exactly the same but are close enough to give the effect of a rhyme.

Rhyming words are also used to link ideas. In addition, rhyme may determine the structure of a poem. For example, a stanza in which the last words in lines 1 and 2 rhyme and the last words in lines 3 and 4 rhyme has a **rhyme scheme** of *aabb*.

Rhythm is the sound pattern that words make when placed together. Think about dancing. When you dance, your body moves to the rhythm of the music. In many poems, words do the same thing. Sometimes the rhythm is so strong and regular you can clap your hands to it. At other times, the rhythm is purposely uneven. A poet may want to capture dissimilar ideas or keep the reader's attention. Instead of rhythm, a poet may use *repetition*—the repeated use of a word or phrase—to make a point.

Another form of rhythm poets use is the placement of text in the poem. Sometimes the physical shape, or the use of selective indents of text, can graphically reinforce the central meaning of the poem. Whenever you see an unusual word spacing or paragraph indent, try to understand how that spacing might contribute to what the words are saying.

Although stanzas, rhyme, and rhythm can be important elements in a poem, some poems do not use all these techniques. When a poem contains irregular rhythm and rhyme, or no rhyme, the structure is called **free verse**. Many modern poets write free verse.

ROAD MAP

- *Rhyme and Rhythm*
- *Understanding Figurative Language*
- *Identifying Theme and Main Idea*

As you read and reread a poem, it can help to ask yourself some questions about it. What is the organization of the poem? Is there repetition of certain words or phrases? How does one sentence and stanza lead to the next? Does the grammar contribute to the meaning of the words? Once you comprehend how a poem is organized and if there's a pattern to the organization, ask yourself why the poet constructed the poem in this way.

EXERCISE 1

Directions: Items 1 and 2 refer to the following poem. As you read this poem, think about how free verse makes the poem effective. Then answer the questions.

What Thoughts Come to the Speaker's Mind?

Line   Do not boast of your speed,
      O blue-green stream running by the hills:
      Once you have reached the wide ocean,
      You can return no more.
5   Why not stay here and rest,
      When moonlight stuffs the empty hills?
      Mountains are steadfast but the mountain streams
      Go by, go by,
      And yesterdays are like the rushing streams,
10   They fly, they fly,
      And the great heroes, famous for a day,
      They die, they die.
      Blue mountains speak of my desire,
      Green waters reflect my lover's love:
15   The mountains unchanging,
      The waters flowing by.
      Sometimes it seems the waters cannot forget me,
      They part in tears, regretting, running away.
      His guests are merry and joking.
20   A distant voyage is like chewing sugar cane,
      Sweetness mixed with bitterness.
      Return, soon I shall return to my home—
      Though beautiful, this is not my land.

—"Do Not Boast of Your Speed" by Hwang Chin-i

1. This poem is primarily about

    (1)   marriage.
    (2)   an athletic event.
    (3)   the birth of a child.
    (4)   the love of nature.
    (5)   the passage of time.

2. Lines 7–12 differ from the rest of the poem because they

    (1)   do not contain any figurative expressions.
    (2)   use rhyme and rhythm to describe the speaker's ancestors.
    (3)   address the ocean directly, as if it were a person.
    (4)   use rhyme and rhythm to describe the passage of time.
    (5)   contain no rhyme or rhythm and quote a different speaker.

Check your answers on page 68.

EXERCISE 2

Directions: Items 1 and 2 refer to the following poem. Consider the rhythm of the poem as you read it. Then answer the questions.

How Do Sounds Help Convey Meaning?

Line Whose woods these are I think I know.
His house is in the village though;
He will not see me stopping here
To watch his woods fill up with snow.

5   My little horse must think it queer
To stop without a farmhouse near
Between the woods and frozen lake
The darkest evening of the year.

He gives his harness bells a shake
10   To ask if there is some mistake.
The only other sound's the sweep
Of easy wind and downy flake.

The woods are lovely, dark and deep,
But I have promises to keep,
15   And miles to go before I sleep,
And miles to go before I sleep.

—"Stopping by Woods on a Snowy Evening" by Robert Frost

1. How do lines 15–16 reinforce the "tone" of the poem?

    (1)   They point out how far the rider must travel.
    (2)   They simulate the sound of a determined horse.
    (3)   They do not reinforce the "mood" of the poem.
    (4)   They are the same for emphasis.
    (5)   They indicate that the rider is already asleep.

2. In lines 1–4, a vowel sound is repeated to suggest

    (1)   that the poem rhymes.
    (2)   the speaker is uncomfortable.
    (3)   the poet's clever use of language.
    (4)   the speaker's intelligence.
    (5)   what it feels like to be there.

Check your answers on page 68.

EXERCISE 3

Directions: Items 1 and 2 refer to the following poem. Note where the various phrases are placed in the poem. Then answer the questions.

What Is Happening to the Speaker?

Line The pennycandystore beyond the El
is where I first
fell in love
with unreality
5 Jellybeans glowed in the semi-gloom
of that september afternoon
A cat upon the counter moved among
the licorice sticks
and tootsie rolls
10 and Oh Boy Gum

Outside the leaves were falling as they died

A wind had blown away the sun

—"The pennycandystore beyond the El" by Lawrence Ferlinghetti

1. In lines 11–12, the speaker is feeling

   (1) as though something has been lost.
   (2) the wonder of nature.
   (3) that it's best to stay in the candy store.
   (4) that it will cost too much money to buy the candy.
   (5) that winter is coming soon.

2. Why are lines 3–4 and 8–10 spaced differently than the rest of the poem?

   (1) The line spacing has nothing to do with the poem's meaning.
   (2) They show that the speaker is going somewhere.
   (3) The poet just wanted those lines to look different.
   (4) They reflect what is going on in the speaker's mind.
   (5) They are meant to keep the reader off guard.

Check your answers on page 68.

EXERCISE 4

Directions: Items 1–3 refer to the following poem. Pay special attention to phrases that are repeated. Then answer the questions.

What Does the Speaker Want?

Line   Do not go gentle into that good night,
     Old age should burn and rave at close of day;
     Rage, rage against the dying of the light.

     Though wise men at their end know dark is right,
5   Because their words had forked no lightning they
     Do not go gentle into that good night.

     Good men, the last wave by, crying how bright
     Their frail deeds might have danced in a green bay,
     Rage, rage against the dying of the light.

10   Wild men who caught and sang the sun in flight,
     And learn, too late, they grieved it on its way,
     Do not go gentle into that good night.

     Grave men, near death, who see with blinding sight
     Blind eyes could blaze like meteors and be gay,
15   Rage, rage against the dying of the light.

     And you, my father, there on the sad height,
     Curse, bless, me now with your fierce tears, I pray.
     Do not go gentle into that good night.
     Rage, rage against the dying of the light.
        —"Do Not Go Gentle into That Good Night" by Dylan Thomas

1. To whom is the speaker talking in this poem?

    (1)   A stranger
    (2)   A friend
    (3)   His child
    (4)   His father
    (5)   Wild men

2. As the speaker talks, someone is

    (1)   dying.
    (2)   watching.
    (3)   dating.
    (4)   sleeping.
    (5)   singing.

3. In line 13, "see with blinding sight" refers to

    (1)   seeing so well it blinds others.
    (2)   being blind and unable to see anything.
    (3)   understanding without the use of eyes.
    (4)   the blinding flash of a meteor.
    (5)   the inability to see anything at all.

Check your answers on page 69.

UNIT 2: UNDERSTANDING FIGURATIVE LANGUAGE

RECOGNIZING ALLITERATION

"Who is the bravest, boldest, and best leader that our beloved country has ever seen?" This question contains four words that begin with *b*. Read it out loud, and notice how the words beginning with *b* catch your attention. Think, too, about how the sound links the leader with the country. Poets often place words that start with the same letter near each other to create this kind of effect. This technique is called alliteration.

PERSONIFICATION, SYMBOLISM, AND IMAGERY

Like other writers, poets sometimes depend on figurative language to communicate ideas and observations. Figurative language is not meant to be taken literally; rather, it compares things in an unusual way. It creates mental images that help readers see ideas in new ways, too.

Symbolism and personification are two more types of figurative language. **Symbolism** is figurative language in which an object, a person, or an event represents something else. For example, a country's flag usually symbolizes its pride and its people. A wedding ring symbolizes long-lasting love. Black clothing often symbolizes mourning. **Personification** takes symbolism one step further. When an object is personified, it is given human qualities. (Just remember: *person*ification = like a *person*.) For example, a building doesn't experience feelings and emotions. Still, a writer might say, "The old building stood its ground bravely against the wrecking ball."

Imagery is the poet's appeal to our senses: the smell of perfume, the sight of a glorious sunset, the thrill of a roller coaster ride, the sound of a cat's meow, the feel of rain on your face. Words that express these images call up sensations that are much greater than the words themselves. They evoke the memories and feelings from our entire lives that go with the sensory images. When you see a verbal image in a poem, try to feel, to sense, to experience the image as you read it. Imagine you are sensing what the poet's words are representing. When a poem refers to "still midnight," try to immerse yourself in the silence of the dark middle of the night. The imagery in a poem offers illuminating signposts directing you to the main idea and theme of the poem. When you let your feelings "step inside" the imagery, you are much closer to understanding and experiencing what the poet is trying to express.

EXERCISE 2

Directions: Items 1–3 refer to the following poem. As you read this poem, consider what new ideas the poet suggests. Then answer the questions.

How Is Death Personified?

Line Because I could not stop for Death,
      He kindly stopped for me;
      The carriage held but just ourselves
      And immortality.
5   We slowly drove, he knew no haste,
      And I had put away
      My labor, and my leisure too,
      For his civility.
          We passed the school where children played
10   At wrestling in a ring;
      We passed the fields of gazing grain,
      We passed the setting sun.
          We paused before a house that seemed
      A swelling of the ground;
15   The roof was scarcely visible,
      The cornice but a mound.
          Since then 'tis centuries; but each
      Feels shorter than the day
      I first surmised the horses' heads
20   Were toward eternity.

—"Because I Could Not Stop for Death" by Emily Dickinson

1. In this poem, death is personified in the form of

   (1) an elderly grandfather.
   (2) a frightening old woman.
   (3) a courteous carriage driver.
   (4) an energetic young man.
   (5) a silent young boy.

2. "We slowly drove, he knew no haste,/And I had put away/My labor, and my leisure too,/For his civility." (lines 5–8)

   Which of the following best restates these thoughts?

   (1) We drove quickly because I was eager to return home.
   (2) Because the driver was rude, I asked to be taken home.
   (3) I was impressed by his politeness but soon felt ready to get back to work.
   (4) We drove hastily toward the setting sun as I enjoyed my leisure.
   (5) I no longer required work or rest, so I was content to move slowly.

3. The house to which the speaker refers in the fourth stanza (lines 13–16) symbolizes

   (1) the earth.
   (2) a small apartment.
   (3) her birthplace.
   (4) a gravesite.
   (5) a mansion.

Check your answers on page 69.

EXERCISE 2

Directions: Items 1 and 2 refer to the following poem. Think about the symbolic meaning of "breaking the string." Then answer the questions.

What is the Speaker Feeling?

Line   These were people
        Who broke the string for me
            Therefore
        This place became like this for me,
5   On account of it.
        Because the string broke for me,
            Therefore
        The place does not feel to me
        As the place used to feel to me,
10   On account of it.
        The place feels as if it stood open before me,
        Because the string has broken for me.
            Therefore
        The place does not feel pleasant to me
15   Because of it.

           —"The String Game" by Dia!kwain, after Xaa-ttin

1. In this poem, the speaker is feeling a sense of

    (1)   happiness.
    (2)   loss.
    (3)   warmth.
    (4)   fun.
    (5)   betrayal.

2. Based on lines 14–15, you can tell the speaker

    (1)   is eager to move on to new things.
    (2)   is usually a happy person.
    (3)   is not comfortable with change.
    (4)   wants to put the string back together.
    (5)   is excited by being at this place.

Check your answers on page 69.

EXERCISE 3

Directions: Items 1 and 2 refer to the following poem. As you read, try to feel what the words suggest. Then answer the questions.

How Do Words Express Emotions?

Line   Night's candles are burnt out, and jocund day
      Stands tiptoe on the misty mountain tops.

          —From "Romeo and Juliet" by William Shakespeare

1. The poet uses alliteration in line 2 to

    (1)   show that the night has ended.
    (2)   point out the mountain in the distance.
    (3)   connect the symbols of candles and mountains.
    (4)   express the sadness and loss of the night.
    (5)   convey the vivid experience of a new day.

2. How is personification is employed here?

    (1)   By showing the night as burning out
    (2)   In the comparison between night and day
    (3)   By having the day act like a person
    (4)   In the description of the mountain tops as misty
    (5)   Through the focus on the tops of the mountains

Check your answers on page 70.

UNIT 3: IDENTIFYING THEME AND MAIN IDEA

As in other kinds of writing, the main idea of a poem is its central point. The theme of a poem, however, is a broader statement or belief about life, relationships, feelings, or behavior. In a poem about reapers, for example, the poet's subject might be "work." The poet's theme might be "the monotony of physical labor." The poet's main idea might be "People can be hypnotized by the routine of their work, becoming blind to the world around them."

The poet's selection of words and imagery can be vital clues in guiding you to the poem's theme and main idea. As you read and reread the poem, ask yourself why the poet chose to use certain words and not others that have a similar meaning. Poets seldom select words randomly or by accident. They use specific words to bring out specific images and feelings. This is one of the ways a poet sets the tone for the poem. The tone, the images, the choice of one word over another—these are all pointers that can help you to identify the poem's theme and main idea.

EXERCISE 3

Directions; Items 1–4 refer to the following poem. As you read, think about the tone of the poem and how you would state its theme. Then answer the questions.

Where Is the Speaker Going?

Line   Farewell, my younger brother!
      From the holy places the gods come for me.
      You will never see me again; but when the showers pass and the thunders peal,
      "There," you will say, "is the voice of my elder brother."
5   And when the harvest comes, of the beautiful birds and grasshoppers you will say,
      "There is the ordering of my elder brother!"

           —"Farewell, My Younger Brother," a traditional Navajo poem

1. Based on line 2, you can assume that the speaker

    (1)   is near death.
    (2)   is not religious.
    (3)   has a brother who is dying.
    (4)   wants to leave town.
    (5)   is afraid.

2. The speaker mentions being remembered in all of the following EXCEPT

    (1)   grasshoppers.
    (2)   rain.
    (3)   springtime flowers.
    (4)   thunder.
    (5)   the time of harvest.

3. Which of the following best states the main idea of this poem?

    (1)   Every harvest is beautiful.
    (2)   Nature should be revered.
    (3)   An elder brother is a good teacher.
    (4)   A person's spirit carries on after death.
    (5)   Brothers should be lifelong friends.

4. If the younger brother applied the theme of this poem to his life, he would most likely become a

    (1)   loving parent.
    (2)   nature photographer.
    (3)   big-game hunter.
    (4)   skilled lumberjack.
    (5)   fiery preacher.

Check your answers on page 70.

EXERCISE 2

Directions: Items 1–4 refer to the following sonnet.

As you read this sonnet, think about how this classical work of literature provides a timeless record of human emotion and about the ways in which you could apply Browning's images and ideas to life today. Then answer the questions.

What Strong Emotions Does This Speaker Express?

Line   How do I love thee? Let me count the ways.
      I love thee to the depth and breadth and height
      My soul can reach, when feeling out of sight
      For the ends of Being and ideal Grace.
5   I love thee to the level of every day's
      Most quiet need, by sun and candlelight.
      I love thee freely, as men strive for Right;
      I love thee purely, as they turn from Praise.
      I love thee with the passion put to use
10   In my old griefs, and with my childhood's faith.
      I love thee with a love I seemed to lose
      With my lost saints,—I love thee with the breath,
      Smiles, tears, of all my life!—and, if God choose,
      I shall but love thee better after death.

         —Sonnet XLIII by Elizabeth Barrett Browning

1. The speaker connects her feelings of love with all of the following EXCEPT

    (1)   purity.
    (2)   freedom.
    (3)   passion.
    (4)   fear.
    (5)   faith.

2. Which of the following literary techniques is used most often in this sonnet?

    (1)   Repetition
    (2)   Falling action
    (3)   Stage directions
    (4)   Foreshadowing
    (5)   Personification

3. If this sonnet were reviewed in a modern-day magazine, the reviewer would most likely characterize it as

    (1)   emotionless.
    (2)   dramatic.
    (3)   dull.
    (4)   manipulative.
    (5)   inexpressive.

4. Which of the following song titles best summarizes the main idea of this sonnet?

    (1)   "Tears of a Clown"
    (2)   "We Are the World"
    (3)   "We Are Family"
    (4)   "Tracks of My Tears"
    (5)   "I Will Always Love You"

Check your answers on page 70.

EXERCISE 3

Directions: Items 1–3 refer to the following poem. Observe how the first stanza differs from the second. Then answer the questions.

What Is He Really Saying?

Line Not to the mother of solitude will I give myself
       Away, not to the mother of art, nor the mother
       Of the ocean, nor the mother of the snake and the fire;
       Nor the mother of conversation, nor the mother
5   Of the downcast face, nor the mother of the solitude of death;
       Not to the mother of the night full of crickets,
       Nor the mother of the open fields, nor the mother of Christ.

       But I will give myself to the father of righteousness, the father
       Of cheerfulness, who is also the father of rocks,
10   Who is also the father of perfect gestures;
       From the Chase National Bank
       An arm of flame has come, and I am drawn
       To the desert, to the parched places, to the landscape of zeros;
       And I shall give myself away to the father of righteousness,
15   The stones of cheerfulness, the steel of money, the father of rocks.

—"A Busy Man Speaks" by Robert Bly

1. In this poem, the speaker associates the qualities of the mother with

    (1) greed.
    (2) formality.
    (3) lack of feeling.
    (4) rocks.
    (5) love.

2. What feeling does the speaker express with words such as "parched," "steel," "stones," and "righteousness?"

    (1) Strength
    (2) Emptiness
    (3) Warmth
    (4) Cheerfulness
    (5) Sincerity

3. In lines 12–13, the speaker indicates he is

    (1) happy to do what he is told.
    (2) joining a friend in his activities.
    (3) being forced to do something.
    (4) making lots of money.
    (5) eager to get to work.

Check your answers on page 71.

EXERCISE 4

Directions: Items 1 and 2 refer to the following poem. Note where the various phrases are placed in the poem. Then answer the questions.

What Does the Speaker Value Most?

Line   My clumsiest dear, whose hands shipwreck vases,
        At whose quick touch all glasses chip and ring,
        Whose palms are bulls in china, burs in linen,
        And have no cunning with any soft thing

5   Except all ill-at-ease fidgeting people:
        The refugee uncertain at the door
        You make at home; deftly you steady
        The drunk clambering on his undulant floor.

        Unpredictable dear, the taxi drivers' terror,
10   Shrinking from far headlights pale as a dime
        Yet leaping before red apoplectic streetcars—
        Misfit in any space. And never on time.

        A wrench in clocks and the solar system. Only
        With words and people and love you move at ease.
15   In traffic of wit expertly manoeuvre
        And keep us, all devotion, at your knees.

—"Love Poem" by John Frederick Nims

1. In this poem, the speaker is saying

    (1)   I wish you were less clumsy.
    (2)   I want you to be more careful and on time.
    (3)   I will leap with you in front of streetcars.
    (4)   I will never get into a taxi with you.
    (5)   I am devoted to your loving nature.

2. How do lines 13–14 express the tone of the poem?

    (1)   They compare clocks and the solar system to words, people, and love.
    (2)   They point out what the speaker feels is most important.
    (3)   They highlight the criticisms of "My clumsiest dear."
    (4)   The word "wrench" is appropriate to the clumsiness referred to elsewhere.
    (5)   These lines are not a good expression of the poem's tone.

Check your answers on page 71.

ANSWERS AND EXPLANATIONS
UNIT 1: RHYME AND RHYTHM
Exercise 1 *(page 57)*

What Thoughts Come to the Speaker's Mind?

1. **The correct answer is (5). (Synthesis)** The reference to a voyage refers to the poet's impending death. The poet is reflecting on the passing of time.

2. **The correct answer is (4). (Analysis)** By repeating the phrases "Go by," "They fly," and "They die," the speaker uses rhyme, rhythm, and repetition to make the point that time passes. Line 9 contains a simile, so choice (1) is incorrect. Choice (2) can be eliminated because the speaker mentions great heroes, not his own ancestors. Choices (3) and (5) are incorrect because the speaker does not mention the ocean in these lines and because he does use rhyme and rhythm.

Exercise 2 *(page 57)*

How Do Sounds Help Convey Meaning?

1. **The correct answer is (2). (Analysis)** These two lines convey the speaker's determination to continue on and keep his promises despite his inclination to linger. Through rhythm and repetition, the speaker expresses his decision to go on and meet his commitments through the horse's resolute trot.

2. **The correct answer is (5). (Synthesis)** The repetition of the "o" sound conveys the feeling of the wind blowing as the speaker stops to gaze at the woods. It is a sense of aloneness, of oneness with the snowy woods, of separation from the needs of civilization, of a love of nature in its pristine, chilling beauty.

Exercise 3 *(page 58)*

What Is Happening to the Speaker?

1. **The correct answer is (1). (Comprehension)** These lines convey the sense that the speaker is on the verge of adolescence and will soon no longer be a child. It is the "childness" that is dying and being blown away, and the speaker feels as though he or she is losing something.

2. **The correct answer is (4). (Analysis)** The spacing in lines 3–4 reflects how the speaker is blissfully moving forward in his or her own mind. However, in lines 8–10, the speaker is moving backward while fantasizing about several delights of childhood that he or she wants to continue to enjoy. This person is not sure whether he or she wants to stay a child.

Exercise 4 *(page 59)*

What Does the Speaker Want?

1. **The correct answer is (4). (Analysis)** In line 16, the speaker addresses "you, my father." The speaker does not say "you" when he refers to others in the poem, such as "wise men," "good men," "wild men," and "grave men."

2. **The correct answer is (1). (Analysis)** There are many references to dying throughout the poem, including "they grieved" (line 11), "Grave men, near death" (line 13), and, indeed, "the dying of the light."

3. **The correct answer is (3). (Synthesis)** The speaker is pointing out that, when the reality of death is near, people can gain penetrating insights and understandings that they were not capable of before. This kind of clear seeing has nothing to do with the use of eyes.

UNIT 2: UNDERSTANDING FIGURATIVE LANGUAGE

Exercise 1 *(page 61)*

How Is Death Personified?

1. **The correct answer is (3). (Comprehension)** Lines 2–5 introduce Death as a courteous carriage driver. There is no evidence of his age, as choices (1), (4), and (5) suggest. Because Death is characterized as male, choice (2) is incorrect.

2. **The correct answer is (5). (Comprehension)** The speaker has "put away" her labor and leisure (work and rest) because her life is over; Death is kind, she is content to move slowly. Choices (1), (2), and (3) are incorrect because they imply that the speaker wants to be taken home. Choice (4) can be eliminated because the speaker says that they drove slowly (line 5).

3. **The correct answer is (4). (Analysis)** The "house" is a gravesite. Choices (2) and (5) are incorrect because the speaker is using a figurative image. It is more specific than the earth as a whole, so choice (1) can be eliminated. There is no evidence to suggest she is at her place of birth, as choice (3) indicates.

Exercise 2 *(page 62)*

What Is the Speaker Feeling?

1. **The correct answer is (2). (Comprehension)** In line 14, the speaker says that the place does not feel pleasant, and this is because the string, which was mentioned earlier in the poem, had been broken. This person has experienced a loss of something or someone important, and this loss has changed the speaker's life.

2. **The correct answer is (3). (Synthesis)** Throughout the poem the speaker is mournful that the string has been broken, which is symbolic of an important change in his or her life. The speaker expresses his or her discomfort most explicitly in lines 14–15, and this discomfort is because of what the breaking of the string represents.

Exercise 3 *(page 66)*

How Do Words Express Emotions?

1. **The correct answer is (5). (Synthesis)** The repetition of the "t" sounds in line 2 helps the reader to feel the excitement and anticipation of the dawning of a new crisp day. It is a stimulating, staccato sound, evoking joyful eagerness.

2. **The correct answer is (3). (Synthesis)** The day acts like a person by being jocund and by standing tiptoe on the mountain tops.

UNIT 3: IDENTIFYING THEME AND MAIN IDEA

Exercise 1 *(page 64)*

Where Is the Speaker Going?

1. **The correct answer is (1). (Synthesis)** From the phrase "the gods come for me" (line 2), it can be assumed that the speaker is near death. The references to "holy places" and "gods" mean the speaker is likely a religious person, so choice (2) can be eliminated. There is no evidence for the other choices.

2. **The correct answer is (3). (Comprehension)** Choice (1) is mentioned in line 5, choices (2) and (4) appear together in line 3, and choice (5) is the subject of line 5.

3. **The correct answer is (4). (Synthesis)** The speaker's point is that his spirit will live on in nature after death. The speaker might agree with the other choices, but these do not relate to the speaker's beliefs about death and spirituality.

4. **The correct answer is (2): (Application)** If the younger brother believes the speaker, he will probably have a greater respect for nature, since the speaker's spirit is a part of nature. Choices (3) and (4) can be eliminated because they suggest a disregard for nature. Choices (1) and (5) are incorrect, respectively, because nothing is suggested about the younger brother's children or about spreading the speaker's message to others.

Exercise 2 *(page 65)*

What Strong Emotions Does This Speaker Express?

1. **The correct answer is (4). (Comprehension)** The speaker never compares her strong feelings to fear or any negative emotion. In lines 7–9, the speaker compares her love to the other choices.

2. **The correct answer is (1). (Analysis)** The speaker repeats the phrase "I love thee . . ." in lines 1, 2, 5, 7, 8, 9, 11, 12, and 14. This brief sonnet does not follow any strict narrative pattern of rising action, crisis, and falling action, so choice (2) is incorrect. Stage directions are used only in drama, so choice (3) can be eliminated. The speaker states that her love will continue after death. This statement does not stand out from the rest of the poem as a foreshadowing of her own death, so choice (4) is not the best answer. The speaker does not personify inanimate objects to describe her feelings, so choice (5) can be eliminated.

3. **The correct answer is (2). (Application)** Phrases such as "I love thee to the depth and breadth and height/My soul can reach . . ." (lines 2–3) and "I love thee with the breath,/Smiles, tears, of all my life!" (lines 12–13) are dramatic statements, full of emotion and exaggeration. Choices (1), (3), and (5) suggest the opposite and can be eliminated. The speaker's tone is one of honesty, not deceit or manipulation, so choice (4) can be eliminated.

4. **The correct answer is (5). (Application)** The speaker states her undying love, so choice (5) is the best answer. Choices (1) and (4) suggest a sad or negative theme and can be eliminated. The speaker is declaring her unity with one other person. Because choices (2) and (3) suggest connection with a larger group of people, they are incorrect.

Exercise 3 *(page 0)*

What Is He Really Saying?

1. **The correct answer is (5). (Comprehension)** In the first stanza, which entirely relates to the mother, the speaker mentions only positive things, such as art, conversation, the night full of crickets, the open fields, and love itself. Though the speaker says he is not giving himself to these things, these are what he cherishes.

2. **The correct answer is (2). (Comprehension)** The speaker uses these words to express the sterility and barrenness of the direction in which he is about to turn. This is especially evident in lines 12–13, where the speaker refers to the "desert," "parched places," and "landscape of zeros."

3. **The correct answer is (3). (Comprehension)** The speaker is clearly being forced by the arm, which is drawing him to "the desert." Reinforcing this feeling is line 15, where "cheerfulness" is paired with "stones," "money" goes with "steel," and "father" corresponds to "rocks."

Exercise 4 *(page 67)*

What Does the Speaker Value Most?

1. **The correct answer is (5). (Comprehension)** The speaker is expressing that it is the loving nature of the person he or she is talking to that is paramount. It is the ability to move at ease with words and people and love that count, not whether or not one is clumsy.

2. **The correct answer is (2). (Comprehension)** A wrench in clocks and the solar system is nowhere near as important to the speaker as the ability to move at ease with words, people, and love. These two lines succinctly summarize the comparison being made throughout the poem, and the results of that comparison set the tone.

GLOSSARY

alliteration: repetition of the initial sound in two or more words in a phrase or in words appearing near one another

free verse: poetry that contains little or no rhyme or rhythm

imagery: the general term for comparisons in figurative language, often appealing to the senses and evocative of memories

personification: figurative language in which something that is not human is given human characteristics

poem: relatively brief, often intense and emotional work of literature

rhyme: the use of words with endings that sound alike

rhyme scheme: a pattern of rhyming sounds that gives structure to a poem

rhythm: the pattern of sounds formed by words

stanza: two or more lines of poetry grouped together

symbolism: figurative language in which an object, person, or event represents a larger, more abstract idea

Drama

UNIT 1: THE WORLD OF A DRAMA

A **drama** is a play that can be read or performed on stage by actors.

When you watch a play, you can see how the actors react to each other. You can see that time passes. A **playwright** has other ways to help you picture these things when you read a play.

UNDERSTANDING SETTING AND STAGE DIRECTIONS

Plays are divided into acts, which are further divided into *scenes*. Each scene advances the time and/or place of the action—that is, changes the setting. The *setting* of a drama is the time and place in which the action occurs. Identifying a play's setting might help you anticipate the action, since time and place can influence what happens. For example, if the setting is a small, cold Alaskan town, the action might focus on how people in the town cope with the long winter.

A playwright provides other clues through **stage directions**, which often appear in *italics*. Stage directions describe how the stage looks and how the actors should stand, move, look, or speak.

In the plays of the best playwrights, stage directions and movements can provide revealing tips on the attitudes of characters, on the relative importance of actions, and indeed on the direction in which the play is heading. You can often gain crucial insights into the prime motivations of characters by the stage directions the playwright attributes to them.

While playwrights usually leave the specific details of physical description and costume up to the director and actors, you can use the few stage directions you are given to expand on your comprehension of the play. It will help you to better understand the significance of the dialogue if you mentally "become a director" yourself. Read as though you were placing the characters on stage where their lines will come across most effectively. "Direct" the characters in their movements, tell them which gestures to make, give them the tone, or manner, with which they should deliver certain lines. Mentally guide them on how to act when they're on stage without lines to deliver. Involving yourself mentally in putting on the play imparts a clearer vision of what the play is about.

RECOGNIZING FORESHADOWING

Foreshadowing is the technique of suggesting an event that will occur later in the play. The foreshadowing may be found in stage directions or in a character's words or actions. For example, if a character wonders out loud when another character might come home after a long absence, the playwright may be foreshadowing this character's return. Watching for foreshadowing helps you understand what is happening—and what will happen—in a drama.

ROAD MAP

- *The World of a Drama*
- *Understanding Comedy and Tragedy*

Try to pay close attention to the words attributed to each character. In a play, words often deliver similar effects to physical actions and movements. A character can sometimes hurt or emotionally destroy another with words just as effectively as with a sword or a gun. Words can also lift the spirits of a character and provide better nourishment than food itself.

A character's physical movements tell us much about his feelings, but his words reinforce and elaborate on those intentions and give us a greater and more subtle understanding of his motivations and future intentions.

ANALYZING CHARACTERS, DIALOGUE, AND CONFLICT

Dialogue, or conversation, is the most important element in a play. By listening closely to dialogue between characters, you can gather information.

A **monologue** is a long speech by one character when another character is on stage. A soliloquy occurs when the character is alone on stage. Monologues and soliloquies are important because characters reveal important feelings or experiences during these long and usually emotional speeches.

As you read, keep in mind that each character in a play has a different perspective to express. The different perspectives often result in a **conflict**, or problem.

The most common types of conflict in drama (and in all types of literature) are:

• conflict between people (such as friends or family members)

• conflict between a person and society (such as a person who opposes prejudice)

• conflict between a person (or people) and an element of nature (such as a hurricane)

• internal conflict—a spiritual or moral disturbance within one character

As you try to understand what a character is about, see if you bring together in your mind any patterns of thoughts that the character consistently expresses. Look for repetitions of statements, or different ways of imparting the same idea. Playwrights will often have a character express his or her innermost motivation clearly and openly at some point in the play. Try to find that point for each of the key characters.

What a character says about another character can provide important information, but it may be biased or incomplete information, reflecting the limitations of the character who is speaking. Often, major characters can offer misleading information, while minor characters can provide penetrating insights. Minor characters are sometimes very single-minded in their motivations. One may serve as the personification of deceit, while another may serve as the sole source of wisdom for a major character who is acting irrationally.

In fact, keep an eye out for contrast between characters. Two characters who are extremely different in viewpoint and motivation can give you a heightened clarity of each of them.

EXERCISE 1

Directions: Items 1 and 2 refer to the following passage. As you read this passage, use the stage directions to imagine the scene and the action. Then answer the questions.

What Brings These Characters Together?

Line *The stage is empty except for a few pale stars. Calorías and Julio enter. Calorías carries the cello on his shoulder.*

Guicho: (*Out of sight*) CA-LO-RIIIIAAS! CAAA-LOOOO-RIIIIAAS!

Guicho appears over a dune. Calorías and Julio stand looking at each other. Guicho
5 *takes out his knife.*

Julio: Hey Guichito.

Calorías: Why Guicho, you comin' with us?

Guicho: No.

Calorías: Ah yes. I see now. You have a knife. (*Approaching*) Perhaps you're
10 angry. Did I hurt a friend of yours? (*He laughs*) Have you come to kill me, little boy?

Guicho shakes his head. He is terrified.

Guicho: I want the guitarrón.

Julio: Ay Guichito. Go away.

15 Calorías: (*Picking up the cello*) This. Ah yes. It is this you want.

Guicho: Just give it to me.

Calorías: If only it were so simple . . . eh? But I can't give it to you. I have to destroy it.

—From *The Guitarrón* by Lynne Alvarez

1. The setting of this passage is

    (1) backstage at an orchestra hall.
    (2) early morning in a Latin American city.
    (3) nighttime in a desert-like place.
    (4) a junkyard.
    (5) late afternoon at the seashore.

2. The stage directions in lines 9–15 show that Calorías is

    (1) foolish.
    (2) eager to make friends with Guicho.
    (3) afraid but hopeful.
    (4) cruel.
    (5) easily misled by Julio.

Check your answers on page 88.

EXERCISE 2

Items 1–4 refer to the following passage. Read the passage. Then answer the questions.

Why Do These Characters Disagree?

Line Troy: Your mama tells me you got recruited by a college football team? Is that right?

Cory: Yeah. Coach Zellman say the recruiter gonna be coming by to talk to you. Get you to sign the permission papers.

5 Troy: I thought you supposed to be working down there at the A&P. Ain't you supposed to be working down there after school?

Cory: Mr. Stawicki say he gonna hold my job for me until after the football season. Say starting next week I can work weekends.

Troy: I thought we had an understanding about this football stuff. You suppose to
10 keep up with your chores and hold that job down at the A&P. Ain't been around here all day on a Saturday. Ain't none of your chores done . . . and now you telling me you done quit your job.

Cory: I'm gonna be working weekends.

Troy: You damn right you are! Ain't no need for nobody coming around here to
15 talk to me about signing nothing.

Cory: Hey, Pop, you can't do that. He's coming all the way from North Carolina.

Troy: I don't care where he coming from. The white man ain't gonna let you get nowhere with that football no way. You go and get your book-learning where you can learn to do something besides carrying people's garbage.

—From *Fences* by August Wilson

1. Which of the following best describes Cory's perspective?

   (1) He wants to own the A&P.
   (2) He wants to give up football.
   (3) He wishes that he were better at football.
   (4) He can work and still play football.
   (5) He does not like the recruiter.

2. Which of the following best describes Troy's perspective?

   (1) He thinks Cory should continue working.
   (2) He is worried about his wife's reaction.
   (3) He wishes that Cory were a better player.
   (4) He admires and respects the recruiter.
   (5) He is jealous of Cory's athletic skill.

3. As a father, Troy could best be described as

  (1) sympathetic.
  (2) wise.
  (3) cruel.
  (4) strict.
  (5) easygoing.

4. Which of the following is not clear by the end of this passage?

  (1) Coach Zellman's perspective
  (2) Cory's desire to play football
  (3) Cory's talent as a football player
  (4) Troy's perspective
  (5) Whether Cory will play college football

Check your answers on page 88.

EXERCISE 3

Directions: Items 1–4 refer to the following passage. As you read, compare how the characters understand the situation. Then answer the questions.

What Do the Characters Understand?

Line TANNER: Enry, why do you think that my friend has no chance with Miss Whitefield?

STRAKER: Cause she's after summun else.

TANNER: Bosh! Who else?

5 STRAKER: You.

TANNER: Me!

STRAKER: Mean to tell me you didn't know? Oh, come, Mr. Tanner!

TANNER: *(in fierce earnest)* Are you playing the fool, or do you mean it?

STRAKER: *(with a flash of temper)* I'm not playin no fool. *(More coolly)* Why, it's
10 as plain as the nose on your face. If you ain't spotted that, you don't know much about these sort of things. Ex-cuse me, you know, Mr. Tanner; but you asked me as man to man; and I told you as man to man.

TANNER: *(wildly appealing to the heavens)* Then I—I am the bee, the spider, the
15 marked down victim, the destined prey.

STRAKER: I dunno about the bee and the spider. But the marked down victim, that's what you are and no mistake.

—From *Man and Superman* by George Bernard Shaw

1. How wise is Tanner in the ways of human nature?

   (1) Extremely wise
   (2) Not very wise
   (3) He knows much about nature
   (4) He understands people
   (5) He plays the fool

2. Straker is telling Tanner that

   (1) Tanner's friend will marry Miss Whitefield.
   (2) Tanner is very clever.
   (3) Miss Whitefield's intentions are unknown.
   (4) Miss Whitefield has her eyes on Tanner.
   (5) it's important to talk man to man.

3. The playwright is suggesting in lines 14–17 that

   (1) what happens between men and women is determined by the heavens.
   (2) Straker doesn't know very much about animals.
   (3) Straker refers to animals when describing human relationships.
   (4) Tanner marks down who he wants to be his victims.
   (5) relationships between men and women are controlled by women.

4. From this passage you can infer that

   (1) Straker is more worldly-wise than Tanner.
   (2) Tanner is smarter than Straker.
   (3) Miss Whitefield is very well educated.
   (4) Straker doesn't like Tanner very well.
   (5) Miss Whitefield tells Straker her confidential thoughts.

Check your answers on page 88.

EXERCISE 4

Directions: Items 1–4 refer to the following passage. See if you can tell what is really being said here. Then answer the questions.

What is the Real Problem?

Line   WILLY: If I had forty dollars a week—that's all I'd need. Forty dollars, Howard.

       HOWARD: Kid, I can't take blood from a stone, I—

       WILLY: *(desperation is on him now)* Howard, the year Al Smith was nominated, your father came to me and—

5   HOWARD: *(starting to go off)* I've got to see some people, kid.

       WILLY: *(stopping him)* I'm talking about your father! There were promises made across this desk! You mustn't tell me you've got people to see—I put thirty-four years into this firm, Howard, and now I can't pay my insurance! You can't eat the orange and throw the peel away—a man is

10   not a piece of fruit! *(After a pause)* Now pay attention. Your father—in 1928 I had a big year. I averaged a hundred and seventy dollars a week in commissions.

       HOWARD: *(impatiently)* Now, Willy, you never averaged—

                              —From *Death of a Salesman* by Arthur Miller

1. Why does Howard hesitate to give Willy forty dollars a week?

   (1) Howard is too busy and has people he must talk to.
   (2) He is not paying attention to what Willy is saying.
   (3) He intends to give Willy a raise next week.
   (4) Howard does not value Willy as an employee.
   (5) Howard doesn't remember the year Al Smith was nominated.

2. From lines 10–12, you can tell that

   (1) Howard will give Willy the raise he is asking for.
   (2) Howard doesn't believe Willy made as much as he says he did.
   (3) Howard's father would have given Willy anything he asked for.
   (4) Howard does not have a very long attention span.
   (5) Willy keeps very accurate records of the commissions he makes.

3. In lines 9–10, Willy is asking Howard to

   (1) keep the peel of the orange he has eaten.
   (2) pay Willy for the success he had in 1928.
   (3) acknowledge Willy's contribution to the firm.
   (4) cover the cost of Willy's insurance payment.
   (5) think of a man as a valuable piece of fruit.

4. Howard's stage directions in lines 5 and 13 indicate that Howard

   (1) likes Willy's company.
   (2) is a relaxed person.
   (3) is committed to the promises his father made.
   (4) is always late for his appointments.
   (5) is trying to avoid Willy.

Check your answers on page 89.

EXERCISE 5

Directions: Items 1–3 refer to the following stage directions. Try to use the directions to help you understand the tone of the scene. Then answer the questions.

What Is About To Happen?

Line Scene: *The room at the* TESMANS'. *The curtains are drawn over the middle doorway, and also over the glass door. The lamp, half turned down, and with a shade over it, is burning on the table. In the stove, the door of which stands open, there has been a fire, which is now nearly burnt out.*

5   MRS. ELVSTED, *wrapped in a large shawl, and with her feet upon a footrest, sits close to the stove, sunk back in the armchair.* HEDDA, *fully dressed, lies sleeping upon the sofa, with a sofa blanket over her.*

—From *Hedda Gabler* by Henrik Ibsen

1. In line 4, the nearly burnt-out fire evokes

   (1) a new beginning.
   (2) a beautiful scene.
   (3) the end of something.
   (4) that it is mid-afternoon.
   (5) a lack of wood in the house.

2. How do you think the room feels?

   (1) Welcoming
   (2) Cheerful
   (3) Warm
   (4) Cold
   (5) Friendly

3. What can you anticipate about the events to come in this scene?

   (1) Fulfillment
   (2) Foreboding
   (3) Love
   (4) Terror
   (5) Amusement

Check your answers on page 89.

UNIT 2: UNDERSTANDING COMEDY AND TRAGEDY

Many plays are categorized as either comedies or tragedies. In a **tragedy,** a major character may suffer great misfortune or ruin, especially as a result of a choice he or she has made. Often the tragic choice involves a moral weakness. Tragedies are designed to evoke strong feelings of sadness and empathy in the audience.

A **comedy** is intended to amuse. It may be lighthearted or hilarious and it usually has a happy ending. Humor is used for many reasons; to break up the tension and conflict in drama, to reveal a character's personality, or to make an audience more receptive to the ideas being presented. Humor is also an important part of life, and drama is usually meant to remind us of elements of our own lives.

Two kinds of comedy are farce and satire. A **farce** contains humorous characterizations and improbable plots. For example, in a farce, two women might dress as men and never be recognized as women. A **satire** makes fun of human characteristics (such as pride or jealousy) or failings (such as being unable to communicate with one's children or being a fool for love). Irony and clever language are often used in satire. In both farce and satire, the characters and their actions are exaggerated to make the drama more entertaining and as a comment on society.

In a comedy, the characters are usually broad, simple types, with little complexity. This is because, in the humorous depiction of life, people are not very complicated.

The characters in comedies are often "types," such as the all-knowing cab driver or bartender, the young lover, or the air-headed tour guide. Often, comic characters single-mindedly seek simple goals, such as a specific woman, food, or money. Just as clearly, their actions toward those goals, while sometimes deliberately disguised by comic confusion and misrepresentation by the playwright, are usually quite straightforward and predictable. A comedy will always have a predictably happy ending.

On the other hand, characters in a tragedy will often have complex and sometimes self-contradictory motives. That is because tragedy portrays peoples' innermost thoughts and feelings, which are usually confused, conflicted, motivated by a combination of values, and anything but straightforward.

In this way, tragic characters seek to reflect what goes on in real life, in real people. The characters are frequently well-rounded and complex, as compared to comic characters, which are often straightforward and flat.

But writers of tragedies want their plays to be effective and their points to be made, so there are usually limits as to how complicated tragic characters will be. A character may be troubled by two or three conflicting motivations, but that is usually about it, although in real life, inner conflict can, and usually does, get much more complicated than that.

In some cases, a tragic character may believe himself to be single-minded, and actually be wracked with an inner conflict. This is often revealed near the end of the play, where the character may gain insight into his conflict, or another character may reveal it, and this can even illuminate for the character the tragic nature of his situation.

EXERCISE 1

Directions: Items 1–4 refer to the following passage. As you read, look for universal themes and situations. Then answer the questions.

What Past Problems Do Lola and Doc Discuss?

Line   Lola: You were so nice and so proper, Doc; I thought nothing we could do together could ever be wrong—or make us unhappy. Do you think we did wrong, Doc?

  Doc: (*consoling*) No, Baby, of course I don't.

5   Lola: I don't think anyone knows about it except my folks, do you?

  Doc: Of course not, Baby.

  Lola: (*follows him in*) I wish the baby had lived, Doc. . . . If we'd gone to a doctor, she would have lived, don't you think?

  Doc: Perhaps. . . . We were just kids. Kids don't know how to look after things.

10   Lola: (*sits on couch*) If we'd had the baby she'd be a young girl now; and then maybe you'd have saved your money, Doc, and she could be going to college—like Marie.

  Doc: Baby, what's done is done.

  Lola: It must make you feel bad at times to think you had to give up being a doctor
15   and to think you don't have any money like you used to.

  Doc: No . . . no, Baby. We should never feel bad about what's past. What's in the past can't be helped. You . . . you've got to forget it and live for the present. If you can't forget the past, you stay in it and never get out.

—From *Come Back, Little Sheba* by William Inge

1. Based on Doc's words in lines 17–19, with which of the following proverbs would he be most likely to agree?

    (1)   Waste not, want not.
    (2)   A stitch in time saves nine.
    (3)   Count your pennies.
    (4)   Don't cry over spilled milk.
    (5)   Little wealth, little care.

2. Which of the following would be the best title for this passage?

    (1)   "A Happy Marriage"
    (2)   "Secrets of the Past"
    (3)   "Saving for College"
    (4)   "How to be a Good Doctor"
    (5)   "A Scary Future"

3. Which of the following best describes the tone of this conversation?

    (1)   Whining
    (2)   Bitter
    (3)   Challenging
    (4)   Apologetic
    (5)   Understanding

4. What does the dialogue between Lola and Doc suggest about their relationship?

    (1)   It is strained and awkward.
    (2)   They enjoy being silly together.
    (3)   It is a close, loving relationship.
    (4)   Everything they say and do seems rehearsed.
    (5)   It is full of frustration.

Check your answers on page 90.

EXERCISE 2

Directions: Items 1–4 refer to the following passage. See if you can pick up the emotions being expressed. Then answer the questions.

Is This Really About Music?

Line   HAMLET: Will you play on this pipe?

GUILDENSTERN: My lord, I cannot.

      HAMLET: I pray you.

GUILDENSTERN: Believe me, I cannot.

5   HAMLET: I do beseech you.

GUILDENSTERN: I know no touch of it, my lord.

      HAMLET: It is as easy as lying. Govern these ventages with your fingers and thumb, give it breath with your mouth, and it will discourse most eloquent music. Look you, these are the stops.

10 GUILDENSTERN: But these cannot I command to any utt'rance of harmony. I have not the skill.

      HAMLET: Why, look you now, how unworthy a thing you make of me! You would play upon me, you would seem to know my stops, you would pluck out the heart of my mystery, you would sound
15   me from my lowest note to the top of my compass; and there is much music, excellent voice, in this little organ, yet cannot you make it speak. 'Sblood, do you think I am easier to be played on than a pipe? Call me what instrument you will, though you can fret me, you cannot play upon me.

—From *Hamlet* by William Shakespeare

1. Why does Hamlet ask Guildenstern to play on the pipe?

    (1)   To make a point
    (2)   To hear nice music
    (3)   To improve Guidenstern's abilities
    (4)   Just to be mean
    (5)   As a joke

2. Hamlet's attitude here can best be described as

    (1)   sad.
    (2)   cheerful.
    (3)   lonely.
    (4)   angry.
    (5)   understanding.

3. In lines 12–19, Hamlet is saying:

    (1)   "this is fun; let's keep going with it."
    (2)   "a person is just like an instrument."
    (3)   "everybody should play the pipes."
    (4)   "you can do it if you try."
    (5)   "I'm onto your game, so stop it."

4. Hamlet sees Guildenstern as a

(1)   friend.
(2)   coworker.
(3)   boss.
(4)   professional.
(5)   spy.

Check your answers on page 90.

EXERCISE 3

Directions: Items 1–3 refer to the following passage. Look for clues that reinforce the mood of the play. Then answer the questions.

What is the Tone of These Words?

Line   CABMAN: Who's your friend?

   MALACHI: Friend!! That's not a friend; that's an employer I'm trying out for a few days.

   CABMAN: You won't like him.

5   MALACHI: I can see you're in business for yourself because you talk about liking employers. No one's ever liked an employer since business began.

   CABMAN: AW—!

   MALACHI: No, sir. I suppose you think *your horse* likes you?

   CABMAN: My old Clementine? She'd give her right feet for me.

10   MALACHI: That's what all employers think. You imagine it. The streets of New York are full of cab horses winking at one another. Let's go in the kitchen and get some whiskey. I can't push people into houses when I'm sober. No, I've had about fifty employers in my life, but this is the most employer of them all. He talks to everybody as though he were
15   paying them.

   CABMAN: I had an employer once. He watched me from eight in the morning until six at night—just sat there and watched me. Oh, dear! Even my mother didn't think I was as interesting as that. (*CABMAN exits through service door*)

20   MALACHI: (*Following him off*) Yes, being employed is like being loved: you know that somebody's thinking about you the whole time.

   —From *The Matchmaker* by Thornton Wilder

1. The mood expressed in this passage would best be described as

(1)   hateful.
(2)   tearful.
(3)   delight.
(4)   charitable.
(5)   comic.

2. How does Malachi feel about employers?

(1) He finds them helpful.
(2) He doesn't like them.
(3) He serves them with pleasure.
(4) He has no opinion.
(5) He thinks they're interesting.

3. In lines 8–11, the Cabman and Malachi

(1) express differing viewpoints.
(2) show their love for horses.
(3) are in complete agreement.
(4) ask Clementine what she thinks.
(5) praise their employers highly.

Check your answers on page 91.

EXERCISE 4

Directions: Items 1–4 refer to the following passage. Use the tone of the dialogue to try to understand what the passage is expressing. Then answer the questions.

What is the Point Being Made?

Line	FIRST VISITOR:	Isn't he wonderful!
	GUIDE:	Forty-five minutes after he finishes a novel we have it printed and assembled and on its way to the movie men.
	FIRST VISITOR:	May we talk to him?
5	GUIDE:	Certainly.
	FIRST VISITOR:	*(To the Novelist)* I've enjoyed your novels very much.
	NOVELIST:	Thank you.
	FIRST VISITOR:	I see you're writing a new one.
	NOVELIST:	Of course. I'm under contract.
10	FIRST VISITOR:	What's that?*(Indicating the book in the Novelist's hand)*
	NOVELIST:	It's my last one.
	FIRST VISITOR:	But weren't you just dictating from it, for your new one?
	NOVELIST:	Yes. They like it that way.
15	GUIDE:	Under the old system they wrote it all new each time. Here—let the gentleman have it as a souvenir.
	FIRST VISITOR:	*(Reading the title)* "Eternal Love." What's your new one called?
	NOVELIST:	"Love Eternal."

—From *Beggar on Horseback* by George S. Kaufman and Marc Connelly

1. The tone of this passage is

   (1) tragic.
   (2) satirical.
   (3) blissful.
   (4) fearful.
   (5) analytic.

2. The passage is intended as

   (1) a statement of admiration for the novelist.
   (2) a description of how movie scripts are written.
   (3) an instruction for guides in companies.
   (4) a condemnation of a way of doing business.
   (5) an explanation of a highly efficient system.

3. In lines 14–15, the passage is pointing out

   (1) the result of a faulty process.
   (2) that a book's title is important.
   (3) that most novels say the same thing.
   (4) the cleverness of the novelist.
   (5) that the novelist is an artist.

4. The passage uses what technique to get its point across?

   (1) Shock
   (2) Horror
   (3) Humor
   (4) Romance
   (5) Repetition

ANSWERS AND EXPLANATIONS
UNIT 1: THE WORLD OF DRAMA

Exercise 1 *(page 75)*

What Brings These Characters Together?

1. **The correct answer is (3). (Literal comprehension)** According to line 1, "a few pale stars" are shining, so choice (5) is incorrect. The fact that Guicho enters over a dune (line 4) suggests a desert or desert-like setting, thus eliminating the other choices.

2. **The correct answer is (4). (Inferential comprehension)** These stage directions call for Calorías to confront Guicho, laugh at him, and then put his hands on Guicho's cello. These actions—especially when added to his words at this point—show his pleasure at causing Guicho distress. There is no evidence for the other choices.

Exercise 2 *(page 76)*

Why Do These Characters Disagree?

1. **The correct answer is (4). (Literal comprehension)** Cory's perspective, or opinion, is that he will be able to play football and continue working on the weekends. The clearest statement of this is in lines 7–8. There is no evidence for the other choices.

2. **The correct answer is (1). (Literal comprehension)** Troy's perspective is that football is not practical and won't make Cory a success. In lines 17–18 Troy states, "The white man ain't gonna let you get nowhere with that football no way." There is no evidence for the other choices.

3. **The correct answer is (4). (Inferential comprehension)** Statements such as, "You damn right you are! Ain't no need for nobody coming around here to talk to me about signing nothing" (lines 14–15) show that Troy is a strict parent. Choice (5) states the opposite. Cruel is too strong a word to describe Troy, so choice (3) is incorrect. Troy may be sympathetic sometimes, but not in this situation, so choice (1) can be eliminated. Troy may be trying to pass along wise advice, as choice (2) suggests, but his emotion undercuts his wisdom.

4. **The correct answer is (5). (Inferential comprehension)** The passage does not resolve what Cory will choose to do. All the other choices describe information that is directly stated or strongly suggested in the passage.

Exercise 3 *(page 77)*

What Do the Characters Understand?

1. **The correct answer is (2). (Synthesis)** Tanner appears to be completely blind to Miss Whitefield's attraction to him, though Straker can see this clearly. Tanner asks Straker if Straker is playing the fool, while the fool here is really Tanner himself.

2. **The correct answer is (4). (Analysis)** In lines 16–17, Straker, who makes it absolutely clear to Tanner that Miss Whitefield has her eyes on Tanner, sees Tanner as a marked down victim.

3. **The correct answer is (5). (Comprehension)** By having Tanner portray himself as the "marked down victim" and "the destined prey" in line 15, the playwright is expressing the viewpoint that it is the woman who calls the shots in man-woman relationships. It is the woman who hunts down and captures the man, her "victim."

4. **The correct answer is (1). (Synthesis)** Judging by his pronounced dialect, it appears as though Straker has much less formal education than Tanner. However, the passage reveals that Straker knows a great deal more than Tanner about human relationships. Tanner had no idea that Miss Whitefield had her sights set on him, while Straker could see this perfectly.

Exercise 4 *(page 79)*

What Is the Real Problem?

1. **The correct answer is (4). (Comprehension)** It is clear from what Howard says that he does not believe that Willy is valuable to the company. Howard is focused on the people he must talk to right now, not on any promises his father may have made to Willy, or on how big a year Willy had in 1928.

2. **The correct answer is (2). (Comprehension)** Howard openly contradicts Willy's claim that Willy averaged $170 a week in commissions in 1928. Howard's attitude throughout the rest of the passage also shows us that Howard is not inclined to accept any positive statements at all about Willy.

3. **The correct answer is (3). (Comprehension)** Willy is pleading for recognition from Howard not only for his long service with the firm but also for his dignity as a human being. He is saying that, even if he isn't that great at his job, he is still a man, and "a man is not a piece of fruit" whose peel you just throw away.

4. **The correct answer is (5). (Analysis)** In line 5, Howard is "starting to go off" and in line 13, he speaks "impatiently." These are the actions of someone who is uncomfortable being where he is and who wants very much to be elsewhere. In this case, Howard does not want to think about giving Willy $40 a week, and the more Willy implores him to listen, the more Howard wants to be somewhere else.

Exercise 5 *(page 80)*

What Is About To Happen?

1. **The correct answer is (3). (Analysis)** The fire is nearly burnt out and approaching its end. There is no hint of any attempt at building a new fire or of wood being available for that.

2. **The correct answer is (4). (Analysis)** Mrs. Elvstead is wrapped in a shawl, sitting close to the stove. Hedda is fully dressed with a blanket over her. These two characters are cold in this room.

3. **The correct answer is (2). (Synthesis)** All of the details of this setting—the dying fire, the closely wrapped-up people—tell of a cool, unwelcoming place. One cannot expect much loving and good to come in this scene. On the contrary, it is very possible that something bad may happen.

UNIT 2: UNDERSTANDING COMEDY AND TRAGEDY

Exercise 1 *(page 82)*

What Past Problems Do Lola and Doc Discuss?

1. **The correct answer is (4). (Application)** Doc believes that "what's in the past can't be helped" (lines 17–18)—a good restatement of the proverb about spilled milk. Choices (1), (2), and (3) apply to being frugal and efficient, not to thoughts about the past. The passage indicates that Doc and Lola do not have a lot of money, as choice (5) suggests, but that choice can be eliminated because they have seen a good bit of care in the past.

2. **The correct answer is (2). (Inferential comprehension)** Lola and Doc are discussing secret events in their past. They seem to have a good marriage, but these memories are sad, so choice (1) is not the best answer. Doc "had to give up being a doctor . . ." (lines 15–16), but they do not discuss this profession, so choice (4) is incorrect. References to college and the future do not suggest ways to succeed, so choices (4) and (5) are not logical.

3. **The correct answer is (5). (Analysis)** The stage direction in line 4 indicates that Doc is "consoling." Lola refers to how Doc must feel at times because he had to give up being a doctor and doesn't have the money he once had (lines 15–16). Both try to be understanding. Doc affectionately refers to Lola as "Baby." Neither whines, so choice (1) is incorrect. Although Lola has regrets (lines 7–8), there is no indication that either she or Doc is bitter, so choice (2) is incorrect. There are no challenges or apologies, so choices (3) and (4) are incorrect.

4. **The correct answer is (3). (Analysis)** Doc and Lola discuss their past problems in a loving manner. She asks him what he thinks (lines –3, 5, and 7–8). He calls her "Baby," consoles her (lines 4, 6, and 14), and encourages her to "live for the present" (lines 18–19). There is no evidence for choices (1) and (4). Although Doc calls Lola "Baby," there is no indication of their acting silly together, so choice (2) is incorrect. They are discussing past problems. There is no evidence that their current relationship is full of frustration, so choice (5) is incorrect.

Exercise 2 *(page 84)*

Is This Really About Music?

1. **The correct answer is (1). (Comprehension)** Hamlet is making his point by giving Guildenstern a bit of his own treatment. Hamlet says that Guildenstern is trying to play Hamlet like an instrument by trying to pry information out of Hamlet, so why shouldn't Guildenstern play the pipe for Hamlet in return?

2. **The correct answer is (4). (Comprehension)** In lines 17–18, Hamlet accuses Guildenstern outright of thinking that Hamlet is "easier to be played on than a pipe." Then he goes on to say, no matter what type of instrument you think I am, "you cannot play upon me." This is anger.

3. **The correct answer is (5). (Comprehension)** Hamlet makes it clear in these lines that he fully understands what Guildenstern has been trying to do, which is to decipher what Hamlet is thinking and feeling. Hamlet tells him it won't work, so Guildenstern may as well quit it.

4. **The correct answer is (5). (Comprehension)** Hamlet believes that Guildenstern is trying to gather information about what Hamlet is thinking. Though Hamlet's words seem to be friendly banter at first, he quickly switches to a stern and angry tone at the end. Hamlet's little verbal deception is meant to match Guildenstern's deception in trying to get information from Hamlet without telling him he's doing so.

Exercise 3 *(page 85)*

What Is the Tone of These Words?

1. **The correct answer is (5). (Synthesis)** The two characters are joking. It is a mood of friendly banter at the expense of employers. The tone of this passage is comic.

2. **The correct answer is (2). (Analysis)** Malachi has no kind words for employers. In line 6, he says that "No one's ever liked an employer since business began." That pretty much sums up Malachi's feelings about employers as well.

3. **The correct answer is (1). (Analysis)** In these lines, the Cabman believes that his horse, Clementine, adores him. However, Malachi considers the Cabman as Clementine's employer, and envisions that all the cab horses on the streets of New York are pretending to love their owners but are making fun of them in secret.

Exercise 4 *(page 86)*

What Is the Point Being Made?

1. **The correct answer is (2). (Comprehension)** This passage is a satire on the business practice of creating art on an assembly line.

2. **The correct answer is (4). (Comprehension)** By showing that the efficiency of business, when it is in total control, can totally suppress the art of novel-writing, the passage brings this damaging process to its logical extension: a novel that is different from its predecessor only in that the words are in reverse order.

3. **The correct answer is (1). (Comprehension)** The passage expresses that, when a faulty system of so-called "business efficiency" is imposed on the creative process, the result is a faulty product.

4. **The correct answer is (3). (Comprehension)** The playwrights effectively criticize the practice they abhor by making fun of it. By using humor to ridicule the object of their venom, they invite the audience to come over to their side and laugh with them at the practice they condemn.

GLOSSARY

comedy: drama that is intended to amuse through its lighthearted approach and happy ending

conflict: a clash of ideas, attitudes, or forces

dialogue: a conversation between characters

drama: a play that can be read or performed

farce: a comedy that contains humorous characterizations and improbable plots

foreshadowing: a technique used to suggest what will happen later

monologue: a long and often emotional speech by one character, often revealing important feelings or events, when another character is present

playwright: the author of a drama

satire: a comedy that makes fun of human characteristics or failings

stage directions: information that describes the stage setting and the movements of the characters in a drama

tragedy: drama that ends in great misfortune or ruin for a major character, especially when a moral issue is involved

Nonfiction

Nonfiction is factual writing about real people, places, and events. Four types of nonfiction passages may be included on the GED: business documents, visual arts, information text, and literary nonfiction. This section will define each of these types and their key features. The exercises will include examples of each type of nonfiction you are likely to encounter on the GED Test.

UNIT 1: BUSINESS DOCUMENTS

When you are working or looking for a job, you read many different types of business documents: employee handbooks, training manuals, and instructions, to name just a few. Business documents are similar to information texts in that you read them to obtain information, but they are different in one key way. When you read a business document, you are looking for specific rules and procedures to follow. For example, a business document may tell you how to apply for a job, how to apply for college, or how to use a word-processing program. Business documents are rule-oriented and organized so that you can find key information easily. They are considered **information text**.

INFORMATION TEXT

Information text is factual material that you read to obtain information. Examples are textbooks, training manuals, and the book you are reading right now. When you read informational text, you are looking for facts and for ways to organize them in a logical way. Each type of information text has a specific purpose, which may be to present information in such a way that the reader is persuaded to take some action or to teach the reader how to do something.

Distinguishing Fact from Opinion

When you read informational text, you should always read critically to separate the author's opinion from facts. In most cases, information text contains a combination of facts and opinions. A **fact** is something that can be proved beyond the point of reasonable argument. For example, "John F. Kennedy was elected President of the United States in 1960" is a fact that can be verified. In contrast, "John F. Kennedy was a great president" is an opinion. Evidence could be produced either to support or deny this statement, and reasonable people might well disagree about whether it is true or false.

Identifying Perspective

A **perspective** is the standpoint from which a person views something. Because your life experiences are different from everyone else's, your perspective will be different as well. When you read, try to identify the perspective of the writer. For example, evaluate the language the writer uses to determine if he or she views the topic favorably. Think about how the language would be different if he or she held a different perspective.

ROAD MAP

- *Business Documents*
- *Visual Information*
- *Glossary*

Cause and Effect

Information text makes frequent use of cause-and-effect relationships. This means that one event (the cause) leads to another event (the effect). Asking questions about why something happens, requiring you to state the cause, often tests knowledge of cause-and-effect relationships.

EXERCISE 1

Directions: Items 1–3 refer to the following informational passage. It comes from the Web site of the Carnegie Institution, a scientific organization in Washington, D.C. As you read the passage, think about the kinds of information it contains and how you can organize this information in your mind so that you can use it most effectively.

What is the Carnegie Institution of Washington?

Line   The Carnegie Institution of Washington, a private, nonprofit organization engaged in basic research and advanced education in biology, astronomy, and the earth sciences, was founded by Andrew Carnegie in 1902 and incorporated by an Act of Congress in 1904. Mr. Carnegie, who provided an initial endowment of $10 million and later gave
5   additional millions, conceived the Institution's purpose "to encourage, in the broadest and most liberal manner, investigation, research, and discovery, and the application of knowledge to the improvement of mankind."

From its earliest years, the Carnegie Institution has been a pioneering research organization, devoted to a field of inquiry that its trustees and staff consider among the
10   most significant in the development of science and scholarship. Its funds are used primarily to support investigations at its own research departments. Recognizing that fundamental research is closely related to the development of outstanding young scholars, the Institution conducts a strong program of advanced education at the predoctoral and postdoctoral levels. Carnegie also conducts distinctive programs for
15   elementary school teachers and children in Washington, D.C. At First Light, a Saturday "hands-on" science school, elementary school students explore worlds within and around them. At summer sessions of the Carnegie Academy for Science Education, elementary school teachers learn interactive techniques of science teaching.

—from the Web site of the Carnegie Institution of Washington

1. According to the passage, the Carnegie Institution's two main functions are

    (1) research and education.
    (2) fundraising and investigation.
    (3) science and scholarship.
    (4) education for teachers and students.
    (5) summer school and Saturday science school.

2. From whose perspective is this passage written?

    (1) Andrew Carnegie's
    (2) A Carnegie Institute employee's
    (3) A jobseeker's
    (4) A student's
    (5) The Carnegie Institute's

3. According to the passage, First Light is a program for

   (1)   elementary school teachers.
   (2)   elementary school students.
   (3)   predoctoral students.
   (4)   postdoctoral students.
   (5)   scientists.

Check your answers on page 130.

EXERCISE 2

Directions: Items 1–4 are based on the following business document, an excerpt from a college admissions guide. Read the passage carefully for information on how to enroll as a student at Lee College. Then answer the questions.

How Do I Become A Student at Lee College?

Admission & Registration

Steps to Enroll

NEW STUDENTS

The state requires the College to charge tuition at the out-of-state rate for students who have resided in Texas less than a year. Out-of-state students must sign an oath if their intent is to become a permanent resident of Texas. Such students will be reclassified as in-state for tuition purposes after one year has elapsed. Proof of residence is also required for in-district status.

Apply for Admission
Obtain New Student Information Card.
Admission & Records Office,
Moler Hall.

Have transcripts sent to Lee College
Arrange for official high school transcripts or GED grade report to be sent to Lee College.

Students transferring from another college must have official transcripts mailed directly to the Lee College Admissions and Records Office or brought in an envelope sealed by the institution. Students who are unable to obtain transcripts prior to submitting their application for admission will be given 2-3 weeks to complete their admissions file.

Apply for Financial Aid
Moler Hall. Refer to page 7 for details.

See a Counselor
Bring New Student Information Card to Counseling Center.
Arrange for TASP *and/or* Placement testing in Counseling. (See pages 8-9.)

Attend New Student Orientation Rundell Hall, July 21 from 8:30 a.m. to 12:00 p.m. See page 16 or inquire in Counseling Center for alternate dates.

Register for classes
Register for classes. See **Registration Options & Payment Deadlines** *on pages 5 & 6.*

Pay Tuition & Fees
If you have financial aid, go to the Financial Aid Office in Moler Hall to process payment. Otherwise pay in Rundell Hall at cashier window. See pages 11-14 for details.

Buy Books
Either online at
www.leecollegebooks.com or in Moler Hall Bookstore. See page 15.

Student Identification Cards
Required for all students. To obtain or update a Lee College ID card after classes start, you will need your paid receipt & a photo ID. During on-campus registration, ID photos can be made in Moler Hall. After on-campus registration IDs will be made at the Library Circulation Desk. During the first week of classes, IDs will be made during regular Library hours. After that, IDs will only be made on Tuesdays and Wednesdays from 10:30-11 :30 a.m. and from 6:30-7:30 p.m. or on Saturdays from Noon-1 p.m. IDs will be made on demand if required to check out Library materials.

1. The author's purpose in writing this passage is to

   (1) persuade students to attend Lee College.
   (2) inform students about programs at Lee College.
   (3) tell students how to apply for financial aid.
   (4) explain admissions procedures at Lee College.
   (5) give student regulations at Lee College.

2. According to the passage, where would you obtain a New Student Information Card?

   (1) Moler Hall Bookstore
   (2) Rundell Hall
   (3) The Counseling Center
   (4) The Library Circulation Desk
   (5) The Admissions and Record Office

3. According to the passage, how many ways of buying books are there?

   (1) 1
   (2) 2
   (3) 3
   (4) 4
   (5) 5

4. It is important to submit proof of residency because students who do not live in the local area

   (1) may not attend Lee College.
   (2) require higher grades to be admitted.
   (3) pay higher tuition.
   (4) must live in on-campus housing.
   (5) must apply for admission in person.

Check your answers on page 130.

EXERCISE 3

Directions: Items 1–3 are based on an excerpt from an employee handbook. Read the passage carefully, and then answer the questions.

How is the Performance of Hourly Employees Evaluated?

Line Hourly staff employees are asked annually to complete a self-appraisal form by April 30th of each year. At the same time the hourly employee receives the self-appraisal form, his/her supervisor will receive a performance appraisal form. These forms are to be filled out by the hourly employee and the supervisor and then discussed.

5   Performance evaluations and supervisory recommendations are to be discussed individually and privately with each Employee. The evaluation is then forwarded to the appropriate Vice President for final decisions regarding a merit increase. Employees are to receive a copy of the evaluation and recommendations and may make written comments regarding their evaluation for inclusion in their personnel

10   files.

      Supervisors will provide additional evaluation opportunities within the first year of an hourly staff member's employment. The initial evaluation, along with continued support and training, provides the best opportunity for successful performance on the part of new hourly staff members, as well as providing adequate information for

15   informed personnel decisions.

—from Personnel Policies and Procedures, Cardinal Stritch University

1. How often do employees complete a self-appraisal form?

   (1) Each week
   (2) Each month
   (3) Every six months
   (4) Each year
   (5) Every two years

2. After the employee and the supervisor fill out their appraisal forms, what is the next step in the evaluation?

   (1) The employee and supervisor discuss the two appraisal forms.
   (2) The supervisor discusses the appraisals with the Vice President.
   (3) The appraisals are sent to the Vice President.
   (4) The employee meets with the Vice President.
   (5) The Vice President decides on the employee's merit increase.

3. Suppose that an employee who has been on the job for three months is not performing as well as expected. What would the supervisor most likely do first?

   (1) Contact the appropriate Vice President and ask to begin a formal evaluation
   (2) Warn the employee
   (3) Fire the employee
   (4) Make a complaint in writing
   (5) Complete an appraisal form and have the employee complete a self-appraisal

Check your answers on page 130.

EXERCISE 4

Directions: Items 1–4 refer to the Web site for Clark College that explains the procedure for international student admission. Read the following information carefully. Then answer the questions.

How do International Students Enroll at Clark College?

International Student Admission

- Message from the President
- New Student Tips
- International Students/Programs
- International Student Admission Application
- Physician Statement
- Affidavit of Support
- Tuition & Fees
- Admissions Exceptions

The college will accept a limited number of international students. To be eligible for admission, you must complete an appropriate preparatory program in your own country, demonstrate competence in the use of the English language, be able to pay the cost of study at the college and give evidence of the ability to succeed in study at Clark College.

Requirements

The Test of English as a Foreign Language (TOEFL) is required of candidates from countries in which English is not the language in general use. Students achieving a score below 520 on the written test, or 200 on the computerized test, will be required to take English as a Non-Native Language classes prior to enrolling in academic classes numbered 100 or above.

Proof of financial security is required of international students. The college reserves the right to require that you place on deposit with the college enough money to ensure payment of educational expenses for one year.

A report of physical examination (using forms acceptable to the college) must be submitted within two weeks of the start of the quarter. Successful applicants must purchase the college-approved health insurance while enrolled at the college.

Prospective students must also submit the following:

- International Student Admission Application
- Physician Statement
- Affidavit of Support
- Official transcripts from previous schooling, including high school and any other colleges, translated into English.

Students transferring from another U.S. college or university must submit the following:

- Verification from the current school showing the student has maintained immigration status and is eligible to transfer.

• A copy of the student's I-20 form from the current school.

You are required to successfully complete a minimum of 12 credit hours per quarter with a minimum GPA of 2.00. If this requirement is not met, you will be out of status with the Immigration and Naturalization Service and may be subject to dismissal from the college

Visas

Clark College issues an I-20 to admitted students. This form can be used to obtain a F-1 or M-1 Visa. For additional information, see the International Students/Programs section.

Clark College
1800 E. McLoughlin Blvd
Vancouver, WA 98663-3598
360-992-2000

1. Based on information in the passage, which one of the following candidates would be required to take the Test of English as a Foreign Language (TOEFL) to enroll at Clark College?

   (1) A student from Australia
   (2) A student from England
   (3) A student from France
   (4) None of the three students would be required to take the TOEFL
   (5) All of the three students would be required to take the TOEFL

2. Based on information in the passage, which of the following candidates would need to take English as a Non-Native Language classes before enrolling in courses numbered 100 or above?

   (1) Only a student from Nigeria who scored 521 on the written TOEFL test
   (2) Only a student from Italy who scored 199 on the computerized TOEFL test
   (3) Only a student from Japan who scored 200 on the written TOEFL test
   (4) Both the student from Italy who scored 199 on the computerized TOEFL test and the student from Japan who scored 200 on the written TOEFL test
   (5) Both the student from Nigeria who scored 521 on the written TOEFL test and the student from Italy who scored 199 on the computerized TOEFL test

3. According to the passage, what is Clark College's policy concerning proof of financial security?

   (1) The college reserves the right to require that all American and international students place on deposit with the college the sum of one year's educational expenses.
   (2) The college reserves the right to require that all international students place on deposit with the college the sum of one year's educational expenses.
   (3) The college requires that all international students place on deposit with the college the sum of one year's educational expenses.
   (4) The college reserves the right to require that all international students place on deposit with the college the sum of two year's educational expenses.
   (5) The college never requires that students place on deposit with the college a sum for educational expenses.

4. Which of the following is NOT required for all international students to submit when applying to Clark College?

(1) Affidavit of support
(2) Official transcripts from previous schooling
(3) International student admission application
(4) Physician statement
(5) A copy of the student's I-20 form

Check your answers on page 131.

Analogy

Writers sometimes illustrate and clarify their points through the use of **analogy**: the extended comparison of things of different kinds. The choice of a comparison can make a significant difference in how the primary topic is viewed. For example, comparing job performance to running a race creates a different effect than comparing job performance to solving a math equation. Comparing a boss to a snake evokes a different image than comparing a boss to a teddy bear. An awareness of analogies and their impact can help to improve reading comprehension.

EXERCISE 5

Directions: Items 1–4 are based on a textbook on sales techniques. Read the passage carefully for information on the "five steps to a sale."

What are the Five Steps to a Sale?

Line   There are five steps through which the salesman must lead the prospective customer in making a sale: (1) gaining attention, (2) arousing interest, (3) building desire, (4) winning conviction, and (5) getting action.

       1. *Gaining attention.* It is obvious that you cannot begin selling until you have
5   the attention of your prospect. The door-to-door salesman appreciates this fact most, since in many cases he cannot finish his opening sentence before the door closes! Attention is gained when a prospective customer is aware that he needs something. The prospect's attention may already have been drawn to the product through an advertisement while the prospect was leisurely reading a magazine, watching a
10 television program, or listening to the radio. Often, however, the salesman must win attention; and he can do so by using a prompt approach, giving a friendly introduction, or having a courteous and businesslike manner. Or he can win attention by doing or saying something unusual.

       2. *Arousing interest.* Interest is aroused by getting the prospect to appreciate
15 fully his need for the product. This step in the sales process, like gaining attention, may have taken place already in the prospect's home or at some time before he has even seen a salesman. If not, it will be necessary for the salesman to arouse the prospect's interest. To accomplish this, the salesman may need to try several different approaches.

20   For example, if the safety features and smart styling of an electric range are being demonstrated and the prospect seems obviously unmoved, the salesman has failed as yet to arouse interest. At this point, he might mention the automatic controls that turn off the heat at a designated time, leaving the customer free to go shopping while the dinner is cooking; or he might mention the even-temperature cooking that
25 lessens the danger of scorching food (a feature he knows many older stoves lack). He

watches for signs of interest and proceeds from one feature to another until he is sure
he has that interest.

    3. *Building desire.* The salesman must build a desire for the prospect to own the
product before he can hope to make a sale. The desire may be built by stressing such
30 qualities as beauty, timesaving features, smartness of design, durability, or economy.
The prospect must want to own the product, or he will not buy it no matter how much
he may be interested in what the salesman tells him about it. If a man has become
interested in a salesman's presentation of a riding-type power lawn mower, he will
purchase it only if the salesman can pinpoint the features that will make him want to
35 own it. It may be the laborsaving features, the fact that his neighbor has one, or merely
an interest in mechanical features.

    4. *Winning conviction.* The prospect may have a desire to own the product, but
often he still needs to be convinced that yours will fit his needs best. At the
"conviction stage" the salesman must be prepared to back up his statements with
40 facts—facts about the advantages claimed for the product, how it measures up to other
products, why it is a smart buy, how easy it is to own, and so on. This is where the
salesman emphasizes the features that aroused the prospect's desire in the first place.

    5. *Getting action.* Even though the prospect may be convinced that a product
will suit him perfectly and he has the desire to own it, he still may not act. The
45 salesman must help him make the decision to buy.

        —John W. Ernest and George M. DaVall, *Salesmanship Fundamentals*

1. The same textbook later states that the sales expert Richard C. Borden draws an
analogy between the function of a match and that of a sales presentation: "Study a
match and what do you see? The tip is made of phosphorus so that it will light at the
first scratch. Right below the tip is the sulfur. The sulfur converts the flash from the
phosphorus into a flame that ignites the main fuel, or wooden shaft, of the match. The
wooden shaft is coated with paraffin so that the match can burn long enough to do its
job, which is to light a fire."

Based on information in the passage, which part of a sales presentation is comparable
to the sulfur stage?

  (1)   Gaining attention
  (2)   Arousing interest
  (3)   Building desire
  (4)   Winning conviction
  (5)   Getting action

2. This passage seems dated because of the use of

  (1)   "salesman."
  (2)   five steps instead of six steps.
  (3)   italicized headings.
  (4)   five steps instead of four steps.
  (5)   "prospect."

3. A salesperson has interested a customer in a particular make of automobile by pointing out its safety features, low price, and stylish look. Now the salesperson provides statistics to demonstrate the safety, economical gas mileage, and popularity of the car. Based on information in the passage, which stage of the sales process is the salesperson at?

   (1) Gaining attention
   (2) Arousing interest
   (3) Building desire
   (4) Winning conviction
   (5) Getting action

Check your answers on page 131.

UNIT 2: VISUAL INFORMATION

Many nonfictional texts have a strong visual component—that is, they rely on detailed descriptions to convey information to the reader. Examples of nonfiction works that include much descriptive information are reviews about art, theater, and film; history books; art books; and works about nature. Even science books can have a strong visual component; for example, a science book or article might describe an experiment, piece of apparatus, animal, or plant in great detail. When you read descriptive text, you should attempt to visualize the scene being described in your mind's eye. This will allow you to understand how the parts relate to the whole and, in general, to understand the author's meaning.

INTERPRETING COMMENTS ON THE VISUAL ARTS

Visual arts include painting, photography, sculpture, and architecture. People enjoy visual arts because such works show them something new about themselves or society.

Some basic information that appears in comments, such as reviews or textbooks, about the visual arts, includes

- the title of the work of art and the name of the artist;
- where the work can be seen;
- the reviewer's opinion; whether the work is of value, and why;
- and how the work was created.

EXERCISE 1

Directions: Items 1–6 refer to the following passage from an art textbook. As you read the passage, concentrate on the historical significance of the painting and the way that it is described.

Line   The lightning changes of style that characterize Picasso's post-Cubist work are too many to record here. Sometimes seemingly incompatible styles appear in the same painting. Sometimes Picasso's art had much in common with Surrealism, but his best-known work of this decade, and in many ways one of the most remarkable
5   pictures involving social protest, is *Guernica*. Picasso executed this mural, twenty-five feet long, to fulfill a commission for the pavilion of the Spanish Republican government at the Paris Exposition of 1937, while the Civil War was still going on in Spain. Intended as a protest against the destruction of the little Basque town of Guernica in April 1937 by Nazi bombers in the service of the Spanish Fascists, the
10   picture has become in retrospect a memorial to all the crimes against humanity in the twentieth century. The painting is not a literal narration in the tradition of Goya, which would have been foreign to Picasso's nature and principles, or even an easily legible array of symbols. As he worked, Picasso seems to have decided, perhaps even subconsciously, to combine images drawn from Christian iconography, such as the
15   Slaughter of the Innocents, with motifs from Spanish folk culture, especially the bullfight, and from his own past. Actual destruction is reduced to fragmentary glimpses of walls and tiled roofs and to flames shooting from a burning house at the right. A bereft mother rushes screaming from the building, her arms thrown wide. Agonized heads and arms emerge from the wreckage. At the left a mother holding her
20   dead child looks upward, shrieking. The implacable bull above her, the adversary in Spanish popular experience, is surely related to the dread Minotaur, adopted by the Surrealists, as an embodiment of the irrational in man, for the title of their periodical in Paris, to which Picasso had contributed designs. If the bull then signifies the forces of Fascism, the dying horse, drawn also from the bullfight ritual, suggests the torment
25   of the Spanish people, and the oil lamp held above it the resistance of humanity against the mechanized eye, whose iris is an electric bulb. The spiritual message of combined terror and resistance is borne, unexpectedly, by Synthetic Cubist aesthetic means stripped of color. Black, white, and gray planes are composed into a giant pyramid, as if triumphant even in destruction.

—Frederick Hartt, *Art: A History of Painting, Sculpture, Architecture*

1. According to the passage, which statement most accurately describes Picasso's artistic style?

    (1) Picasso's style changed rapidly before he completed his Cubist works.
    (2) Picasso attempted to emulate Goya's style of literal narration.
    (3) Picasso's style was most influenced by Surrealism.
    (4) Picasso experimented with many different styles in his post-Cubist works.
    (5) Picasso's most important influence was Christian iconography.

2. According to the passage, what did Picasso intend his painting *Guernica* to express?

    (1) A memorial to all twentieth-century crimes against humanity
    (2) Support for the Spanish Fascists during the Spanish Civil War
    (3) A tribute to the Paris Exposition of 1937
    (4) A protest against the Nazi bombing of the town of Guernica
    (5) Support for the Basque movement

3. According to the passage, which emotions are most strongly conveyed in the painting?

    (1) Horror and defeat
    (2) Horror and resistance
    (3) Triumph and jubilation
    (4) Misery and apathy
    (5) Anger and cowardice

4. The reviewer's opinion of *Guernica* is best described as

    (1) respectful.
    (2) confused.
    (3) terrified.
    (4) critical.
    (5) disgusted.

5. Which sentence from the passage includes examples of symbolism?

    (1) "If the bull then signifies the forces of Fascism, the dying horse, drawn also from the bullfight ritual, suggests the torment of the Spanish people, and the oil lamp held above it the resistance of humanity against the mechanized eye, whose iris is an electric bulb."
    (2) "Sometimes seemingly incompatible styles appear in the same painting."
    (3) "The painting is not a literal narration in the tradition of Goya, which would have been foreign to Picasso's nature and principles, or even an easily legible array of symbols."
    (4) "At the left a mother holding her dead child looks upward, shrieking."
    (5) "Picasso executed this mural, twenty-five feet long, to fulfill a commission for the pavilion of the Spanish Republican government at the Paris exposition of 1937."

6. In the Spanish Civil War, Fascists led by Generalissimo Francisco Franco attacked Republican forces loyal to the newly elected government. Based on information in the passage, what side did Picasso support?

    (1) He was politically neutral.
    (2) He supported the Republican government.
    (3) He supported the Fascists.
    (4) He supported neither side.
    (5) He supported German intervention in the war.

Check your answers on page 132.

ALLUSIONS

Allusions are unacknowledged references that a work makes to other sources that relate to it. These older sources lend meaning to a work when used in a new context. It can help you to understand a text if you are aware of the allusions that the author is making and the way that they pertain to the text.

EXERCISE 2

Directions: Items 1–3 refer to the following movie review. Read the passage carefully, noting the allusions the reviewer refers to, and answer the following questions.

What is this Reviewer's Opinion?

Line   From the nursery to the boutique is now a very short path; "Yellow Submarine" travels with it with charm and ease. The Beatles, represented by cartoon, go to the rescue of the people of Pepperland and save them from the Blue Meanies, their weapons being (who'd have guessed it?) music and love—but what is so pleasant
5   about "Yellow Submarine" is its lighthearted, throwaway quality, and the story seems as disposable as the banter and the images. If the movie tried to be significant, if it had "something to say," it might be a disaster. One of the best characters is a gluttonous consumer with a vacuum snout, who devours the universe, yet the movie itself sucks up an incredible quantity of twentieth-century graphics. If "Yellow Submarine" were
10   not so good-natured and—despite all the "artistic" effects—unpretentious, one would be embarrassed; its chic style can't support much more than the message of "love." You could almost make a game of how many sources you can spot, but, because of the giddy flower-childishness of it all, this not only seems all right but rather adds to one's pleasure. The eclecticism is so open that it is in itself entertaining—we have the fun of
15   a series of recognitions. A little Nolde here, a bit of Klimt there, the hotel corridor from "The Blood of a Poet," with "The Mysteries of China" now become Indian, and good old Birnam Wood moving once again—it's like spotting the faces in Tchelitchew's "Cache-Cache."
            The movie is extravagantly full of visual puns and transformations, but not too
20   full (though there are places where one might wish for an extra instant to savor what is going by). The Beatles' non-singing voices are not their own, but they're good. The verbal jokes invite comparison with Edward Lear but can't sustain it. The movie seems to get its spirit back each time one of the Beatles' songs (sung by the Beatles) comes on (there are ten, three of them new), and this is not just because of the richer
25   verbal texture but because the animation, ingenious as it is, is not much more than a shifting series of illustrations. The movie works best when the images (even though they don't quite connect with the meaning of the lyrics) are choreographed to the music.

                              —Pauline Kael, "Metamorphosis of the Beatles," *Going Steady*

1. The reviewer refers to several allusions she found in *The Yellow Submarine*. For example, she points out that the film includes "a little Nolde here, a bit of Klimt there, the hotel corridor from 'The Blood of a Poet,' with 'The Mysteries of China' now become Indian, and good old Birnam Wood moving once again—it's like spotting the faces in Tchelitchew's 'Cache-Cache.'" In order to grasp the reviewer's point, it is helpful to have more information. For example, Emile Nolde was a German expressionist painter. Gustav Klimt was an Austrian painter. *The Blood of a Poet* is a fantasy film by Jean Cocteau. Birnam Wood appears to be moving in William Shakespeare's play *Macbeth* because soldiers are using the trees as camouflage. Tchelitchew was a Russian Surrealist artist who painted *Cache-Cache* (*Hide and Seek*), a picture with hidden faces in it. Which of the following statements best sums up the meaning of the reviewer's statement?

   (1) Recognizing the references to art, film and literature in *The Yellow Submarine* is like spotting the faces in the painting *Cache-Cache*.
   (2) *The Yellow Submarine* has too many distracting references to other works in it.
   (3) Tchelitchew's painting *Cache-Cache* has the faces of Nolde, Klimt, and Birnam Wood in it.
   (4) *The Yellow Submarine* should have included more original material.
   (5) Recognizing the references to astronomy, archeology, and psychology in *The Yellow Submarine* is like spotting the faces in the painting *Cache-Cache*.

2. Which of the following best sums up the reviewer's attitude toward the film?

   (1) *The Yellow Submarine* should be more serious in tone.
   (2) *The Yellow Submarine*'s lighthearted tone suits it.
   (3) *The Yellow Submarine* is too serious in tone.
   (4) *The Yellow Submarine*'s tone is uneven and hence confusing.
   (5) *The Yellow Submarine* fittingly has an uneven tone.

3. The reviewer says that in *The Yellow Submarine*, "The verbal jokes invite comparison with Edward Lear but can't sustain it." Edward Lear was a nineteenth-century writer and artist known for his humorous nonsense verses and limericks. What point is the reviewer making with her comparison?

   (1) *The Yellow Submarine*'s humor is not as clever as Lear's.
   (2) *The Yellow Submarine*'s humor is more suitable for a contemporary audience than Lear's.
   (3) *The Yellow Submarine*'s humor was strongly influenced by Lear.
   (4) *The Yellow Submarine*'s humor is cleverer than Lear's.
   (5) *The Yellow Submarine* should not have borrowed humorous effects from Lear.

Check your answers on page 132.

EXERCISE 3

Directions: Items 1–3 refer to the following excerpt from a 1941 movie review of *Citizen Kane*. As you read the passage, concentrate on what the reviewer has to say about the public reaction to the film as well as the film itself.

What is this Film About?

Line Within the withering spotlight as no other film has ever been before, Orson Welles's
Citizen Kane had its world premiere at the Palace last evening. And now that the
wraps are off, the mystery has been exposed, and Mr. Welles and the RKO directors
have taken the much-debated leap, it can be safely stated that suppression of this film
5   would have been a crime. For, in spite of some disconcerting lapses and strange
ambiguities in the creation of the principal character, Citizen Kane is far and away the
most surprising and cinematically exciting motion picture to be seen here in many a
moon. As a matter of fact, it comes close to being the most sensational film ever made
in Hollywood.

10   Count on Mr. Welles; he doesn't do things by halves. Being a mercurial fellow,
with a frightening theatrical flair, he moved right into the movies, grabbed the medium
by the ears, and began to toss it around with the dexterity of a seasoned veteran. Fact
is, he handled it with more verve and inspired ingenuity than any of the elder
craftsmen have exhibited in years. With the able assistance of Gregg Toland, whose
15   services should not be overlooked, he found in the camera the perfect instrument to
encompass his dramatic energies and absorb his prolific ideas. Upon the screen he
discovered an area large enough for his expansive whims to have free play. And the
consequence is that he has made a picture of tremendous and overpowering scope, not
in physical extent so much as in its rapid and graphic rotation of thoughts. Mr. Welles
20   has put upon the screen a motion picture that really moves.

             As for the story which he tells—and which has provoked such an uncommon
fuss—this corner frankly holds considerable reservation. Naturally we wouldn't know
how closely—if at all—it parallels the life of an eminent publisher, as has been
somewhat cryptically alleged. But that is beside the point in a rigidly critical appraisal.
25   The blamable circumstance is that it fails to provide a clear picture of the character
and motives behind the man about whom the whole thing revolves.

             As the picture opens, Charles Kane lies dying in the fabulous castle he has
built—the castle called Xanadu, in which he has surrounded himself with vast
treasures. And as death closes his eyes his heavy lips murmur one word, "Rosebud."
30   Suddenly the death scene is broken; the screen becomes alive with a staccato
March-of-Time-like news feature recounting the career of the dead man—how, as a
poor boy, he came into great wealth, how he became a newspaper publisher as a young
man, how he aspired to political office, was defeated because of a personal scandal,
devoted himself to material acquisition, and finally died.

1. The character of Charles Kane is patterned after the publishing mogul William Randolph Hearst, who used his control of the newspapers and the influence of the gossip columnist Louella Parsons to try to pressure film industry executives to stop release of *Citizen Kane*. How does the reviewer handle the controversy surrounding the film?

   (1) He criticizes the film for misrepresenting William Randolph Hearst.
   (2) He praises the film for exposing the corrupt business practices of "an eminent publisher."
   (3) He praises the film for exposing William Randoph Hearst's underhanded political maneuverings.
   (4) He diplomatically doesn't name William Randolph Hearst and praises the film for its artistic merits.
   (5) He is afraid to name William Randolph Hearst but praises the film for its accurate portrayal of a certain "eminent publisher."

2. Based on information in the passage, what does the reviewer's opinion of censorship appear to be?

   (1) Potentially offensive films should not be shown to the public.
   (2) Films of great artistic merit should be shown to the public.
   (3) Censorship is wrong and should not be allowed.
   (4) Slanderous works should not be shown to the public.
   (5) Movie studio executives should decide whether to release a director's film.

3. The poet Samuel Taylor Coleridge's poem "Kubla Khan," includes the lines, "In Xanadu did Kubla Khan / A stately pleasure dome decree" (lines 1–2). Kubla Khan was the thirteenth-century founder of the Mongol dynasty in China. According to the review, the main character in *Citizen Kane*, Charles Kane (note the resemblance to Khan), names his castle Xanadu. What does this suggest about Kane?

   (1) Samuel Taylor Coleridge is Kane's favorite poet.
   (2) Kane prefers Eastern architecture.
   (3) Kane would like to live in the thirteenth century.
   (4) Kane is of Mongol descent.
   (5) Kane likes to think of himself as rich and powerful.

Check your answers on page 133.

EXERCISE 4

Directions: Items 1–3 refer to the following excerpt from a classic book about nature. This detailed description of a small feature of the natural world vividly conveys the writer's sense of wonder and delight.

What Makes this Place Special?

Line A dawn wind stirs on the great marsh. With almost imperceptible slowness it rolls a bank of fog across the wide morass. Like the white ghost of a glacier the mists advance, riding over phalanxes of tamarack, sliding across bogmeadows heavy with dew. A single silence hangs from horizon to horizon.

5   Out of some far recess of the sky a tinkling of little bells falls soft upon the listening land. Then again silence. Now comes a baying of some sweet-throated hound, soon the clamor of a responding pack. Then a far clear blast of hunting horns, out of the sky into the fog.

High horns, low horns, silence, and finally a pandemonium of trumpets, rattles,
10   croaks, and cries that almost shakes the bog with its nearness, but without yet disclosing whence it comes. At last a glint of sun reveals the approach of a great echelon of birds. On motionless wings they emerge from the lifting mists, sweep a final arc of sky, and settle in clangorous descending spirals to their feeding grounds. A new day has begun on the crane marsh.

—Aldo Leopold, *A Sand County Almanac*

1. What is the main thing that is happening in this passage?

    (1)   Hunters with dogs are killing cranes.
    (2)   Dawn is breaking over the marsh.
    (3)   The writer has killed a crane.
    (4)   The cranes have flown away from the marsh.
    (5)   The sun has set and all is still.

2. Which sentence from the passage includes an example of alliteration?

    (1)   A dawn wind stirs on the great marsh.
    (2)   A single silence hangs from horizon to horizon.
    (3)   Then a far clear blast of hunting horns.
    (4)   Now comes a baying of some sweet-throated hound.
    (5)   A new day has begun on the crane marsh.

3. What is the best way to describe the author's perspective on the scene he describes in this passage?

    (1)   Fear
    (2)   Distancing
    (3)   Joy
    (4)   Anger
    (5)   Awe

Check your answers on page 133.

EXERCISE 5

Directions: Items 1–4 refer to this descriptive passage from a history book. Read the passage carefully and attempt to visualize the subject in your mind. Then answer the questions.

Why Did A City Grow Here?

Line   Geography was destiny. From prehistoric times, Britain's grandest river ran through a broad valley, fed by streams from wooded hills now called Highgate and Hampstead and from higher ground beyond Camberwell, down to the North Sea. The Thames was wider and shallower than now; marshes and mud-flats abounded, and islands appeared
5   at low tide—names like Battersea and Bermondsey commemorate former islands. (The Angle-Saxon *ea* means island, so Battersea is Peter's Island.) The Thames valley offered hospitable terrain for pastoralists, and Neolithic sites sprang up; but though settlements have been discovered—at Runnymede, Staines, and Heathrow, for instance—there is no proof that central London was permanently settled by the Celts
10   before the Romans. Nevertheless, geology and geography foreordained that it would, in time, become a choice place of habitation.

Strategic considerations and physical features marked this spot as suitable for civilization. It was the lowest point where the Thames could be forded and bridged. Here, forty miles from the sea, the river was blessed with a gravel bed. In contrast to
15   treacherous mudbanks, gravel subsoil provided safe landings for trading craft crossing the Channel and venturing up the Thames.

—Roy Porter, *London, A Social History*

1.   According to the passage, gravel subsoil allows

   (1)   people to ford the river.
   (2)   people to build bridges.
   (3)   boats to land safely.
   (4)   animals to drink from the river.
   (5)   people to build houses.

2.   Which sentence states the main idea of the passage?

   (1)   Geography was destiny.
   (2)   The Thames was wider and shallower than now.
   (3)   Anglo-Saxon *ea* means island.
   (4)   It was the lowest point where the Thames could be forded.
   (5)   The river was blessed with a gravel bed.

3.   Of the following place names, which probably means "island"?

   (1)   Kent
   (2)   Thames
   (3)   Camberwell
   (4)   Hammondsey
   (5)   Staines

4. "London grew astonishingly in the nineteenth century, with its hordes of labourers and landlords, its pen-pushers and porters. Between 1841 and 1851 alone, some 330,000 migrants flooded into the capital . . ."

This passage from later in the same book tells you that

    (1)   the Thames valley included good farmland.
    (2)   London's destiny was eventually fulfilled.
    (3)   the gravel beds allowed for boat moorings.
    (4)   there was plenty of water for flocks.
    (5)   people traveled up the river to settle there.

Check your answers on page 134.

EXERCISE 6

Directions: Items 1–3 refer to the following passage from an anatomy textbook. It describes a condition that affects the eyes of many elderly people. Read the passage carefully, visualize the descriptive material, and answer the questions that follow.

What Causes Cataracts?

Line   The transparency of the lens depends on a precise combination of structural and biochemical characteristics. When the balance becomes disturbed the lens loses its transparency, and the abnormal lens is known as a cataract. Cataracts may result from drug reactions, injuries, or radiation, but senile cataracts are the most common form.

5   Over time, the lens takes on a yellowish hue, and eventually it begins to lose its transparency. As the lens becomes "cloudy," the individual needs brighter and brighter reading lights, and visual clarity begins to fade. If the lens becomes completely opaque, the person will be functionally blind, even though the retinal receptors are normal. Modern surgical procedures involve removing the lens, either intact or in

10   pieces, after shattering it with high frequency sound. The missing lens can be replaced by an artificial substitute, and vision can then be fine-tuned with glasses or contact lenses.

—Frederick Martini, *Fundamentals of Anatomy and Physiology*

1. In a person who has cataracts, the lens of the eye becomes

    (1)   cloudy.
    (2)   thick.
    (3)   soft.
    (4)   brittle.
    (5)   dark.

2. A person who is developing cataracts would be likely to make the comment:

    (1)   "It seems very warm in here."
    (2)   "Please speak up."
    (3)   "My soup isn't hot enough."
    (4)   "My feet are cold."
    (5)   "The light seems very dim."

3. According to the passage, the most common cause of cataracts is

   (1)   disease.
   (2)   radiation.
   (3)   old age.
   (4)   drug reactions.
   (5)   surgery.

Check your answers on page 134.

EXERCISE 7

Directions: Items 1–4 refer to the following passage from a book on the history of the senses that describes a condition called *synesthesia*. As you read, pay particular attention to the way in which synesthesia is described, and answer the questions that follow.

What is Synesthesia?

Line   In time, the newborn learns to sort and tame all its sensory impressions, some of which have names, many of which will remain nameless to the end of its days. Things that elude our verbal grasp are hard to pin down and almost impossible to remember. A cozy blur in the nursery vanishes into the rigorous categories of common sense. But
5   for some people, that sensory blending never quits, and they taste baked beans whenever they hear the word "Francis," as one woman reported, or see yellow on touching a matte surface, or smell the passage of time. The stimulation of one sense stimulates another: *synesthesia* is the technical name, from the Greek *syn* (together) + *aisthanesthai* (to perceive). A thick garment of perception is woven thread by
10   overlapping thread. A similar word is *synthesis*, in which the garment of thought is woven together idea by idea, and which originally referred to the light muslin clothing worn by the ancient Romans.

         Daily life is a constant onslaught on one's perceptions, and everyone experiences some intermingling of the senses. According to Gestalt psychologists,
15   when people are asked to relate a list of nonsense words to shapes and colors they identify certain sounds with certain shapes in ways that fall into clear patterns. What's more surprising is that this is true whether they are from the United States, England, the Mahali peninsula, or Lake Tanganyika. People with intense synesthesia tend to respond in predictable ways, too. A survey of two thousand synesthetes from various
20   cultures revealed many similarities in the colors they assigned to sounds. People often associate low sounds with dark colors and high sounds with bright colors, for instance. A certain amount of synesthesia is built into our senses. If one wished to create instant synesthesia, a dose of mescaline or hashish would do nicely by exaggerating the neural connections between the senses. Those who experience intense synesthesia
25   naturally on a regular basis are rare—only about one in every five hundred people—and neurologist Richard Cytowic traces the phenomenon to the limbic system, the most primitive part of the brain, calling synesthetes "living cognitive fossils," because they may be people whose limbic system is not entirely governed by the much more sophisticated (and more recently evolved) cortex. As he says,
30   "synesthesia . . . may be a memory of how early mammals, saw, heard, smelled, tasted and touched."

—Diane Ackerman, *A Natural History of the Senses*

1. In his autobiography *Speak, Memory*, the Russian writer Vladimir Nabokov writes that he often sees a color when he sounds out a letter of the alphabet: "The long *a* of the English alphabet . . . has for me the tint of weathered wood, but a French *a* evokes polished ebony. This black group also includes hard *g* (vulcanized rubber) and *r* (a sooty rag being ripped)." What does this quotation indicate about Nabokov's experience of synesthesia?

   (1)   Synesthetic responses can be subtle and complex.
   (2)   Synesthesia never blends sound, color, and texture.
   (3)   Synesthesia is not an international phenomenon.
   (4)   Nabokov is ashamed of his experiences of synesthesia.
   (5)   Nabokov speaks many different languages.

2. Synesthesia can be defined as

   (1)   an intermingling of the senses.
   (2)   the limbic system of the brain.
   (3)   sensations from the cortex of the brain.
   (4)   light muslin clothing worn by the ancient Romans.
   (5)   an onslaught on one's perceptions.

3. A person who has synesthesia might make the comment,

   (1)   "The light is very bright."
   (2)   "The music is too loud."
   (3)   "The food is delicious."
   (4)   "The music is bright."
   (5)   "The fire is warm."

4. Which sentence from the passage includes an example of metaphor?

   (1)   "Things that elude our verbal grasp are hard to pin down and almost impossible to remember."
   (2)   "But for some people, that sensory blending never quits, and they taste baked beans whenever they hear the word 'Francis,' as one woman reported . . ."
   (3)   "A thick garment of perception is woven thread by overlapping thread."
   (4)   "People often associate low sounds with dark colors and high sounds with bright colors, for instance."
   (5)   "A certain amount of synesthesia is built into our senses."

Check your answers on page 135.

THESIS STATEMENTS

A **thesis statement** is a declarative sentence that states the main point of an essay. Not all nonfiction has a thesis statement, but many works of nonfiction do. A thesis statement provides a focus for a text, and identifying a thesis can help you to understand and analyze a passage.

TOPIC SENTENCES

A **topic sentence** states the main point of a paragraph and supports the thesis of a nonfiction work. Identifying the topic sentence of a paragraph can help you to comprehend the material better.

IDENTIFYING DIFFERENT FORMS OF DEVELOPMENT

Different forms of development are used in structuring nonfiction. An awareness of these different modes of development will help you to understand a writer's purpose and increase your comprehension of the material. Different ways of developing paragraphs and essays are listed below.

- **Cause and effect** shows the reasons why something occurs (cause) and the results of the occurrence (effect). For example, a cause and effect paper might focus on the causes of schizophrenia and/or the effects of schizophrenia. A writer might also deal with absence of cause: what might prevent the effect from occurring. For example, in the case of schizophrenia, absence of cause might be a particular medication.

- **Comparison/contrast** shows the similarities (comparison) and differences (contrast) between subject matter of the same kind. For example, two athletes could be compared or two beaches could be compared.

- **Analogy** is an extended comparison that shows the similarities between subject matter of different kinds. For example, life might be compared to a river, or a man might be compared to an ape.

- **Process analysis** describes how some kind of action is performed. An **informational process analysis** aims at giving readers a sense of what it is like to perform a certain action. A **directional process analysis** aims at giving readers the ability to perform a certain action. For instance, an informational process analysis might describe the experience of skydiving. A directional process analysis might instruct a reader on how to install his or her new DVD player.

- **Definition** explains how the writer conceptualizes a word or phrase. For instance, a writer might try to define what love is, or power, or freedom.

- **Classification/division** divides a topic into different categories. A writer might divide a group of people such as moviegoers or pet owners into different types, for example.

- **Argumentation** examines an issue and advances the writer's opinion based on the available evidence. For instance, a writer might argue for or against funding for a new local sports arena.

- **Narration** relates an experience and follows a temporal order. A writer might describe an experience he or she had while camping, for example.

- **Description** conveys an experience and follows a spatial order. For instance, a writer might describe what a river looks like while one is walking next to it, or swimming in it, or flying over it.

EXERCISE 8

Directions: Items 1–3 refer to the following passage from a humanities textbook discussing Gothic cathedrals. As you read, visualize the differences between Notre Dame and Chartres Cathedral, and answer the questions that follow.

What is a Gothic Cathedral?

Line   The Gothic cathedral has been described as the perfect synthesis of intellect, spirituality, and engineering. The upward, striving line of the Gothic arch makes a simple yet powerful statement of medieval people's striving to understand their earthly relation to the spiritual unknown. Even today the simplicity and grace of that design
5   have an effect on most who view a Gothic cathedral.

The four-square power of Notre Dame, Paris, reflects the strength and solidarity of an urban cathedral in Europe's largest city of the age. Its careful composition is highly mathematical—each level is equal to the one below it, and its tripartite division is clearly symbolic of the trinity. Arcs (whose radii are equal to the width of the
10   building) drawn from the lower corners, meet at the top of the circular window at the second level. Careful design moves the eye inward and slowly upward. The exterior structure clearly reveals the interior space.

Chartres Cathedral stands in remarkable contrast. Chartres is a country cathedral raised above the center of a small city. Just as its sculptures illustrate a progression of
15   style, so does its architectural design. Our first encounter leads us to wonder why its cramped entry portal is so small in comparison with the rest of the building. The reason is that Chartres represents a cumulative building effort over many years, as fire destroyed one part of the church after another. The main entry portal and the windows above it date back to its Romanesque beginnings. The porch of the south transept (the
20   portal holding the statues of the warrior saints) is much larger and more in harmony with the rest of the building. Finally, as our eyes rise upward, we wonder at the incongruity of the two unmatched spires. Fire was again responsible. The early spire on the right illustrates faith in a simple upward movement that rises, unencumbered, to disappear at the tip into the ultimate mystery—space. The later spire, designed in
25   psychological balance with the other, is more ornate and complex. The eye travels upward with increasing difficulty, its progress halted and held earthbound by decoration and detail. Only after some pause does the eye reach the tip of the spire, the point of which symbolizes the individual's escape from the earthly known to the unknown.

—Dennis J. Sporre, *Reality through the Arts*

1. What primary form of development is used in the passage?

    (1) Cause and effect
    (2) Argumentation
    (3) Classification and division
    (4) Comparison/contrast
    (5) Narration

2. Which sentence best describes the author's attitude toward his subject matter?

    (1) Notre Dame is architecturally superior to Chartres Cathedral.
    (2) Chartres Cathedral is architecturally superior to Notre Dame.
    (3) The author does not imply that one design is better than another.
    (4) Notre Dame and Chartres Cathedral are very similar in construction.
    (5) The Gothic style is inferior to baroque style.

3. Based on information in the passage, which of the following sentences best describes the differences in design between Notre Dame and Chartres Cathedral?

    (1) Notre Dame has a strong, balanced design whereas Chartres has a varied, asymmetrical design.
    (2) Notre Dame has an ethereal, ornate design whereas Chartres has a sturdy, Romanesque design.
    (3) Notre Dame has a strong, balanced design whereas Chartres has a classical, harmonious design.
    (4) Notre Dame has an urban, avant-garde design whereas Chartres has a rural, modest design.
    (5) Notre Dame has a varied, asymmetrical design whereas Chartres has a strong, balanced design.

Check your answers on page 135.

EXERCISE 9

Directions: Items 1–3 refer to the following passage from the slave narrative of Frederick Douglass in which he describes a turning point in his life. As you read the passage, visualize the experience he describes and then answer the questions that follow.

What Makes this Experience Important?

Line   He asked me if I meant to persist in my resistance. I told him I did, come what might; that he had used me like a brute for six months, and that I was determined to be used so no longer. With that, he strove to drag me to a stick that was lying just out of the stable door. He meant to knock me down. But just as he was leaning over to get the
5   stick, I seized him with both hands by his collar, and brought him by a sudden snatch to the ground. By this time, Bill came. Covey called upon him for assistance. Bill wanted to know what he could do. Covey said, "Take hold of him, take hold of him!" Bill said his master hired him out to work, and not to help to whip me; so he left Covey and myself to fight our own battle out. We were at it for nearly two hours.
10   Covey at length let me go, puffing and blowing at a great rate, saying that if I had not resisted, he would not have whipped me half so much. The truth was, that he had not whipped me at all. I considered him as getting entirely the worst end of the bargain; for he had drawn no blood from me, but I had from him. The whole six months afterwards, that I spent with Mr. Covey, he never laid the weight of his finger upon me
15   in anger. He would occasionally say, he didn't want to get hold of me again. "No," thought I, "you need not; for you will come off worse than you did before."

     This battle with Mr. Covey was the turning-point in my career as a slave. It rekindled the few expiring embers of freedom, and revived within me a sense of my own manhood. It recalled the departed self-confidence, and inspired me again with a
20   determination to be free. The gratification afforded by the triumph was a full

compensation for whatever else might follow, even death itself. He only can understand the deep satisfaction which I experienced, who has himself repelled by force the bloody arm of slavery. I felt as I never felt before. It was a glorious resurrection, from the tomb of slavery, to the heaven of freedom. My long-crushed
25   spirit rose, cowardice departed, bold defiance took its place; and I now, resolved that, however long I might remain a slave in form, the day had passed forever when I could be a slave in fact.

—Frederick Douglass, *Narrative of the Life of Frederick Douglass*

1. Based on information in the passage, Covey does not lay his finger on Frederick Douglass again after their encounter because

   (1)   Covey is ashamed of himself for mistreating Douglass.
   (2)   Covey has become friends with Douglass.
   (3)   Covey is afraid of Douglass.
   (4)   Covey is against slavery.
   (5)   Covey has a deep respect for Douglass.

2. According to the passage, what is the most significant change Douglass undergoes after he confronts Covey?

   (1)   Douglass realizes how physically strong he is.
   (2)   Douglass is freed from slavery and leaves Covey.
   (3)   Douglass gains a new respect for Covey.
   (4)   Douglass's self-confidence and self-respect are revived.
   (5)   Douglass's self-confidence and self-respect are shattered.

3. Which of the following phrases from the passage is an example of metaphor?

   (1)   ". . . he had used me like a brute . . ."
   (2)   ". . . a sudden snatch to the ground . . ."
   (3)   ". . . the tomb of slavery . . ."
   (4)   ". . . determination to be free."
   (5)   ". . . the weight of his finger . . ."

Check your answers on page 136.

EXERCISE 10

Directions: Items 1–5 refer to the following passage about an experience the author had in the badlands of South Dakota. As you read the passage carefully, visualize the descriptive material, and then answer the questions that follow.

What Makes this Experience Special?

Line   It was then that I saw the flight coming on. It was moving like a little close-knit body of black specks that danced and darted and closed again. It was pouring from the north and heading toward me with the undeviating relentlessness of a compass needle. It streamed through the shadows rising out of monstrous gorges. It rushed over towering

5   pinnacles in the red light of the sun or momentarily sank from sight within their shade. Across that desert of eroding clay and windworn stone they came with a faint wild twittering that filled all the air about me as those tiny living bullets hurtled past into the night.

    It may not strike you as a marvel. It would not, perhaps, unless you stood in the

10   middle of a dead world at sunset, but that was where I stood. Fifty million years lay under my feet, fifty million years of bellowing monsters moving in a green world now gone so utterly that its very light was traveling on the farther edge of space. The chemicals of all that vanished age lay about me in the ground. Around me still lay the shearing molars of dead titanotheres, the delicate sabers of soft-stepping cats, the

15   hollow sockets that had held the eyes of many a strange, outmoded beast. Those eyes had looked out upon a world as real as ours: dark, savage brains had roamed and roared their challenges into the steaming night.

    Now they were still here, or, put it as you will, the chemicals that made them were here about me in the ground. The carbon that had driven them ran blackly in the

20   eroding stone. The stain of iron was in the clays. The iron did not remember the blood it had once moved within, the phosphorus had forgotten the savage brain. The little individual moment had ebbed from all those strange combinations of chemicals as it would ebb from our living bodies into the sinks and tunnels of oncoming time.

    I had lifted up a fistful of that ground. I held it while that wild flight of

25   south-bound warblers hurtled over me into the oncoming dark. There went phosphorus, there went iron, there went carbon, there beat the calcium in those hurrying wings. Alone on a dead planet I watched that incredible miracle speeding past. It ran by some true compass over field and waste land. It cried its individual ecstasies into the air until the gullies rang. It swerved like a single body, it knew itself,

30   and, lonely, it bunched close in the racing darkness, its individual entities feeling about them the rising night. And so, crying to each other their identity, they passed away out of my view.

—Loren Eiseley, "The Judgment of the Birds," *The Immense Journey*

1. Which of the following quotations from the passage uses personification?

   (1) "It was moving like a little close-knit body of black specks that danced and darted and closed again."
   (2) "It swerved like a single body. . ."
   (3) "The iron did not remember the blood it had once moved within, the phosphorus had forgotten the savage brain."
   (4) "It was pouring from the north and heading toward me with the undeviating relentlessness of a compass needle."
   (5) "It rushed over towering pinnacles in the red light of the sun or momentarily sank from sight within their shade."

2. The author's style can best be described as

   (1) a blend of poetry and exaggeration.
   (2) a blend of science and fiction.
   (3) a blend of poetry and fiction.
   (4) a blend of poetry and science.
   (5) a blend of fiction and nonfiction.

3. Based on the content of the passage, the writer's other vocations would most likely be which of the following?

   (1) A naturalist and anthropologist
   (2) An anthropologist and physicist
   (3) A physicist and psychologist
   (4) An anthropologist and psychologist
   (5) A naturalist and performer

4. Which of the following statements best sums up the connection the author makes between the dinosaurs and the birds?

   (1) Birds are descended from dinosaurs.
   (2) Birds are very different creatures than dinosaurs.
   (3) Birds can adapt to the environment better than dinosaurs can.
   (4) Birds will eventually become a part of the ground, just as dinosaurs have.
   (5) The existence of birds after dinosaurs is an example of survival of the fittest.

5. In *A Sand County Almanac*, Aldo Leopold describes a flock of cranes in the following way: "On motionless wings they emerge from the lifting mists, sweep a final arc of sky, and settle in clangorous descending spirals to their feeding grounds." In the passage above, Loren Eiseley describes a flock of warblers: "It swerved like a single body, it knew itself, and, lonely, it bunched close in the racing darkness, its individual entities feeling about them the rising night."

   Which of the following states the most significant difference between the ways the flocks of birds are described?

   (1) Leopold describes the flock in the afternoon while Eiseley describes the flock at night.
   (2) Leopold uses a simile in his description while Eiseley does not.
   (3) Leopold's tone is one of awe whereas Eiseley's tone is not.
   (4) Leopold describes only what the flock does whereas Eiseley also describes how the flock feels.
   (5) Leopold's attitude toward the flock is much more judgmental than Eiseley's attitude.

Check your answers on page 136.

EXERCISE 11

Directions: Items 1–3 refer to the following passage from an essay describing mangroves. As you read, visualize the trees and the natural processes the author describes.

What are Mangroves?

Line If survival is an art, then mangroves are artists of the beautiful: not only that they exist at all—smooth-barked, glossy-leaved, thickets of lapped mystery—but that they can and do exist as floating islands, as trees upright and loose, alive and homeless on the water.

5   I have seen mangroves, always on tropical ocean shores, in Florida and in the Galapagos. There is the red mangrove, the yellow, the button, and the black. They are all short, messy trees, waxy-leaved, laced all over with aerial roots, woody arching buttresses, and weird leathery berry pods. All this tangles from a black muck soil, a black muck matted like a mud-sopped rag, a muck without any other plants, shaded,
10   cold to the touch, tracked at the water's edge by herons and nosed by sharks.

      It is these shoreline trees which, by a fairly common accident, can become floating islands. A hurricane flood or a riptide can wrest a tree from the shore, or from the mouth of a tidal river, and hurl it into the ocean. It floats. It is a mangrove island, blown.

15   There are floating islands on the planet; it amazes me. Credulous Pliny described some islands thought to be mangrove islands floating on a river. The people called these river islands *the dancers*, "because in any consort of musicians singing, they stir and move at the stroke of the feet, keeping time and measure."

      Trees floating on rivers are less amazing than trees floating on the poisonous
20   sea. A tree cannot live in salt. Mangrove trees exude salt from their leaves; you can see it, even on shoreline black mangroves, as a thin white crust. Lick a leaf and your tongue curls and coils; your mouth's a heap of salt.

      Nor can a tree live without soil. A hurricane-born mangrove island may bring its own soil to the sea. But other mangrove trees make their own soil—and their own
25   islands—from scratch. These are the ones which interest me. The seeds germinate in the fruit on the tree. The germinated embryo can drop anywhere—say, onto a dab of floating muck. The heavy root end sinks; a leafy plumule unfurls. The tiny seedling, afloat, is on its way. Soon aerial roots shooting out in all directions trap debris. The sapling's networks twine, the interstices narrow, and water calms in the lee. Bacteria
30   thrive on organic broth; amphipods swarm. These creatures grow and die at the trees' wet feet. The soil thickens, accumulating rainwater, leaf rot, seashells, and guano; the island spreads.

—Annie Dillard, "Sojourner," *Teaching a Stone to Talk*

1. Which of the following quotations from the passage is an example of a simile?

    (1) "If survival is an art, then mangroves are artists of the beautiful: not only that they exist at all—smooth-barked, glossy-leaved, thickets of lapped mystery—but that they can and do exist as floating islands. . ."
    (2) "Soon aerial roots shooting out in all directions trap debris."
    (3) "Bacteria thrive on organic broth."
    (4) "These creatures grow and die at the trees' wet feet."
    (5) "All this tangles from a black muck soil, a black muck matted like a mud-sopped rag . . ."

2. The author refers to Pliny as "credulous" because

    (1)   he believes that mangroves can become floating islands.

    (2)   he refers to river islands as *the dancers*.

    (3)   he writes about mangroves.

    (4)   he writes that the mangrove islands will keep time to music.

    (5)   he writes that mangroves will not keep time to music.

3. What is the best way to describe the author's perspective on the topic?

    (1)   A combination of amazement and matter-of-factness

    (2)   A combination of disgust and matter-of-factness

    (3)   A combination of amazement and romanticization

    (4)   A strong sense of reverence

    (5)   A strong sense of confusion

Check your answers on page 137.

POINT OF VIEW

In order to interpret a passage successfully, it is helpful to be aware of the influence of point of view. Point of view is the perspective from which a narrative is told. **First-person** point of view relates a narrative from the perspective of "I" or "we." **Second-person** point of view narrates from the perspective of "you." **Third-person** point of view narrates from the perspective of "he," "she," "it," or "they." **Omniscient** point of view relates not only what occurs but also what the characters are thinking. **Objective** point of view relates only what occurs without entering the minds of any characters.

EXERCISE 12

Directions: Items 1–4 refer to this descriptive passage from a book on Oregon rivers. As you read the passage carefully, visualize the subject in your mind, paying special attention to the point of view used. Then answer the questions.

Where Does the Rogue River Begin?

Line   Start at any of these sources, let water lead you, and eventually you will stand where a river empties into the Pacific or a desert lake. The story isn't hard to follow. But start at the mouth and trace the story back, and your journey may involve more questions. Trace the Rogue River, to choose one. From its outlet at Gold Beach on the southern

5   coast, follow it back through its wild canyon in the Klamath Mountains, through its broad valley between Grants Pass and Medford, and up past Lost Creek Reservoir into the Cascades. Climb alongside through the volcanic landscape, where at one point the river hurls itself into a lava tube and churns out of sight for two hundred feet. Follow still higher, until the Rogue is nothing but a creek joined by other creeks, all issuing

10   from mountain springs, all small and white and fast. You could follow any of them. *Here*, says the river, *here* and *here*.

     Stay with the blue line your map calls the Rogue and you'll arrive, on foot, at a place called Boundary Springs, high in the northwest corner of Crater Lake National Park. But even here you'll face choices. There are several springs, each of them bright

15   with moss and rushing water. Where is the Rogue River now? The largest spring? Take off your boots, douse your feet. Watch how lucid water springs forth among shaggy stones and cascades lightly away. Watch how it flows. It does not gather and then begin to move. It is born in motion, a gesture already underway. This spring is only the place where a river emerges from the deep cold joints of an exploded

20   mountain, a subterranean wilderness fed by seepings out of Crater Lake, which by itself is fed by underground springs, which themselves are fed by snowmelt sinking into the soil.

     Snowfall, then, is the source of the Rogue. But snow is only an expression of winter storms. And the storms are swirling eddies of a vast air mass that flows out of

25   Siberia, soaks up moisture south of the Aleutians, and delivers barrages of weather to our West Coast. It is known as the Pacific maritime polar airstream, one of seven such atmospheric tendencies that shape the North American climate. The headwaters of the Rogue, the headwaters of every stream on Earth, is a river in the sky.

—John Daniel, "Beginnings," *Oregon Rivers*

1. What is the main point of view used in the passage?

    (1)   First person
    (2)   Second person
    (3)   Third person
    (4)   First-person omniscient
    (5)   Third-person objective

2. Based on the passage, what is the psychological effect on a reader when the author uses second-person point of view?

(1)   It tends to distance the reader from the text.
(2)   It tends to draw the reader into the text.
(3)   It tends to confuse the reader.
(4)   It tends to sound very formal.
(5)   It tends to be objective.

3. Which of the following sentences from the passage is an example of personification?

(1)   "Trace the Rogue River, to choose one."
(2)   "Watch how it flows."
(3)   "You could follow any of them."
(4)   "But even here you'll face choices."
(5)   "*Here*, says the river, *here* and *here*."

4. The focus of the passage is best described as

(1)   a search for the origins of the Rogue River.
(2)   a search for the origins of humanity.
(3)   a search for the origin of Crater Lake.
(4)   a meteorological study of Oregon.
(5)   an indictment of the pollution of the Rogue River.

Check your answers on page 137.

EXERCISE 13

Directions: Items 1–3 refer to the following passage from a book in which the author returns to his grandmother's home to discover more about his heritage as a Native American after she passes away. In the passage he reminisces about his grandmother, Aho. As you read, pay particular attention to what the author says about the history of the Kiowas. Then answer the questions.

Who Were the Kiowas?

Line   I like to think of her as a child. When she was born, the Kiowas were living the last great moment of their history. For more than a hundred years they had controlled the open range from the Smoky Hill River to the Red, from the headwaters of the Canadian to the fork of the Arkansas and Cimarron. In alliance with the Comanches,
5   they had ruled the whole of the southern Plains. War was their sacred business, and they were among the finest horsemen the world has ever known. But warfare for the Kiowas was preeminently a matter of disposition rather than of survival, and they never understood the grim, unrelenting advance of the U.S. Cavalry. When at last, divided and ill-provisioned, they were driven onto the Staked Plains in the cold rains
10   of autumn, they fell into panic. In Palo Duro Canyon they abandoned their crucial stores to pillage and had nothing but their lives. In order to save themselves, they surrendered to the soldiers at Fort Sill and were imprisoned in the old stone corral that now stands as a military museum. My grandmother was spared the humiliation of those high gray walls by eight or ten years, but she must have known from birth the
15   affliction of defeat, the dark brooding of old warriors.

Her name was Aho, and she belonged to the last culture to evolve in North America. Her forebears came down from the high country in western Montana nearly

three centuries ago. They were a mountain people, a mysterious tribe of hunters whose language has never been positively classified in any major group. In the late
20 seventeenth century they began a long migration to the south and east. It was a journey toward the dawn, and it led to a golden age. Along the way the Kiowas were befriended by the Crows, who gave them the culture and religion of the Plains. They acquired horses, and their ancient nomadic spirit was suddenly free of the ground. They acquired Tai-me, the sacred Sun Dance doll, from that moment the object and
25 symbol of their worship, and so shared in the divinity of the sun. Not least, they acquired the sense of destiny, therefore courage and pride. When they entered upon the southern Plains they had been transformed. No longer were they slaves to the simple necessity of survival; they were a lordly and dangerous society of fighters and thieves, hunters and priests of the sun. According to their origin myth, they entered the
30 world through a hollow log. From one point of view, their migration was the fruit of an old prophecy, for indeed they emerged from a sunless world.

—N. Scott Momaday, *The Way to Rainy Mountain*

1. According to the passage, the Kiowas were

   (1) the last culture to evolve in North America.
   (2) the first Native Americans to practice the religion of the Plains.
   (3) the first Native Americans to form the culture of the Plains.
   (4) the first Native Americans to migrate from the southern Plains to the high country of western Montana.
   (5) the last culture to practice the sacred Sun Dance.

2. What does the author mean when he says that the Kiowas "emerged from a sunless world?"

   (1) The Kiowas emerged from the high gray walls of Fort Sill.
   (2) The Kiowas emerged through a hollow log.
   (3) The Kiowas emerged from the southern Plains.
   (4) The Kiowas emerged from Palo Duro Canyon.
   (5) The Kiowas emerged from the high country in western Montana.

3. Based on information in the passage, which of the following statements best describes how the writer depicts the temperament of the Kiowas?

   (1) They were pacifists who refused to fight.
   (2) They were pacifists who were forced to fight.
   (3) They were warriors who fought to annihilate their enemies.
   (4) They were warriors who fought through inclination.
   (5) They were fierce enemies of the Crows and allies of the Apaches.

Check your answers on page 138.

EXERCISE 14

Directions: Items 1–4 refer to a passage from an essay in which the author describes an experience he has fly-fishing. As you read, visualize the scene that the author is describing and note the emotions that he conveys. Then answer the following questions.

What Does the Fisherman Experience?

Line I step, half-lost, into the river. I ease the trout into my hands, unhook the fly. The fish
streaks for the depths with every appearance of purpose. I stand in the shallows with
nothing of the sort.

   There are no rises on the glide now. My rainbow's leaping has spooked things
5 for a time. If I were a younger man I'd say the show here was over and rush, before
light failed, to the next likely water or showing fish. But there are desires the vaunted
energy of youth conceals. What I often want now is to be more present where I am.
There are tricks to this, as to any kind of fishing. Here is one . . .

   When trout rise in rivers the rings drift quickly downstream. For this reason a
10 fisherman must cast not to visible rise-rings, but to an invisible memory of where rings
first appear. I've heard this called "the memory point." I knew of this point when I
was young. What I did not know, then, was that one's best casts to it are not
necessarily made with one's rod. Leaning mine against an osier, using eyes along, I
cast to a memory point now:

15   In the last hours of a September day, you can't see down into the waters of the
Clark Fork. The sun is too low, the light too acutely angled. In the last hours of day the
river's surface grows reflective, shows you blue sky and red clouds, upside-down
pines, orange water-birch, yellow cottonwoods. Deer hang as if shot, but their feet, yet
keep browsing bright grasses. Ospreys fly beneath you. Everything is swirling. In a
20 snag, way down deep, you might spot a flycatcher. It's hard to believe that these
clouds and trees, deer and birds, colored grasses are a door. It's hard to believe fish
live behind it. Yet it was the clouds at my feet the rainbow troubled by rising. It was
into the downward sky that I cast the mahogany mayfly. It was out of inverted pines
and cottonwoods that the trout then flew, shattering all reflection, three times speaking
25 its leaping word.

   Not every cast hits the memory point. But when one does, this word just goes on
speaking. It says that death is like the Clark Fork, late in the day. It says true words are
eternal. It says eternity passes through doors as it pleases.

—David Duncan, "A Door," *River Teeth*

1. According to the passage, what does the author do with the rainbow trout?

   (1) He is unable to catch it.
   (2) He catches it and takes it home.
   (3) He catches it and releases it back into the water alive.
   (4) He catches it and releases it back into the water dead.
   (5) He catches it, cooks, and eats it.

2. How does the author define a memory point?

    (1) As the rings that appear when a fish rises in a river
    (2) As the remembrance of where the rings first appeared when a fish rises in a river
    (3) As the rings that drift downstream when a fish rises in a river
    (4) As the remembrance of where the rings drifted downstream after a fish rises in a river
    (5) As the remembrance of where a fish is caught in a river

3. Based on information in the passage, as the narrator has grown older he has

    (1) lost his energy and enthusiasm.
    (2) learned a lot about life through experience.
    (3) become aware of a desire to fully appreciate the moment.
    (4) become obsessed with death.
    (5) developed problems with his vision.

4. In the passage, how does the author cast to a memory point?

    (1) With a rod
    (2) With an osier
    (3) With his imagination
    (4) With his eyes
    (5) He doesn't cast to a memory point

Check your answers on page 138.

EXERCISE 15

Directions: Items 1–3 refer to the following passage from an essay in which the author describes the results after she created a pond in the yard of her Tucson, Arizona, home. Visualize the animals she describes as you read, and then answer the questions that follow.

What Visitors Come to the Pond?

Line   I'm tempted to believe in spontaneous generation. Rushes have sprung up around the edges of my pond, coyotes and javelinas come down to drink and unabashedly wallow, nighthawks and little brown bats swoop down at night to snap insects out of the air. Mourning doves, smooth as cool gray stones, coo at their own reflections.

5   Families of Gambel's quail come each and every spring morning, all lined up puffed and bustling with their seventeen children, Papa Quail in proud lead with his ridiculous topknot feather boinging out ahead of him. Water lilies open their flowers at sunup and fold them, prim as praying hands, at dusk. A sleek male Cooper's hawk and a female great horned owl roost in the trees with their constant predators' eyes on

10   dim-witted quail and vain dove, silently taking turns with the night and day shifts.

     For several years that Cooper's hawk was the steadiest male presence in my life. I've stood alone in his shadow through many changes of season. I've been shattered and reassembled a few times over, and there have been long days when I felt my heart was simply somewhere else—possibly on ice, in one of those igloo coolers that show

15   up in the news as they are carried importantly onto helicopters. "So what?" life asked, and went on whirling recklessly around me. Always, every minute, something is eating or being eaten, laying eggs, burrowing in mud, blooming, splitting its seams, dividing itself in two. What a messy marvel, fecundity.

20   That is how I became goddess of a small universe of my own creation—more or less by accident. My subjects owe me their very lives. Blithely they ignore me. I stand on the banks, wide-eyed, receiving gifts in every season. In May the palo verde trees lean into their reflections, so heavy with blossoms the desert looks thick and deep with golden hoarfrost. In November the purple water lilies are struck numb with the first frost, continuing to try to open their final flowers in slow motion for the rest of the

25   winter. Once, in August, I saw a tussle in the reeds that turned out to be two bull snakes making a meal of the same frog. Their dinner screeched piteously while the snakes' heads inched slowly closer together, each of them engulfing a drumstick, until there they were at last, nose to scaly nose. I watched with my knuckles in my mouth, anxious to see if they would rip the frog in two like a pair of pants. As it turned out,

30   they were nowhere near this civilized. They lunged and thrashed, their long bodies scrawling whole cursive alphabets into the rushes, until one of the snakes suddenly let go and curved away.

—Barbara Kingsolver, "Reprise," *High Tide in Tucson*

1. Which of the following phrases from the passage is an example of a metaphor?

    (1)   ". . . smooth as cool gray stones . . ."
    (2)   ". . . prim as praying hands . . ."
    (3)   ". . . their long bodies scrawling whole cursive alphabets . . ."
    (4)   ". . . rip the frog in two like a pair of pants . . ."
    (5)   ". . . the purple water lilies are struck numb . . ."

2. Based on information in the passage, what can be inferred about the writer's social life?

    (1)   She was single for many years but has a male partner now.
    (2)   She has been single for many years.
    (3)   She has been married for many years.
    (4)   She has been married for a few years.
    (5)   She has recently gotten divorced.

3. The author's tone is mainly one of

    (1)   vulnerability.
    (2)   loneliness.
    (3)   enjoyment.
    (4)   disgust.
    (5)   independence.

Check your answers on page 139.

ONOMATOPOEIA

An awareness of the different figurative uses of words can help to increase reading comprehension of both nonfiction and fiction. **Onomatopoeia** is the use of naturalistic sounding words that mimic what they represent, for example, "woof," "meow," and "cheep."

EXERCISE 16

Directions: Items 1–3 refer to the following passage from an essay in which the author describes a visit to a cave. Visualize the place as she describes it, and answer the questions that follow.

What is this Place Like?

Line There is a holy place in the salt desert, where egrets hover like angels. It is a cave near the lake where water bubbles up from inside the earth. I am hidden and saved from the outside world. Leaning against the back wall of the cave, the curve of the rock supports the curve of my spine. I listen:

5   *Drip. Drip-drip. Drip. Drip. Drip-drip.*

My skin draws moisture from the rocks as my eyes adjust to the darkness.

    Ancient murals of ceremonial art bleed from the cavern walls. Pictographs of waterbirds decorate the interior of the cave. Herons, egrets, and cranes. Tadpoles and serpents stain the walls red. Human figures dance wildly, backs arched, hips thrust
10 forward. A spear-thrower lunges toward fish. Beyond him stands a water-jug maiden faintly painted above ferns. So lucent are these forms on the weeping rocks, they could be smeared without thought.

    I kneel at the spring and drink.

    This is the secret den of my healing, where I come to whittle down my losses. I
15 carve chevrons, the simple image of birds, on rabbit bones cleaned by eagles. And I sing without the embarrassment of being heard.

    The men in my family have migrated south for one year to lay pipe in southern Utah.

    My keening is for my family, fractured and displaced.

—Terry Tempest Williams, "Birds-of-Paradise,"
Refuge: An Unnatural History of Family and Place

1. Which of the following phrases from the essay is a simile?

    (1) ". . . egrets hover like angels."
    (2) ". . . water bubbles up . . ."
    (3) "I am hidden and saved . . ."
    (4) "My skin draws moisture . . ."
    (5) "Ancient murals of ceremonial art bleed . . ."

2. The book that this passage is taken from describes the way that the author, her mother, and their family and friends deal with her mother's illness from breast cancer. Shortly before this passage, we learn that her mother has died. What does knowledge of this event add to the passage?

    (1)   It lends a sense of bleakness and futility to the oppressive atmosphere of the cave.

    (2)   It adds poignancy to the therapeutic and spiritual atmosphere of the cave.

    (3)   It lends a sense of anger to the sadness of the scene.

    (4)   It adds a sense of guilt and sadness to the ugliness of the scene.

    (5)   It adds a sense of calm and hope to the beauty of the scene.

3. Which of the following words from the passage is an example of onomatopoeia?

    (1)   Angels

    (2)   Chevrons

    (3)   Drip

    (4)   Skin

    (5)   Listen

Check your answers on page 139.

ANSWERS AND EXPLANATIONS

UNIT 1: BUSINESS DOCUMENTS

Exercise 1 *(page 94)*

What is the Carnegie Institution of Washington?

1. **The correct answer is (1). (Comprehension)** The answer is stated in the first sentence of the passage. All the other choices are phrases from the passage, but they are not the Institution's purpose. Choice (3) is close to the correct answer, but it is vague rather than precise, so choice (1) is the better choice.

2. **The correct answer is (5). (Analysis)** Because all the language used in the passage is highly favorable to the Institution, it is written from the perspective of the Institution itself.

3. **The correct answer is (2). (Comprehension)** The answer is stated directly in the next-to-last sentence of the passage. The other choices are groups mentioned in the passage as participating in other Carnegie programs.

Exercise 2 *(page 95)*

How Do I Become a Student at Lee College?

1. **The correct answer is (4). (Analysis)** Although the passage mentions where to find information about financial aid, choice (3), its main purpose is to give admissions procedures. Choices (1), (2), and (5) are not supported by the passage.

2. **The correct answer is (5). (Comprehension)** This is stated in the second section, under the heading "Apply for Admission." Although the passage also states that the bookstore is in Moler Hall, you would not apply for admission in that part of the building.

3. **The correct answer is (2). (Comprehension)** Under the heading "Buy Books," the passage states that you may either buy books online or go to Moler Hall.

4. **The correct answer is (3). (Comprehension)** In the first paragraph of the passage, under the heading, "New Students," it states that students must submit proof of residency in order to be eligible for in-state fees.

Exercise 3 *(page 97)*

How Is the Performance of Hourly Employees Evaluated?

1. **The correct answer is (4). (Comprehension)** The passage states that employees complete a self-appraisal form by April 30 of each year.

2. **The correct answer is (1). (Comprehension)** This step is listed, in order, in the first paragraph of the passage. The other choices that occur later in the process.

3. **The correct answer is (5). (Application)** The last paragraph states that supervisors should provide additional opportunities for evaluation during the first year of employment. This implies that if a new employee is experiencing difficulties, the first step would be to begin a formal evaluation by completing the two appraisal forms.

Exercise 4 *(page 98)*

How Do International Students Enroll at Clark College?

1. **The correct answer is (3). (Application)** The Web site says that the TOEFL is required only of students from countries in which English is not the chief language.

2. **The correct answer is (4). (Application)** Since candidates must achieve a score of at least 520 on the written TOEFL test or a minimum score of 200 on the computerized TOEFL test in order to enroll in academic classes numbered 100 or above, both the Japanese student and the Italian student would need to take English as a Non-Native Language classes prior to enrolling in 100-level courses.

3. **The correct answer is (2). (Comprehension)** The Web site states that the college can request international students to make a year's deposit for educational expenses. Choice (1) is incorrect because that requirement does not apply to American students. Choice (3) is incorrect because a deposit is not mandatory in all cases. Choice (4) is wrong because the time span for deposits is limited to one year. Choice (5) is contradicted by the information in the passage.

4. **The correct answer is (5). (Comprehension)** The Web site states that choices (1) through (4) are required of all international students. A copy of the student's I-20 form is required only if the student is transferring from another U.S. college or university. Clark College issues an I-20 form to a student upon admission.

Exercise 5 *(page 100)*

What Are the Five Steps to a Sale?

1. **The correct answer is (2). (Synthesis)** Having gained the prospect's attention (the phosphorus), the salesperson must raise interest in the product (the sulfur). Choices (3), (4), and (5) can be equated respectively with the main fuel, keeping the main fuel burning, and lighting a fire.

2. **The correct answer is (1). (Analysis)** A contemporary textbook would use the term "salesperson" instead of "salesman." Choices (2) and (4) are incorrect because there is no indication that the five steps have been replaced by four or six steps. Choices (3) and (5) are incorrect because italicized headings and the word "prospect" are not old-fashioned.

3. **The correct answer is (4). (Application)** According to the passage, the salesperson supports his or her claims with facts at the "winning conviction" stage. The other answers are not supported by the passage.

UNIT 2: VISUAL INFORMATION

Exercise 1 *(page 103)*

What Is This Painting About?

1. **The correct answer is (4). (Comprehension)** The first sentence of the passage states that Picasso's post-Cubist work is characterized by "lightning changes of style," and *Guernica* is described as an amalgamation of many different styles. The passage offers no support for choice (1) because it doesn't comment on changes in style in Picasso's pre-Cubist works. The passage directly contradicts choice (2) because it says that Picasso did not follow in the tradition of Goya. Choices (3) and (5) are incorrect because while the passage does state that Picasso's work was influenced by Surrealism and Christian iconography, it does not state that either was his most important influence.

2. **The correct answer is (4). (Comprehension)** The passage states that the painting was created as a protest against the bombing of Guernica. Choice (1) is incorrect because although the passage does say that *Guernica* in retrospect has been viewed as a protest against twentieth-century atrocities, Picasso meant it as a protest against specific events at Guernica. Choice (2) is contradicted by the passage because it points out that the Nazis were in league with the Fascists when they bombed Guernica. Choice (3) is incorrect because although Picasso was commissioned by the Spanish Republican government to paint a mural for the Paris Exhibition, the painting is a condemnation of what transpired at Guernica. Choice (5) is incorrect because although the passage says the town of Guernica was Basque, the painting refers to the Spanish Civil War and has no connection with the Basque movement.

3. **The correct answer is (2). (Comprehension)** The passage states that the painting conveys both terror and resistance. None of the other answers are supported by the passage.

4. **The correct answer is (1). (Synthesis)** The reviewer speaks in positive terms of the painting throughout the passage with a tone of admiration, so the other choices can be eliminated as unsupported by the passage.

5. **The correct answer is (1). (Analysis)** Choice (1) includes three examples of images in the passage that are said to represent something else. Choice (4) might have symbolic value, but what it might represent is not made explicit, and it is only one example. The other choices are incorrect because they provide information about the painting that is unrelated to symbolism.

6. **The correct answer is (2). (Synthesis)** Since Picasso painted *Guernica* to protest the bombing of Guernica by Nazis in the service of the Spanish Fascists, it can be inferred that his sympathies did not lie with these groups and that he was not politically apathetic.

Exercise 2 *(page 105)*

What Is This Reviewer's Opinion?

1. **The correct answer is (1). (Synthesis)** The reviewer's examples refer to art, film, and literature. Choice (5) is incorrect because the reviewer's examples do not refer to astronomy, archeology, and psychology. Choices (2) and (4) are incorrect because the reviewer's observation is not negative. Choice (3) is wrong because although Nolde, Klimt, and Birnam Wood are all referred to, the reviewer does not say that their faces appear in the painting *Cache-Cache*. Also, Birnam Wood is a place, not a person.

2. **The correct answer is (2). (Comprehension)** The reviewer says that *Yellow Submarine* is a charming, pleasant film, and if the movie were not so "unpretentious, one would be embarrassed."

3. **The correct answer is (1). (Synthesis)** The reviewer's point is that some of the humor in the film is reminiscent of Lear's humor, but it is not as consistently clever as Lear's humor. Choices (2) and (4) are incorrect because the reviewer is making an unfavorable comparison to Lear. Choice (3) is incorrect because it is an overstatement to say that the film's humor is *strongly* influenced by Lear. Choice (5) is wrong because the reviewer does not criticize the resemblance to Lear's humor; she just says that the humor in the film does not live up to Lear's.

Exercise 3 *(page 107)*

What Is This Film About?

1. **The correct answer is (4). (Synthesis)** The reviewer doesn't call William Randolph Hearst by name, referring to him as "an eminent publisher." He praises the film for its artistry, saying *Citizen Kane* is "the most surprising and cinematically exciting motion picture to be seen here in many a moon." Choices (1) and (3) are incorrect because he never names William Randolph Hearst. Choices (2) and (5) are incorrect because the reviewer does not give an opinion as to the accuracy of the portrayal of Hearst but says that "it fails to provide a clear picture of the character" and his motives.

2. **The correct answer is (2). (Application)** The reviewer says of *Citizen Kane* that "suppression of this film would have been a crime" because of its artistic merit. Choice (1) is incorrect because the reviewer says nothing in support of censorship. Choice (3) is incorrect because the reviewer makes no general statement about censorship; hence this is an overstatement. Choice (4) is contradicted by the reviewer's statement that whether the film accurately parallels a person's life is "beside the point in a rigidly critical appraisal." Choice (5) is incorrect because the reviewer says nothing about movie executives and appears to support the director of the film, Orson Welles.

3. **The correct answer is (5). (Synthesis)** The fact that Kane would name his castle after the opulent estate of a powerful ruler suggests that he enjoys thinking of himself as rich and powerful. Choice (1) is incorrect because although it might be surmised that Kane admires Coleridge's poem, there is no support for the idea that Coleridge is his favorite poet. Choice (2) is incorrect because although Kane names his home after an Eastern estate, all we know of the design is that Kane lives in a "castle." Choices (3) and (4) are not supported by the passage.

Exercise 4 *(page 109)*

What Makes This Place Special?

1. **The correct answer is (2). (Synthesis)** The passage describes the dawn on the marsh, from the first faint signs until the cranes arrive to feed. Although hunters and hunting dogs are mentioned, there is no evidence for choices (1) or (3). Choices (4) and (5) are not supported by the passage.

2. **The correct answer is (2). (Analysis)** Alliteration refers to the repetition of sounds at the beginning of words. This sentence repeats both the "s" sound in "single silence" and the "h" sound in "horizon to horizon." None of the other choices use this technique.

3. **The correct answer is (5). (Synthesis)** You can determine the correct answer to this question by considering the author's tone and choice of language throughout the passage; also, you can eliminate the other choices as unsupported by the language. The language is calm but elevated, deliberate and cadenced, almost poetic. The overall effect is quiet awe at the wonder of the scene.

Exercise 5 *(page 110)*

Why Did a City Grow Here?

1. **The correct answer is (3). (Comprehension)** This item is related to cause and effect, but the answer is stated in the last paragraph of the passage. Although choices (1) and (2) are mentioned in the passage, they are not the reason that gravel banks are advantageous. Choices (4) and (5) are not supported by the passage.

2. **The correct answer is (1). (Analysis)** The main idea is stated in the first sentence of the first paragraph, and the rest of the passage is mostly detail.

3. **The correct answer is (4). (Application)** The passage states that "*ea*" meant island, and it gives an example of a name, Bermondsey, that is parallel with the correct answer, Hammondsey. There is no support for the other choices in the passage.

4. **The correct answer is (2). (Synthesis)** The main passage describes a place that is still unsettled yet destined for greatness by its geography. The excerpt depicts a time when vast numbers of people are pouring into the city—its destiny fulfilled. There is no support for the other choices in the main passage. Choice (5) is incorrect because by the 1840's people would have arrived in London by railroad and coach, not by boat.

Exercise 6 *(page 111)*

What Causes Cataracts?

1. **The correct answer is (1). (Comprehension)** The correct answer is stated directly in the second paragraph (line 6).

2. **The correct answer is (5). (Application)** The passage states that the person would need brighter and brighter light in order to see; therefore, the person would be likely to mention that the light seemed dimmer than usual. The other choices are not supported by the passage.

3. **The correct answer is (3). (Comprehension)** The passage states that senile cataracts, or cataracts related to old age, are the most common form. Choices (1), (2), and (4) are incorrect because these are all mentioned as minor causes, while the question asks for the most common cause. Choice (5), surgery, is mentioned in the passage as a cure, not a cause.

Exercise 7 *(page 112)*

What Is Synesthesia?

1. **The correct answer is (1). (Synthesis)** Nabokov goes so far as to discriminate between different shades of black and different textures. Choice (2) is incorrect because he does associate different sounds, colors, and textures together. Choice (3) is incorrect because Nabokov points out that he experiences synesthesia with both the English and French alphabets. Choice (4) is wrong because Nabokov gives no indication that he is embarrassed that he has synesthesia and appears to talk freely about it. Choice (5) is inaccurate because while it is apparent that Nabokov speaks Russian, English, and French, the question is directed at Nabokov's experience of synesthesia, not his mastery of languages.

2. **The correct answer is (1). (Comprehension)** The correct answer is stated directly in the first sentence of the second paragraph. Choices (2) and (3) are incorrect because, according to the passage, synesthesia results from sensations in the limbic system of the brain. Choice (4) is incorrect because the passage states that light muslin clothing worn by the ancient Romans was called synthesis, not synesthesia. Choice (5) is wrong because the passage says that life itself, not synesthesia, is "an onslaught on one's perceptions."

3. **The correct answer is (4). (Application)** The passage states that synesthesia means that more than one sense is stimulated, and in choice (4) both the auditory and visual senses are aroused. The other choices are not supported by the passage.

4. **The correct answer is (3). (Analysis)** A metaphor is figurative language that makes a comparison in which two things are described as the same without the use of the words *like* or *as*. None of the other choices make this comparison, so they can be ruled out.

Exercise 8 *(page 115)*

What Is a Gothic Cathedral?

1. **The correct answer is (4). (Analysis)** The passage is organized around a comparison/contrast of Notre Dame and Chartres Cathedral. The other choices do not describe the main pattern of organization used in the passage.

2. **The correct answer is (3). (Analysis)** The author does not express a preference for one of the cathedrals, so choices (1) and (2) are incorrect. Choice (4) is directly contradicted in the passage when the author states that "Chartres Cathedral stands in remarkable contrast" to Notre Dame. Choice (5) is incorrect because the writer does not discuss baroque style in the passage.

3. **The correct answer is (1). (Comprehension)** The passage emphasizes the difference between the solid, mathematical structure of Notre Dame and the amalgamation of a number of styles found in Chartres due to its reconstruction after a number of fires. The other answers are not supported by the passage.

Exercise 9 *(page 116)*

What Makes This Experience Important?

1. **The correct answer is (3). (Comprehension)** Douglass states that Covey does not touch him again after their fight because Covey knows that he "will come off worse" than he did before. Choices (1), (2), (4), and (5) are incorrect because there is no evidence in the passage that Covey has become a better person through his encounter with Frederick Douglass.

2. **The correct answer is (4). (Comprehension)** Douglass says that his struggle with Covey "revived within me a sense of my own manhood. It recalled the departed self-confidence . . ." Choice (1) is incorrect because, although Douglass may have a new awareness of how physically strong he is, the most significant change he undergoes involves emotional strength. Choice (2) is directly contradicted by the passage because Douglass states that he spent six more months with Covey and was still "a slave in form." Choice (3) is unsupported by the passage, and choice (5) is directly contradicted by the passage.

3. **The correct answer is (3). (Analysis)** Slavery is directly and implicitly compared to a tomb, so it is a metaphor. Choice (1) is incorrect because it is a simile, an explicit comparison using the signal word "like." Choices (2), (4), and (5) are incorrect because they are literal rather than figurative.

Exercise 10 *(page 118)*

What Makes This Experience Special?

1. **The correct answer is (3). (Analysis)** Personification means describing something that is not human in human terms. Choice (3) says that "the iron did not remember" and "the phosphorus had forgotten," actions that apply only to humans, so it is the correct choice.

2. **The correct answer is (4). (Synthesis)** Phrases such as "there went phosphorus, there went iron, there went carbon, there beat the calcium in those hurrying wings" incorporate both scientific and poetic language. Since the passage is nonfiction, the other choices can be ruled out.

3. **The correct answer is (1). (Application)** The author writes about natural phenomena such as the migration of the birds, and he relates his observations to the human condition. Choice (5) is incorrect because he does not indicate that he is a performer, and choices (2), (3), and (4) are incorrect because they do not include his interest in the study of nature.

4. **The correct answer is (4). (Application)** In the passage, the author draws a comparison between the wondrous yet ephemeral world of the dinosaurs, still a part of the landscape surrounding him, and the wondrous migration of birds that will also eventually be reduced to chemicals. Choices (1) and (5) are incorrect because the author does not discuss evolution. Choices (2) and (3) are incorrect because the author is not concentrating on the differences between birds and dinosaurs.

5. **The correct answer is (4). (Synthesis)** Both Leopold and Eiseley describe what the flock looks like and does, but only Eiseley also describes what the flock feels with details such as "it knew itself" and it is "lonely," with "its individual entities feeling about them the rising night." Choice (1) is incorrect because there is nothing in Leopold's sentence that suggests it is afternoon. Choice (2) is incorrect because the reverse is actually true: Leopold does not use a simile, a figure of speech in which two things are compared through the use of the words "like" or "as." Eiseley does use a simile when he says that the flock "swerved like a single body." Choices (3) and (5) are incorrect because both authors convey admiration and appreciation of the birds rather than any negative emotions.

Exercise 11 *(page 120)*

What Are Mangroves?

1. **The correct answer is (5). (Analysis)** Since a simile is an explicit comparison that contains the signal word "like" or "as," the other choices can be ruled out.

2. **The correct answer is (4). (Application)** The author calls Pliny credulous, or gullible, because he appears to believe that the mangrove islands can keep time to music: "they stir and move at the stroke of the feet, keeping time and measure." Choice (1) is incorrect because Pliny is correct in his belief that mangroves can become floating islands. Choice (2) is wrong because the passage says that "the people," not Pliny, referred to the river islands as *the dancers*. Choice (3) is incorrect because, although Pliny does write about mangroves, this does not indicate that he is credulous. Choice (5) is directly contradicted by the passage.

3. **The correct answer is (1). (Synthesis)** This answer can be arrived at by considering her tone and choice of words. She says that the thought of mangrove islands "amazes me," yet her descriptions include words such as "muck," "rot," and "guano." The other choices are not supported by the passage because they fail to encompass a perspective of awe and realism.

Exercise 12 *(page 122)*

Where Does the Rogue River Begin?

1. **The correct answer is (2). (Analysis)** The author uses second-person point of view throughout most of the passage, for example, "Take off your boots, douse your feet." The other choices are not supported by the passage.

2. **The correct answer is (2). (Synthesis)** A point of view that addresses the reader directly tends to involve readers in what they are reading by including them in the scene. Choices (1) and (4) are incorrect because the second-person point of view in this passage is conversational in tone. Choice (3) is not supported by the text. Choice (5) is incorrect because the second-person point of view draws readers into the text and encourages them to have a subjective response.

3. **The correct answer is (5). (Analysis)** Personification is the attribution of human qualities to nonhuman things. In this passage, the river is given a human voice. The other choices are not supported by the text.

4. **The correct answer is (1). (Analysis)** The focus of the passage is on the beginnings of rivers. Choice (2) is wrong because the emphasis is on rivers rather than people. Choice (3) is incorrect because, although the setting is partially at Crater Lake, the focus is on the Rogue River and its origins. Choice (4) is incorrect because the main focus of the passage is not on weather patterns. Choice (5) is not supported by the passage.

Exercise 13 *(page 123)*

Who Were the Kiowas?

1. **The correct answer is (1). (Comprehension)** The passage states that Aho, a Kiowa, "belonged to the last culture to evolve in North American. Choices (2) and (3) are incorrect because the passage says that the Kiowas adopted the religion and culture of the Plains from the Crows. Choice (4) is incorrect because the information is reversed: the Kiowas migrated from the high country of western Montana to the southern Plains. Choice (5) is false because while the passage says that the Kiowas practiced the sacred Sun Dance, it does not say that the Kiowas were the last culture to do so.

2. **The correct answer is (5). (Comprehension)** Based on the chronology of the passage, the author is referring to the migration of the Kiowas from the cold mountains of western Montana to the warm southern plains. Choices (1) and (4) are incorrect because even though the Kiowas did emerge from these places, these locations belong to different time frames than the one the author is referring to. Choice (2) is incorrect because only mythologically speaking did the Kiowas emerge from a hollow log. Choice (3) is incorrect because the Kiowas reached a sunny world when they arrived in the southern Plains.

3. **The correct answer is (4). (Comprehension)** The author says that "warfare for the Kiowas was preeminently a matter of disposition . . ." Choices (1) and (2) are incorrect because the Kiowa are not described as pacifists. In another section of the passage they are called "a lordly and dangerous society of fighters and thieves, hunters and priests of the sun." Choice (3) is incorrect because the Kiowa are contrasted with the white soldiers: "But warfare for the Kiowas preeminently a matter of disposition rather than of survival, and they never understood the grim, unrelenting advance of the U.S. Cavalry." Choice (5) is contradicted by the passage because the Kiowa are described as "in alliance with the Comanches" and "befriended by the Crows."

Exercise 14 *(page 125)*

What Does the Fisherman Experience?

1. **The correct answer is (3). (Comprehension)** The author says that he unhooks the fly and "the fish streaks for the depths . . ." The other answers are not supported by the passage.

2. **The correct answer is (2). (Comprehension)** The author says that since the rings drift downstream when fish leap, fishermen must cast "to an invisible memory of where rings first appear," and this is "the memory point." The other answers are not supported by the text.

3. **The correct answer is (3). (Application)** The author says that when he was younger, he would rush to catch more fish, but "what I often want now is to be more present where I am." This statement can be taken to apply to more than just fishing and suggests that he desires to slow down and savor life. Choice (1) is incorrect because he has not lost his energy, but has other priorities, and he still exhibits enthusiasm. Choice (2) is incorrect because the passage doesn't address the issue of knowledge. Choice (4) is incorrect because he does not appear to be obsessed with death, although he mentions it. Choice (5) is incorrect because the unusual sights he sees are reflections in the water.

4. **The correct answer is (4). (Comprehension)** The author describes himself casting to a memory point "using eyes alone." Choices (1) and (2) are incorrect because he leans his rod against an osier before he casts to the memory point. Choice (3) is incorrect because in the passage he is at the scene, not remembering it. Choice (5) is contradicted by information in the passage.

Exercise 15 *(page 126)*

What Visitors Come to the Pond?

1. **The correct answer is (3). (Analysis)** Metaphors are direct, implicit comparisons of unlike things. In this case the snakes' bodies are equated with cursive alphabets. Choices (1), (2), and (4) are similes, explicit comparisons of unlike things that use the signal words "like" or "as." Choice (5) is a personification, attributing human qualities to nonhuman things.

2. **The correct answer is (1). (Application)** The author says that "for several years that Cooper's hawk was the steadiest male presence in my life." This suggests that she had been single for many years, but "was" makes this past tense and suggests that she now has a male partner. The other choices are not supported by the passage.

3. **The correct answer is (3). (Application)** The author takes pleasure in watching the animal and plant life around her pond, and she speaks of "receiving gifts in every season." Choices (1), (2), and (5) are incorrect because even though she mentions periods where her heart felt like it was "on ice," the main point is that the wondrous animal life "went on whirling recklessly around me," regardless of how she felt. Choice (4) is incorrect because she seems more fascinated than disgusted when watching two snakes eat a frog.

Exercise 16 *(page 128)*

What Is This Place Like?

1. **The correct answer is (1). (Analysis)** A simile is an explicit comparison between unlike things using the signal words "like" or "as." The other choices are not supported by the text.

2. **The correct answer is (2). (Synthesis)** The tone and word choice suggest this refuge has some healing qualities. It is described as "a holy place," where the author is "hidden and saved from the outside world." It is the den of the author's "healing." Knowledge of her mother's death adds sadness and need to the scene and intensifies the sense of loss when she comments that the men in her family have temporarily moved away and her family is "fractured and displaced." The therapeutic connotation of some words is interspersed with the sadness of "bleed" and "weeping." The other choices are not supported by the emotions that the tone and word choice convey. Choices (1) and (4) are incorrect because the cave is described as a wondrous place. Choice (3) is incorrect because no anger is shown. Choice (5) is incorrect because it describes a scene that is content, without the sadness of the loss of a loved one.

3. **The correct answer is (3). (Analysis)** The paragraph that reads, *"Drip. Drip-drip. Drip. Drip. Drip-drip,"* mimics what the author hears as she sits in the cave. The other choices are incorrect because they do not sound like what they represent.

GLOSSARY

allusions: unacknowledged references that a work makes to other sources that relate to it

analogy: the extended comparison of things of different kinds

fact: something that can be proved to be true

first person: point of view that relates a narrative from the perspective of "I" or "we"

information text: a document that is organized so that you can find key information quickly

objective: point of view that relates only what occurs without entering the minds of any characters

omniscient: point of view that relates not only what occurs but also what the characters are thinking

onomatopoeia: the use of words that sound like what they represent

opinion: a belief that cannot be proved absolutely but that can be supported with evidence

perspective: a way of looking at people, places, and events

second person: point of view that narrates from the perspective of "you"

thesis statement: a declarative sentence that states the main point of an essay

third person: point of view that narrates from the perspective of "he," "she," "it," or "they"

topic sentence: sentence that states the main point of a paragraph and supports the thesis of a nonfiction work

Practice Test 1

Directions: Read each passage; then answer the questions that follow. Choose the *one best answer* to each question.

Items 1–8 refer to the following excerpt from a novel.

ROAD MAP

- *Practice Test 1*
- *Answers and Explanations*

How Are the Mothers at Grand Isle Depicted?

Line It would have been a difficult matter for Mr. Pontellier to define to his own satisfaction or any one else's wherein his wife failed in her duty toward their children. It was something that he felt rather than perceived, and he never voiced the feeling without subsequent regret and ample atonement.

If one of the little Pontellier boys took a tumble whilst at play, he was not apt to rush crying to his mother's arms for comfort; he would more likely pick himself up, wipe the water out of his eyes and the sand out of his mouth, and go on playing. Tots as they were, they pulled together and stood their ground in childish battles with doubled fists and uplifted voices, which usually prevailed against the other mother-tots. The quadroon nurse was looked upon as a huge encumbrance, only good to button up waists and panties and to brush and part hair, since it seemed to be a law of society that hair must be parted and brushed.

In short, Mrs. Pontellier was not a mother-woman. The mother-women seemed to prevail that summer at Grand Isle. It was easy to know them, fluttering about with extended, protecting wings when any harm, real or imaginary, threatened their precious brood. They were women who idolized their children, worshipped their husbands, and esteemed it a holy privilege to efface themselves as individuals and grow wings as ministering angels.

Many of them were delicious in the role; one of them was the embodiment of every womanly grace and charm. If her husband did not adore her, he was a brute, deserving of death by slow torture. Her name was Adele Ratignolle. There are no words to describe her save the old ones that have served so often to picture the bygone heroine of romance and the fair lady of our dreams.

—From *The Awakening* by Kate Chopin

1. The setting of this passage is most likely a

    (1)   steamy hot city.
    (2)   relaxed vacation site.
    (3)   bustling overcrowded train.
    (4)   grand old mansion.
    (5)   formal hotel.

2. When Mr. Pontellier criticizes his wife's care of their children, he apologizes because

    (1)   he knows he has not been a good father.
    (2)   the children don't care about what she does.
    (3)   he thinks the nurse cares for them adequately.
    (4)   he couldn't explain what her inadequacy was.
    (5)   she loves them in spite of her lack of attention to them.

3. Which of the following best characterizes Mrs. Pontellier as a mother?

   (1) Warm and loving
   (2) Strict yet comforting
   (3) Cruel and abusive
   (4) Somewhat distant
   (5) Overprotective

4. "... it seemed to be a law of society that hair must be parted and brushed."

   Which of the following best describes the tone of this statement?

   (1) Serious
   (2) Respectful
   (3) Social
   (4) Studious
   (5) Exaggerated

5. Based on paragraph 2, the Pontellier children could best be described as

   (1) sheltered.
   (2) immature.
   (3) loving.
   (4) foolish.
   (5) independent.

6. Based on the last sentence in paragraph 3, what is the meaning of *efface*?

   (1) Erase
   (2) Strengthen
   (3) Condemn
   (4) Praise
   (5) Support

7. What do the first two sentences of paragraph 4 suggest about Adele Ratignolle?

   (1) She exemplified the "mother-women" that summer.
   (2) She was frequently spoiled by her family and friends.
   (3) She was envied by the other women.
   (4) She cooked delicious meals for her family.
   (5) Her husband never treated her well.

8. An early reviewer of this novel wrote, "At the very outset of the story, one feels that the heroine [Mrs. Pontellier] should pray for deliverance from temptation . . . It is not a healthy book; if it points to any particular moral or teaches any lesson, the fact is not apparent."

   —"Notes from Bookland," *St. Louis Daily Globe-Democrat*

   Based on the passage from the novel, a reader can conclude that this reviewer thinks the novel is unhealthy because

   (1) Adele Ratignolle is contrasted with Mrs. Pontellier.
   (2) the children are not always obedient.
   (3) Mrs. Pontellier does not behave the way a mother ought to.
   (4) Mr. Pontellier is an immoral person.
   (5) people relax behavioral standards when on vacation.

Items 9–13 refer to the following excerpt from a contract.

What Rights Does This Credit Card Give You?

Billing Rights Summary

Line   In case of errors or questions about your bill: If you think your bill is wrong or if you
need more information about a transaction on your bill, write us on a separate sheet of
paper at the billing error notice address shown on the front where annual percentage
rates are displayed, as soon as possible. We must hear from you no later than 60 days
5   after we sent you the first bill on which the error or problem appeared. You can
telephone us, but doing so will not preserve your rights. In your letter, give us the
following information:

    1. your name and account number
    2. the dollar amount of the suspected error
10   3. Describe the error and explain, if you can, why you believe there is an error.
       If you need more information, describe the item you are unsure about.

After we receive your letter, we cannot try to collect any amount you question or
report you as delinquent. We can continue to bill you for the amount you question,
including finance charges, and we can apply any unpaid amount against your credit
15   limit. You do not have to pay any questioned amount while we are investigating, but
you are still obligated to pay the parts of your bill that are not in question.

Special Rule for Credit Card Purchases

If you have a problem with the quality of goods or services that you purchased with a
credit card, and you have tried in good faith to correct the problem with the merchant,
you may not have to pay the remaining amount due on the goods or services. You
20   have this protection only when the purchase price was more than $50 and the purchase
was made in your home state or within 100 miles of your mailing address. (If we own
or operate the merchant, or if we mailed you the advertisement for the goods or
services, all purchases are covered regardless of amount or location of purchase.)

—From Terms and Conditions of Credit Card Account

9. If you think there is an error on your bill, you should send a letter to the

    (1)   address where you send your payments.
    (2)   annual percentage rate location.
    (3)   address listed for billing error notices.
    (4)   credit card company's corporation address.
    (5)   collection agency asking you for payment.

10. On your credit card bill, there is a charge for $350 from Classy Pants. You bought one
pair of jeans, which cost $35, at that store. The best thing to do would be to

    (1)   call Classy Pants to complain.
    (2)   write to Classy Pants asking them to correct the error.
    (3)   close your credit card account.
    (4)   write to the credit card company explaining the error.
    (5)   return the jeans to Classy Pants.

11. The tone of this Billing Rights Summary is best described as

    (1) informative.
    (2) threatening.
    (3) friendly.
    (4) humorous.
    (5) thoughtful.

12. You have a problem with an item you charged on your card, but the store where you bought it will neither give you a refund nor exchange the item. In such a case, you

    (1) are always protected from paying the amount due.
    (2) can make a claim only if the item cost more than $50.
    (3) can make a claim only if you bought the item in your home state.
    (4) are always protected from paying if the credit card company owns that store.
    (5) cannot be sued by the owner of the store.

13. Your credit card bill shows a purchase of $75 from United General Merchandisers.

    You have never heard of this company. You should

    (1) telephone United General Merchandisers to ask what they sell.
    (2) write to United General Merchandisers asking for an explanation.
    (3) telephone the credit card company asking for an explanation.
    (4) write to the credit card company asking for more information.
    (5) file a legal complaint against United General Merchandisers.

Items 14–19 refer to the following poem.

How Does This Speaker Feel about Work?

Work

Line   I don't have to work.
        I don't have to do nothing
        but eat, drink, stay black, and die.
        This little old furnished room's
5   so small I can't whip a cat
        without getting fur in my mouth
        and my landlady's so old
        her features is all run together
        and God knows she sure can overcharge—
10   which is why I reckon I does
        have to work after all.

—From *Necessity* by Langston Hughes

14. From this poem, what can be concluded about the speaker?

    (1) He owns a house.
    (2) He resents the freedom of animals.
    (3) He admires his landlady.
    (4) He rents an apartment.
    (5) He has two jobs.

15. If the poem ended at line 3, the speaker might have to

  (1) leave this apartment.
  (2) rent a larger apartment.
  (3) eat more food.
  (4) sue his landlady.
  (5) buy a house.

16. "This little old furnished room's/so small I can't whip a cat/without getting fur in my mouth." The tone of this figurative statement could best be described as

  (1) exaggerated.
  (2) cruel.
  (3) angry.
  (4) proud.
  (5) embarrassed.

17. ". . . my landlady's so old/her features is all run together." This figurative description reveals that the landlady's skin is

  (1) smooth and firm.
  (2) damaged by the sun.
  (3) a soft tan color.
  (4) wrinkled and sagging.
  (5) covered with freckles.

18. This poem's structure is best described as a

  (1) narrative.
  (2) description.
  (3) comparison.
  (4) problem and solution.
  (5) situation and realization.

19. The main idea of this poem could best be stated as

  (1) people are lazy.
  (2) old women are greedy.
  (3) work is a necessity.
  (4) idleness is desirable.
  (5) ethnicity cannot be changed.

Items 20–24 refer to the following excerpt from a magazine article.

What Makes This Artist's Work Distinctly American?

Line   Winslow Homer (1836–1910) is today universally embraced as a powerful visual poet whose fluid brushwork and bold compositions created big metaphors for the contested relationship between Man and Nature . . .

The critics regularly differed among themselves, but a certain constancy does
5   emerge. In deciding what was putatively American about American art, in general, and about Homer's art in particular, two issues loomed large. One concerned subject matter, the other technique.

A lovely picture like "The Cotton Pickers" . . . could be seen as American on its face. Two black women, represented with a solemn dignity and not a trace of
10   sentimentality, stand before the agrarian landscape like humble Nikes, their heads wreathed in farmer's bonnets and with baskets of cotton as their palm branches. African Americans were frequently subjects of Homer's oils and watercolors, and these include some of the most compelling works in the show.

Sometimes the presumed American-ness of the subject is more submerged. In
15   the radiant light-infused interior of a one-room schoolhouse, for instance, the unprecedented American pledge of universal education as a linchpin for functional democracy is implied. In the classic picture of farm boys at play, "Snap the Whip" (1872)—and indeed in the general abundance of Homer's relaxed, candid, unsentimental images of children, both white and black—the promise of America's
20   future is unfurled.

Technique was an equally slippery issue. Homer, especially because of his gifts as a watercolorist, was regularly lambasted for paintings that looked sketchy and unfinished. Like their compatriots in the French Academy, many American observers perceived a sketch to be an incomplete and unrefined idea . . .
25   Homer increasingly portrayed the fading theme of Man and Nature, for which he would be remembered.

"Breezing Up (Fair Wind)" (1876) is a knockout early example, the best painting in the show. The choppy sea, sky, and clouds are wide horizontal expanses of mottled color. No middle ground is depicted—just a silhouetted boat in the
30   background, and dramatic sloop commanding the foreground. Homer typically composed on a grid, adding dynamism by tipping major elements 90 degrees. Here, he also tilts the sailboat in space, creating an ample volume of luminous air at the picture's core.

A man guiding the sail's ropes is accompanied by three boys who lean against
35   the wind, their backs carved out of light. Pulling together, a generational tableau stabilizes the little vessel in choppy water, enacting fundamental lessons in survival.

—From "The Ideas Bristle" by Christopher Knight

20. Based on this passage, the most likely of the following to be a subject of a painting by Winslow Homer would be

    (1)   the Eiffel Tower in France.
    (2)   harvesting wheat in Kansas.
    (3)   planting rice in Japan.
    (4)   a self-portrait.
    (5)   a still-life of apples and pears in a bowl.

21. In discussing what was American about American art, the critics considered

    (1)   the theme of man and nature.
    (2)   subjects such as a schoolhouse and children playing.
    (3)   what was painted and how it was painted.
    (4)   what appeared in the foreground and background of the composition.
    (5)   how the paint was applied to the canvas.

22. According to paragraph 3, all of these elements appear in "The Cotton Pickers" EXCEPT

    (1)   two women.
    (2)   baskets.
    (3)   palm branches.
    (4)   a cotton field.
    (5)   bonnets.

23. The critic thinks "Breezing Up (Fair Wind)" is the best picture in the show because of its

    (1)   subject.
    (2)   coloring.
    (3)   size.
    (4)   composition.
    (5)   Americanism.

24. The critic mentions Homer's use of children in his pictures in order to

    (1)   show that Homer loved children.
    (2)   emphasize the American elements in Homer's work.
    (3)   criticize the French Academy.
    (4)   praise Homer's skill as an artist.
    (5)   prove he is a patriot as well as a critic.

Items 25–29 refer to the following excerpt from a short story.

How Does This Narrator Recall Her Past?

Line   I was fifteen and away from home for the first time. My parents had made the effort and sent me to high school for a year, but I didn't like it. I was shy of strangers and the work was hard; they didn't make it nice for you or explain the way they do now.

At the end of the year, the averages were published in the paper, and mine came
5   out at the very bottom . . . My father said that's enough and I didn't blame him. The last thing I wanted, anyway, was to go on and end up teaching school. It happened the very day the paper came out with my disgrace in it. Dr. Peebles was staying at our place for dinner, having just helped one of the cows have twins, and he said I looked smart to him and his wife was looking for a girl to help. He said she felt tied down,
10   with the two children, out in the country. I guess she would, my mother said, being polite, though I could tell from her face she was wondering what on earth it would be like to have only two children and no barn work, and then to be complaining.

When I went home, I would describe to them the work I had to do, and it made everybody laugh. Mrs. Peebles had an automatic washer and dryer, the first I ever saw.
15   I have had those in my own home for such a long time now it's hard to remember how much of a miracle it was to me, not having to struggle with the wringer and hang up and haul down. Let alone not having to heat water. Then there was practically no baking. Mrs. Peebles said she couldn't make piecrust, the most amazing thing I ever heard a woman admit. I could, of course, and I could make light biscuits and white
20   cake and dark cake, but they didn't want it; she said that they watched their figures. The only thing I didn't like about working there, in fact, was feeling half hungry a lot of the time.

—From "How I Met My Husband" by Alice Munro

25. From the passage, it is clear that Dr. Peebles is a

    (1)   dermatologist.
    (2)   psychologist.
    (3)   surgeon.
    (4)   veterinarian.
    (5)   vegetarian.

26. The purpose of the first three sentences in paragraph 2 is to

    (1)   show how her employers lived.
    (2)   contrast herself then and now.
    (3)   indicate her family was poor.
    (4)   explain why she worked for the Peebles.
    (5)   criticize the Peebles' extravagance.

27. What adds irony to Dr. Peebles saying the speaker looked smart to him?

    (1)   He just met her.
    (2)   She failed in high school.
    (3)   She was shy around strangers.
    (4)   His wife wanted to hire someone to help with housework.
    (5)   He was eating dinner with her family.

28. Since the speaker thinks Mrs. Peebles's admission she can't make piecrust is, "the most amazing thing I ever heard a woman admit," the reader can conclude that she

   (1)   enjoyed baking.
   (2)   disliked Mrs. Peebles.
   (3)   assumed all women could bake.
   (4)   didn't get enough to eat.
   (5)   planned to teach Mrs. Peebles to bake.

29. From the tone of this passage, the speaker's attitude toward her younger self could best be described as

   (1)   disgust.
   (2)   distrust.
   (3)   anger.
   (4)   respect.
   (5)   amusement.

Items 30–35 refer to the following excerpt from a play.

How Does This Young Woman React?

Husband: Well, how are we today? *[Young Woman—no response]*

Nurse: She's getting stronger!

Husband: Of course she is!

Nurse: *[Taking flowers]* See what your husband brought you.

Husband: Better put 'em in water right away. *[Exit Nurse.]* Everything OK? *[Young Woman signs "No."]* Now see here, my dear, you've got to brace up, you know! And—and face things! Everybody's got to brace up and face things! That's what makes the world go round. I know all you've been through but—[Young Woman signs "No."] Oh, yes I do! I know all about it! I was right outside all the time! *[Young Woman makes violent gesture of "no." Ignoring]* Oh yes! But you've got to brace up now! Make an effort! Pull yourself together! Start the uphill climb! Oh I've been down—but I haven't stayed down. I've been licked but I haven't stayed licked! I've pulled myself up by my own bootstraps, and that's what you've got to do! Will power! That's what conquers. Look at me! Now you've got to brace up! Face the music! Stand the gaff! Take life by the horns! Look it in the face! Having a baby's natural! Perfectly natural thing—why should—[Young Woman chokes—points wildly to door. Enter nurse with flowers in a vase.]

Nurse: What's the matter?

Husband: She's gagging again—like she did the last time I was here. *[Young Woman gestures him out.]*

Nurse: Better go, sir.

Husband: *[At door]* I'll be back. *[Young Woman gasping and gesturing.]*

Nurse: She needs rest.

Husband: Tomorrow then. I'll be back tomorrow—tomorrow and every day—goodbye.

                        —From *Machinal* by Sophie Treadwell

30. Based on the setting of this passage and on the husband's comments, you can infer that this young woman

    (1) is resting quietly at home.
    (2) has been through childbirth.
    (3) is in love with her husband.
    (4) will never be able to walk again.
    (5) was in a serious car accident.

31. The stage directions that describe the young woman's actions show that she is

    (1) upbeat and hopeful.
    (2) sincere and well-intentioned.
    (3) generous and noble.
    (4) afraid and timid.
    (5) depressed and upset.

32. As the passage continues, the young woman becomes

    (1) increasingly uncertain.
    (2) more dependent on her husband.
    (3) more panic-stricken.
    (4) increasingly ashamed.
    (5) intensely serious.

33. The function of the nurse in this scene is to

    (1) encourage the husband's behavior.
    (2) care for the baby.
    (3) help and protect the young woman.
    (4) pretend that there is no problem.
    (5) call for aid in an emergency.

34. In his long speech to the young woman, the husband's tone is

    (1) pitying.
    (2) tender and loving.
    (3) sarcastic.
    (4) scolding.
    (5) humorous.

35. When the husband returns the next day, the young woman most likely will

    (1) greet him with a warm smile.
    (2) ask the nurse to show him the baby.
    (3) get out of bed and hit him.
    (4) shout at him angrily.
    (5) refuse to speak to him.

Items 36–40 refer to the following excerpt from a novel.

What Are This Speaker's Feelings for His Wife?

Line   Oh, my love. Yes. Here we sit, on warm broad floorboards, before a fire, the children
between us, in a crescent, eating. The girl and I share one-half pint of French-fried
potatoes; you and the boy share another; and in the center, sharing nothing, making
simple reflections within himself like a jewel, the baby, mounted in an Easybaby,
5   sucks at his bottle.

Three children, five persons, seven years. Seven years since I wed wide warm
woman, white-thighed. Wooed and wed. Wife. A knife of a word that for all its final
bite did not end the wooing. To my wonderment.

We eat meat, meat I wrestled warm from the raw hands of the hamburger girl in
10   the diner a mile away, a ferocious place, slick with savagery, wild with chrome; young
predators snarling dirty jokes menaced me; old men reached for me with
coffee-warmed paws; I wielded my wallet, and won my way back. The fat brown bag
of buns was warm beside me in the cold car; the smaller bag holding the two tiny
cartons of French-fries emitted an even more urgent heat. Back through the black
15   winter air to the fire, the intimate cave, where halloos and hurrahs greeted me, the
deer, mouth agape and its cotton throat gushing, stretched dead across my shoulder.
And now you, beside the white O of the plate upon which the children discarded with
squeals of disgust the rings of translucent onion that came squeezed into the
hamburgers—you push your toes an inch closer to the blaze. . .
20   Who would have thought, wide wife, back there in the white tremble of the
ceremony (in the corner of my eye I held, despite the distracting hails of ominous
vows, the vibration of the cluster of stephanotis clutched at your waist), that seven
years would bring us no distance, through all those warm beds, to the same trembling
point, of beginning?

—From *Wife Wooing* by John Updike

36. The main idea of this passage is best described as

    (1)   the joys of fatherhood.
    (2)   the struggle for survival.
    (3)   the persistence of romantic love.
    (4)   eating dinner with the family.
    (5)   thinking about the past.

37. When the narrator refers to "the deer, mouth agape, and its cotton throat gushing,
    stretched dead across my shoulders," he is referring to

    (1)   a deer he shot.
    (2)   the venison burgers they were eating.
    (3)   a leather jacket he wears.
    (4)   his cotton neck scarf.
    (5)   living in a forest.

38. When the speaker says "wife" is a "knife of a word," he is emphasizing

    (1) that marriage ends the emotions of single life.
    (2) the cruelty of leaving one's family to marry.
    (3) how difficult it is to have a happy marriage.
    (4) the sharpness of the emotions he feels.
    (5) his wife's possessiveness.

39. The description of buying the hamburgers and bringing them home shows the speaker wants to think of himself as

    (1) dutiful.
    (2) patriotic.
    (3) youthful.
    (4) efficient.
    (5) heroic.

40. Based on the passage, if the husband starts to talk to the wife later in the evening, the conversation might be about

    (1) a life insurance policy.
    (2) the children's health.
    (3) memories of their honeymoon.
    (4) what to have for dinner tomorrow.
    (5) buying a new car.

ANSWERS AND EXPLANATIONS
How Are the Mothers at Grand Isle Depicted? *(page 141)*

1. **The correct answer is (2). (Synthesis)** The passage mentions sand, water, and summer, so the setting is probably a vacation site—seashore or an island. Choices (1) and (3) can be eliminated because they describe crowded, stressful situations. Although families may be staying in large old homes or even hotels, there is no evidence to support these ideas; therefore, choices (4) and (5) can be eliminated.

2. **The correct answer is (4). (Comprehension)** The first sentence says he could not "define" how she "failed." His regret is about criticizing her, not about his behavior toward the children, so choice (1) is not correct. Nothing in the passage states his attitude toward the nurse or the children's attitude toward their mother, so choices (2) and (3) can be eliminated. While one might guess Mrs. Pontellier loves her children even if she does not "idolize" them as the mother-women do, that cannot be assumed from the information in the passage; thus choice (5) is not a good answer.

3. **The correct answer is (4). (Synthesis)** Since Mrs. Pontellier's child is "not apt to rush crying to his mother's arms for comfort," she is probably a somewhat distant mother. Choices (1) and (5) suggest the opposite, whereas choice (3) is too strongly negative a description based on the passage. There is no evidence that Mrs. Pontellier is or is not strict, but the speaker does indicate she is not comforting, so choice (2) is incorrect.

4. **The correct answer is (5). (Analysis)** Since hair parting cannot be an actual law, the speaker is humorously exaggerating its importance to the characters in this passage. Choices (1), (2), and (4) suggest that the speaker is serious. Although the speaker is describing a social custom or standard, her tone could not be characterized as social; therefore, choice (3) can be eliminated.

5. **The correct answer is (5). (Synthesis)** The passage states a child would pick himself up and continue to play if he fell rather than going to his mother, and the children join with each other and win childish arguments against others. Choices (1), (2), and (4) are descriptions implying weakness, which is contradicted by the description of their behavior. While their banding together may indicate they love each other, "loving" is too general a term to describe their character from the limited description in the passage, so choice (3) is not a good answer.

6. **The correct answer is (1). (Synthesis)** The point of the statement is that women direct so much of their energy toward their husbands and children that their own personalities are nearly erased, or *effaced* . Choices (2), (4), and (5) are incorrect because they suggest that the women are building up, not erasing their own personalities. Choice (3) is not the best choice because the women are not criticizing or condemning themselves—they simply aren't paying any attention to their own needs.

7. **The correct answer is (1). (Synthesis)** As the "embodiment of every womanly grace and charm," Adele is the model, or perfect example, of the "mother-woman." Choices (2), (3), and (4) may be true, but they are not supported by the passages. Adele's husband is not described, so choice (5) is incorrect.

8. **The correct answer is (3). (Synthesis)** From the passage, the only character described with whom the reviewer might find fault is Mrs. Pontellier. While choice (1) accurately describes the structure of the passage, it does not present a reason for a moral judgment. Choice (5) is contradicted by the reference to "laws of society," which are maintained even when on vacation. There is no moral basis for judging Mr. Pontellier or the children in the passage, so choices (2) and (4) can be eliminated.

What Rights Does This Credit Card Give You? (page 143)

9. **The correct answer is (3). (Comprehension)** The passage explicitly states the letter should be sent to the "billing error notice address," which is located at the same place where the "annual percentage rates" are shown, but the annual percentage rate location is not an address, so choice (2) is incorrect. Choices (1), (4), and (5) are incorrect because the instructions do not make reference to any of these addresses.

10. **The correct answer is (4). (Application)** The passage assumes that the credit card company, not the merchant, will correct billing errors, so choices (1), (2), and (5) would not correct the billing error. Choice (3) would neither correct the error nor relieve the customer of the responsibility of paying the amount allegedly due.

11. **The correct answer is (1). (Analysis)** While the passage explains what will happen in various situations, it does not threaten any action against the customer, so choice (2) is incorrect. While the passage is serious, "thoughtful," choice (5), suggests discussions of complicated ideas, which the passage does not do. Choices (3) and (4) are inappropriate for business communications and do not describe the tone of this passage.

12. **The correct answer is (4). (Comprehension)** This is explicitly stated in the last sentence of the passage. Choices (2) and (3) are incorrect because of the exception noted in that sentence. Choice (1) is incorrect because the passage states you "may" not have to pay. The passage does not discuss what the store owner's rights may be, so choice (5) is not a good answer.

13. **The correct answer is (4). (Application)** This situation is an example of what the passage means by "If you need more information, describe the item you are unsure about." Choice (3) is not a good answer because the passage states that telephoning will not protect the customer's rights. While telephoning the company to ask what merchandise they sell, choice (1), might satisfy curiosity, it will do nothing to solve the problem, nor will writing to the company, choice (2). Filing a legal complaint is too strong a reaction at this point in time, therefore choice (5) is not appropriate.

How Does This Speaker Feel about Work? (page 144)

14. **The correct answer is (4). (Synthesis)** The speaker mentions that his landlady overcharges; thus he does not own a home, as choice (1) suggests. The speaker's feelings about animals in general cannot be inferred from his mention of one cat; so choice (2) can be eliminated. Since he resents his landlady, choice (3) is incorrect. Choice (5) can be eliminated because the specifics of the speaker's work situation are not given.

15. **The correct answer is (1). (Application)** At the end of line 3, the speaker has not yet decided that work is essential. Without working, he could not afford the rent and might have to move. Without working, he probably could not rent a larger apartment, eat more, or buy a house as stated in choices (2), (3), and (5). By the end of line 3, the speaker has not yet mentioned a grievance against his landlady, as choice (4) suggests.

16. **The correct answer is (1). (Analysis)** The speaker does not actually "whip a cat" to prove how small his apartment is, so this figurative statement is humorous, and choice (2) is incorrect. Though the apartment is very small, the speaker does not seem especially angry, proud, or embarrassed by that fact; thus, choices (3), (4), and (5) can be eliminated.

17. **The correct answer is (4). (Analysis)** If the landlady's features look as though they run together, her skin must be wrinkled and sagging. Choice (1) suggests the opposite. The color of the landlady's skin and freckles are not mentioned, so choices (3) and (5) can be eliminated. Her skin may be damaged by the sun, but this is not stated in the poem; thus, choice (2) is incorrect.

18. **The correct answer is (5). (Analysis)** The poem does not tell a story in order of events as choice (1) suggests, nor is the entire poem a physical description, so choice (2) is incorrect. While the speaker changes his mind during the course of the poem, his realization about work comes from his thoughts, rather than merely contrasting his earlier idea, so choice (3) is not a good answer. The speaker does not think he has a problem until the poem's last two lines, so choice (4) is not a good answer.

19. **The correct answer is (3). (Synthesis)** All of the other choices, while they may be inferred from one or more lines in the poem, do not describe the entire poem's theme as well as choice (3).

What Makes This Artist's Work Distinctively American?

(page 146)

20. **The correct answer is (2). (Application)** The passage states Homer painted American subjects with the theme of Man and Nature. This is the only choice that meets both of those criteria. While a self-portrait could be an American subject since Homer was an American, it would not illustrate the theme of Man and Nature, so choice (4) is not a good choice. Choices (1) and (3) have to do with nature but in other countries. Choice (5) has to do with nature but not with America.

21. **The correct answer is (3). (Comprehension)** The passage states that critics considered "subject matter" (what was painted) and "technique" (how it was painted). Choice (5) paraphrases only the idea of technique, but it does not include subject matter; nor does choice (4). Choices (1) and (2) mention elements in Homer's paintings, but not the critics' general criteria.

22. **The correct answer is (3). (Comprehension)** Paragraph 3 states that baskets of cotton substitute for the palm branches that would be in the hands of a Nike, not that the painting portrays the palm branches. Choices (1), (2), (4), and (5) are all mentioned as being in the painting.

23. **The correct answer is (4). (Composition)** Paragraphs 7 and 8, which describe this picture, discuss how its elements are related to each other on the canvas. There is no mention of the picture's size, so choice (3) is incorrect. The color and subject, choices (2) and (1), are mentioned, but they are not the focus of the description. The American element of the painting is not analyzed in this description, so choice (5) is not a correct answer.

24. **The correct answer is (2). (Analysis)** The passage does not state that Homer liked children, choice (1). While the French Academy, choice (3), is mentioned in paragraph 5, it is not related to children in the pictures. While the whole review praises Homer's skill as an artist, choice (4), in this paragraph it is not mentioned in connection with the children in his pictures, so it is not a good answer. Choice (5) is a statement about the critic, not about Homer, and thus it would not be an appropriate answer.

How Does This Narrator Recall Her Past? *(page 148)*

25. **The correct answer is (4). (Comprehension)** Since he has just helped a cow deliver twins, he is clearly an animal doctor. Choices (1), (2), and (3) are not doctors who ordinarily treat animals, so they are incorrect. There is nothing in the passage about his eating habits, so choice (5) is not appropriate.

26. **The correct answer is (2). (Analysis)** While choice (1) is an accurate statement about what the sentences do, it does not explain their function in the paragraph. Choice (3) is not a good choice, because although her family lived on a farm, we cannot assume they were poor. Choice (4) is contradicted by the account of her hiring in the first paragraph. There is nothing to indicate a critical tone in the sentences, so choice (5) is not correct.

27. **The correct answer is (2). (Analysis)** While all of the other choices are true statements based on this passage, none of them makes his statement about her intelligence ironic.

28. **The correct answer is (3). (Synthesis)** The word "amazing" indicates surprise at Mrs. Peebles's inability, which would result from assuming all women could bake. While she may enjoy baking, choice (1), and she indicates that she was hungry often, choice (4), neither of these is related to her reactions to Mrs. Peebles's admission. There is nothing in the passage to indicate she dislikes Mrs. Peebles, choice (2), or that she plans to teach her to bake, choice (5).

29. **The correct answer is (5). (Synthesis)** The speaker, in recounting her past, presents details that show how naive and sheltered she was. She does not seem upset by this, so choices (1) and (3) are incorrect. Since she admits her simplicity, she does not "distrust" her younger self, choice (4). But she clearly does not think she knew very much, so choice (4), respect, is not a good answer.

How Does This Young Woman React? *(page 149)*

30. **The correct answer is (2). (Synthesis)** The husband states, "Having a baby is natural!" The young woman is in a hospital, so choice (1) is incorrect. She does not want to see her husband there, so choice (3) is not necessarily true. There is no evidence for choices (4) and (5).

31. **The correct answer is (5). (Analysis)** Choices (1), (2), and (3) indicate a positive mood that is clearly contradicted by the woman's refusal to speak to the husband. Because she makes a "violent" gesture and points "wildly" toward the door, it can be assumed she is not afraid and timid, choice (4).

32. **The correct answer is (3). (Synthesis)** The woman's gestures increase in intensity, until she is so upset that she starts to choke. Her behavior does not show increasing uncertainty, choice (1), nor shame about her feelings, choice (4). At no point is she dependent on her husband, so choice (2) is incorrect. The situation may be a serious one, but her attitude is equally serious from the beginning to the end of the scene, so choice (5) is incorrect.

33. **The correct answer is (3). (Analysis)** In her first two speeches, the nurse encourages the woman, which would seem to indicate she wants to help the husband. But when the woman is upset by the husband, the nurse tells him to go and that the woman needs rest, so choice (1) is incorrect. Choices (2) and (5) present actions that are not part of this scene. Choice (4) is contradicted by the nurse's last two speeches to the husband.

34. **The correct answer is (4). (Analysis)** The husband repeatedly tells the wife what he thinks she needs to do and insists that if he can do it, she can also. Although the situation seems to call for kindness, the husband is neither pitying, choice (1), nor tender and loving, choice (2). Neither the situation nor his language are funny, so choice (5) can be eliminated. While there is anger implicit in his speech, he does not intend to hurt her, so sarcastic, choice (3), is not a good choice.

35. **The correct answer is (5). (Application)** There is no evidence to suggest anything will change before the husband's next visit. Because choices (3) and (4) imply strong and angry actions rather than the depression and panic the woman seems to be suffering, although they would be negative reactions to his visit, they are not good choices. In choices (1) and (2), the suggested happiness at the husband's visit is inconsistent with the woman's behavior as indicated in the passage. They are, therefore, incorrect.

What Are This Speaker's Feelings for His Wife? *(page 151)*

36. **The correct answer is (3). (Analysis)** In the first paragraph, he states that marriage did not end his wooing of her, and in the last paragraph, he states that after seven years, they are back at the point where they began. While the speaker is thinking about the past, it is in the context of his present feelings for his wife, so choice (5) is not the best answer. His description of getting the hamburgers is comic and not literal, so the struggle for survival, choice (2), is not a good choice. Choice (4) describes the situation rather than stating what the idea of the passage is, and although the speaker seems to enjoy eating dinner with his children, his focus is on his wife, so choice (1) is incorrect.

37. **The correct answer is (3). (Comprehension)** This description is in the passage where the narrator is describing himself figuratively as a hunter or caveman. Thus, choices (1), (2), and (5), which suggest he literally hunted for deer in a forest, are not correct. Since the deer is "stretched across his shoulders," the description is of a jacket, not a scarf, so choice (4) is incorrect.

38. **The correct answer is (1). (Analysis)** He says the word has a "final bite," meaning that it ends something. There is no evidence for choices (2), (3), or (5). While his emotions throughout the passage are sharp, in the context of the entire sentence, he is referring only to marriage, so choice (4) is not a good answer.

39. **The correct answer is (5). (Synthesis)** Because the speaker uses figurative language to portray himself as a man in a dangerous situation, he is trying to see himself as a hero. None of the other choices explain why he exaggerates in this way.

40. **The correct answer is (3). (Application)** The speaker's major feeling in the passage is wonder that he still loves his wife as he did when they were first married. Thus, he is wooing her as he did then. None of the other choices would be appropriate for a conversation intended to make his wife feel romantic.

Practice Test 2

Directions: Read each passage; then answer the questions that follow. Choose the *one best answer* to each question.

Items 1–6 refer to the following excerpt from a play.

What Does This Conversation Reveal?

Amanda: Resume your seat, little sister—I want you to stay fresh and pretty—for gentleman callers.

Laura: I'm not expecting any gentleman callers.

Amanda: *(Crossing to kitchenette. Airily):* Sometimes they come when they are least expected. Why I remember one Sunday afternoon in Blue Mountain—*(Enters kitchenette)*

Tom: I know what's coming!

Laura: Yes, but let her tell it.

Tom: Again?

Laura: She loves to tell it.
(Amanda returns with a bowl of dessert.)

Amanda: One Sunday afternoon in Blue Mountain—your mother received—*seventeen!*—gentleman callers! Why sometimes there weren't chairs enough to accommodate them all.

Laura: *(Rising)* Mother, let me clear the table.

Amanda: No, dear, you go in front and study your typewriter chart. Or practice your shorthand a little. Stay fresh and pretty!—It's almost time for our gentlemen callers to start arriving. *(She flounces girlishly toward the kitchenette)* How many do you suppose we're going to entertain this afternoon?

(Tom throws down the paper and jumps up with a groan.)

Laura: *(Alone in the dining room)* I don't believe we're going to receive any, Mother.

Amanda: *(Reappearing airily)* What? No one—not one? You must be joking. *(Laura nervously echoes her laugh. She slips in a fugitive manner through the half-open portieres and draws them gently behind her. A shaft of very clear light is thrown on her face against the faded tapestry of the curtains.)* Not one gentleman caller? It can't be true! There must be a flood; there must have been a tornado!

Laura: It isn't a flood; it's not a tornado, Mother. I'm just not popular like you were in Blue Mountain . . . *(Tom utters another groan. Laura glances at him with a faint, apologetic smile. Her voice catches a little.)* Mother's afraid I'm going to be an old maid.

—From *The Glass Menagerie* by Tennessee Williams

ROAD MAP

- *Practice Test 2*
- *Analysis Chart*
- *Answers and Explanations*

1. Which of the following best describes Laura's behavior toward her mother?

    (1) Cruel
    (2) Kind
    (3) Flirtatious
    (4) Mocking
    (5) Impatient

2. According to this passage, what does Amanda expect is going to happen?

    (1) They will eat dinner.
    (2) Laura will practice her shorthand.
    (3) Tom will announce he is moving.
    (4) Male admirers will visit Laura.
    (5) Laura will become upset.

3. The stage directions describing Tom's actions suggest that he

    (1) loves his sister.
    (2) is about to go out.
    (3) will finish reading the paper.
    (4) does not have a job.
    (5) is impatient with his mother.

4. "A shaft of very clear light is thrown on [Laura's] face against the faded tapestry of the curtains." In a live performance, the most important result of this stage direction would be that the audience could

    (1) focus on Laura's face as she speaks.
    (2) see that it is not yet dark.
    (3) see that Laura is hiding from Amanda and Tom.
    (4) focus on Tom's reaction to Amanda's words.
    (5) see that the family is not wealthy.

5. When Amanda says, "There must be a flood; there must have been a tornado," she is

    (1) literally commenting about the weather.
    (2) figuratively implying only a disaster could prevent gentleman callers.
    (3) exaggerating the number of gentleman callers she had one afternoon.
    (4) explaining her feelings about Tom and Laura.
    (5) complaining about Laura's lack of popularity.

6. If you were the costume designer for this play, your best choice for Laura's costume would be

    (1) bathing suit.
    (2) pants and a tee shirt.
    (3) housedress and an apron.
    (4) blouse and skirt.
    (5) long evening gown.

Items 7–11 refer to the following excerpt from a brochure.

What Warranties Does the Manufacturer Offer on Its Washing Machine?

GE Washer Warranty

Line   All warranty service is provided by our Factory Service Centers or an authorized Customer Care technician. For service, call 1-800-GE-CARES.

For The Period of:	We Will Replace:
5 One Year	Any part of the washer that fails due to defect in materials or workmanship. During this full one-year warranty, GE will also provide, free of charge, all labor and in-home service to replace the defective part.
Two Years 10	Any part of the washer that fails due to a defect in materials or workmanship. During this additional one-year limited warranty, you will be responsible for any labor or in-home service costs.
Five years 15	The suspension and spring assembly, if any of these parts should fail due to a defect in materials or workmanship. GE will also replace the washer lid or cover, if they should rust under operating conditions. During this additional four-year limited warranty, you will be responsible for any labor or in-home service costs.
Ten Years 20	The transmission and washer tank, if any of these parts should fail due to a defect in materials or workmanship. During this additional nine-year limited warranty, you will be responsible for any labor or in-home service costs.
Lifetime	The washer basket, if it should fail due to a defect in materials or workmanship. During this lifetime-limited warranty, you will be responsible for any labor or in-home service costs.

25 All warranty periods are calculated from the date of the original purchase of the washing machine.

This warranty is extended to the original purchaser and any succeeding owner for products purchased for home use within the USA. In Alaska, the warranty excludes the cost of shipping or service calls to your home.

—From *GE Appliance—Profile Washers*

7. The best description of the organization of this warranty is

    (1)   from part to whole.
    (2)   comparison and contrast.
    (3)   customer's and manufacturer's rights.
    (4)   time sequence.
    (5)   specific to general.

8. For how long is labor covered as part of the warranty on the washing machine?

    (1)   One year
    (2)   Two years
    (3)   Five years
    (4)   Ten years
    (5)   Lifetime

9. Your neighbor sold her house and moved away, and you bought her GE washing machine that she had purchased three years earlier. Something goes wrong with the machine. Under the terms of this warranty, you

    (1)   would have to pay for any repairs to the machine.
    (2)   would not have to pay for the parts to repair the transmission.
    (3)   would not have to pay for parts or labor to replace the washer basket.
    (4)   could only claim the warranty rights if you live in Alaska.
    (5)   can sue your neighbor for selling you a defective machine.

10. This warranty applies if the machine is repaired by

    (1)   service technicians employed by the store where you bought it.
    (2)   you, since you are an excellent worker.
    (3)   taking it to the local hardware and fix-it store.
    (4)   any authorized GE dealer.
    (5)   Factory Service Centers or authorized technicians.

11. From this warranty, you can conclude that GE

    (1)   does not want to admit it makes products that may have defects.
    (2)   finds the cost of labor more expensive than the cost of parts.
    (3)   wants to have its customers buy more GE products.
    (4)   advertises heavily in newspapers about product reliability.
    (5)   realizes that customers may not use the machine properly.

Items 12–17 refer to the following excerpt from a speech.

Why Is the Word *No* Important to This Speaker?

Line Brief, solid, affirmative as a hammer blow, this is the virile word, which must enflame lips and save the honor of our people, in these unfortunate days of anachronistic imperialism. . . .

5 We do not know how to say "no," and we are attracted, unconsciously, like a hypnotic suggestion, by the predominant *si* of the word on thought, of the form on essence—artists and weak and kindly, as we have been made by the beauty and generosity of our land. Never, in general terms, does a Puerto Rican say, nor does he know how to say "no": "We'll see," "I'll study the matter," "I'll decide later"; when a Puerto Rican uses these expressions, it must be understood that he does not want to;

10 at most, he joins *si* with the *no*. . . .

We have to learn to say "no," raise our lips, unburden our chest, put in tension all our vocal muscles and all our will power to fire this *o* of *no*, which will resound perhaps in America and the world, and will resound in the heavens with more efficacy than the rolling of cannons.

—From "No" by José De Diego

12. Based on this passage, you can infer that the speaker's heritage is

    (1)   African American.
    (2)   Puerto Rican.
    (3)   Haitian.
    (4)   Mexican.
    (5)   European.

13. According to this speaker, in what manner does the Puerto Rican citizen say "no"?

    (1)   In a tone of voice that cannot be misunderstood
    (2)   With faith that justice will be done
    (3)   In a tone of voice that may offend others
    (4)   With expressions that might sound like "yes" to others
    (5)   With a firm, resounding voice that cannot be questioned

14. The speaker wishes that his people would learn to say "no" so that they might

    (1)   find better jobs.
    (2)   be stricter parents.
    (3)   save their environment.
    (4)   help end political oppression.
    (5)   increase their exports.

15. Based on lines 8–10, the speaker believes that his homeland is

    (1)   cruel.
    (2)   unattractive.
    (3)   nurturing.
    (4)   forgotten.
    (5)   hopeless.

16. "We have to learn to say no, . . . to fire this *o* of *no* . . . " (lines 17–19)

The speaker compares the sound of the word *no* to gunfire in order to

   (1)   stress that war is imminent.
   (2)   encourage the Puerto Rican people to revolt.
   (3)   support gun control.
   (4)   show that he is not afraid.
   (5)   emphasize the power of this word.

17. It can be inferred from the passage that "si" (line 7) means

   (1)   we'll see.
   (2)   I'll decide later.
   (3)   yes.
   (4)   maybe.
   (5)   never.

Items 18–22 refer to the following excerpt from a nonfiction book.

What Were the Qualities of Greek Art?

Line Erected between 447 and 431 B.C., the Parthenon was the crowning achievement of the great rebuilding program undertaken on the Acropolis by Pericles. This famous temple was not nearly so simple a building as it appeared to be, for it was designed to look exactly right to the spectator standing in front of it. By means of many subtle

5   distortions, it created the illusion of perfection. The columns inclined slightly inward, so that they would look more stable; their diameter was not constant but increased very slightly in the middle of the shaft, for otherwise they might have seemed concave; and the corner columns were a little thicker than the others, to stress their proportionately greater importance to the structure as a whole.

10   The columns of the Parthenon rose directly from the floor of the building and ended at the top in simple block capitals; their surface was "fluted," divided into a series of shallow curved depressions. They represented the Doric order, the plainest style of Greek architecture. In the more elaborate Ionic order, the columns were more slender, the fluting separated by narrow ribbons of stone, and their capitals were

15   "volute," that is ornamented with simple curlicues. In the Corinthian order, an elaboration of the Ionic, acanthus leaves encrusted the capital.

       The Parthenon is now a ruin, and the other masterpieces of Greek architecture have suffered cruelly since the Age of Pericles. So has Greek sculpture, a good deal of which is known only through Roman copies or descriptions. The celebrated "Venus de

20   Milo" (the correct Greek title is "Aphrodite of Melos") and the Winged Victory, which we now think of as Greek, actually date from the later Hellenistic age. The three giant statues by Phidias (*c.* 490–432)—the Zeus at Olympia and two Athenas for the Acropolis—no longer exist. However fragments of the sculpture with which Phidias decorated the gables of the Parthenon do remain. They must have been wonderfully striking in

25   their original state, when they were apparently colored with golden tint against blue-paint gables. Most Greek statues were colored, to minimize the white glare of pure marble in the bright Mediterranean sunshine. We do not know the exact color scheme, but experts conjecture that the artists used a kind of suntan color for the body, a deep red for the hair, lips, eyebrows, and the irises of the eyes, and black for the pupils.

—From *A History of Civilization* by Crane Brinton,
John B. Christopher, Robert Lee Wolff

18. The structure of the first paragraph of this passage is best described as

    (1)   spatial.
    (2)   chronological.
    (3)   comparison and contrast.
    (4)   idea and examples.
    (5)   from parts to whole.

19. The Parthenon creates its effect of perfection for the viewer by

    (1)   using Doric columns.
    (2)   dignity and simplicity.
    (3)   deceiving the eye.
    (4)   rebuilding the Acropolis.
    (5)   having unstable columns.

20. Most Greek statues were originally

    (1)   created in the Hellenistic Age.
    (2)   used as decoration on buildings.
    (3)   copied by the Romans.
    (4)   left as pure white marble.
    (5)   painted or tinted.

21. The best word to describe the authors' feelings about the art they describe is

    (1)   admiration.
    (2)   astonishment.
    (3)   regret.
    (4)   confusion.
    (5)   truthfulness.

22. Why does the passage give the correct name of the "Venus de Milo"?

    (1)   The original statue has been destroyed.
    (2)   Like the Zeus at Olympia, it is a statue representing a religious figure.
    (3)   The statue's hair was painted red.
    (4)   Another Hellenic statue is named the "Winged Victory."
    (5)   The name change emphasizes that it is a copy.

Items 23–28 refer to the following excerpt from a poem.

How Does This Man Remember His Father?

My Papa's Waltz

Line   The whiskey on your breath
        Could make a small boy dizzy;
        But I hung on like death,
        Such waltzing was not easy.

5   We romped until the pans
        Slid from the kitchen shelf;
        My mother's countenance
        Could not unfrown itself.

        The hand that held my wrist
10   Was battered on one knuckle;
        At every step you missed
        My right ear scraped a buckle.

        You beat time on my head
        With a palm caked hard by dirt,
15   Then waltzed me off to bed
        Still clinging to your shirt.

             —*My Papa's Waltz* by Theodore Roethke

23. The mother's reaction to the scene is best described as

    (1) hatred.
    (2) amusement.
    (3) disapproval.
    (4) enjoyment.
    (5) sadness.

24. Theodore Roethke's father owned and operated a large greenhouse. This suggests the speaker's father may have had battered knuckles and dirty hands because he

    (1) was an alcoholic.
    (2) frequently beat his son.
    (3) worked with plants and earth.
    (4) was too lazy to wash his hands.
    (5) danced clumsily.

25. Which quality of the encounter is emphasized by the language of the poem?

    (1) Fear
    (2) Shyness
    (3) Noise
    (4) Playfulness
    (5) Abnormality

26. The figure of speech, "but I held on like death," suggests

    (1) that the father was a brutal man.
    (2) that the mother didn't play with the boy.
    (3) the speaker had no brothers or sisters.
    (4) the father's terminal illness.
    (5) the speaker didn't want to let go.

27. In a poem by Robert Hayden, "Those Winter Sundays," he writes, "Sundays too, my father got up early/ and put his clothes on in the blue-black cold,/ then with cracked hands that ached/ from labor in the weekday weather made/ banked fires blaze. No one ever thanked him." What is the difference between these lines and "My Papa's Waltz"?

    (1) The speaker's father doesn't work outdoors.
    (2) The speaker's poem is about what happened on Sundays.
    (3) The father and son seem distant from one another.
    (4) The son wishes he had been more appreciative of his father.
    (5) The mother disapproves of the father's actions with the son.

28. "My Papa's Waltz" is a poem that would be most appealing to

    (1) men who remember playing with their fathers.
    (2) women who had good relationships with their fathers.
    (3) children under the age of 10.
    (4) battered women.
    (5) children of alcoholics.

Items 29–34 refer to the following excerpt from a novel.

How Is This Woman Spending Her Life?

Line   "Nearly twenty years since I set out to seek my fortune. It has been a long search, but I think I have found it at last. I only asked to be a useful, happy woman, and my wish is granted, for I believe I am useful; I know I am happy."

    Christie looked so as she sat alone in the flower parlor one September afternoon,
5   thinking over her life with a grateful, cheerful spirit. Forty today, and pausing at that halfway house between youth and age, she looked back into the past without bitter regret or unsubmissive grief, and forward into the future with courageous patience. For three good angels attended her, and with faith, hope, and charity to brighten life, no woman need lament lost youth or fear approaching age. Christie did not, and
10   though her eyes filled with quiet tears as they were raised to the faded cap and sheathed sword hanging on the wall, none fell . . .

    A few evenings before, she had gone to one of the many meetings of working women, which had made some stir of late . . . The workers poured out their wrongs and hardships, passionately or plaintively, demanding or imploring justice, sympathy,
15   and help, displaying the ignorance, incapacity and prejudice which make their need all the more pitiful, their relief all the more imperative.

    —From *Work: A Story of Experience* by Louisa May Alcott

29. Christie's mood in this passage is one of

    (1) contentment.
    (2) unhappiness.
    (3) laziness.
    (4) ambition.
    (5) sympathy.

30. Based on this passage, you can assume that Christie

    (1) is a wealthy woman.
    (2) frequently argues with her husband.
    (3) is a working woman.
    (4) does not approve of working women.
    (5) is happily married.

31. In paragraph 2, Christie's sadness most likely results from

    (1) remembering a sad first marriage.
    (2) remembering a loved one who has died.
    (3) her failure to find her fortune.
    (4) the realization that she is 40 years old.
    (5) sympathizing with the working women.

32. Which of the following statements best captures the theme of this passage?

    (1) A middle-aged woman has good reason to fear the approach of old age.
    (2) Caring for a family is harder work than most people believe it to be.
    (3) All workers deserve justice, sympathy, and hope.
    (4) Middle age is a time to reflect upon past events and look forward with hope.
    (5) At the age of 40, this woman is happy.

33. Based on this passage, which of the following events is most likely to happen later?

    (1) Christie's husband will divorce her.
    (2) The working women will arrive at Christie's house.
    (3) Christie will lose hope regarding the future.
    (4) Christie will regret being a mother.
    (5) Christie will attend another meeting.

34. The figurative statement that Christie is "... pausing at that halfway house between youth and age" suggests that she

    (1) believes that halfway houses can help people.
    (2) is afraid that time will pass quickly.
    (3) has been longing for her youth.
    (4) is at a reflective point in her life.
    (5) has decided to move.

Items 35–40 refer to the following excerpt from a novel.

During the Depression, many midwestern farmers lost their land. They piled their belongings and families into cars or trucks and set out for California where they believed jobs were plentiful. In the passage below, one such family of migrants stops at a roadside diner.

What Does the Passage Show about These Families and the People They Encounter?

Line   Mae said, "You can't get no loaf a bread for a dime. We only got fifteen-cent loafs."

From behind her Al growled, "God almighty, Mae, give 'em bread."

"We'll run out 'fore the bread truck comes."

"Run out, then, Goddamn it," said Al. . .

5   She held the screen door open and the man came in, bringing a smell of sweat with him. The boys edged in behind him and they went immediately to the candy case and stared in—not with craving or with hope or even with desire, but just with a kind of wonder that such things could be. They were alike in size and their faces were alike. One scratched his dusty ankle with the toenails of his other foot. The other whispered

10   some soft message, and they straightened their arms so that their clenched fists in the overall pockets showed through the thin blue cloth . . .

"Go ahead—Al says to take it." . . .

When he put [the dime] on the counter he had a penny with it. He was about to drop the penny back into the pouch when his eye fell on the boys frozen before the

15   candy counter. He moved slowly down to them. He pointed in the case at big long sticks of striped peppermint. "Is them penny candy, ma'am?"

Mae moved down and looked in. "Which ones?"

"There, them stripy ones."

The little boys raised their eyes to her face and they stopped breathing; their

20   mouths were partly opened, their half-naked bodies were rigid.

"Oh—them. Well, no—them's two for a penny."

"Well gimme two then, ma'am." He placed the copper cent carefully on the counter. The boys expelled their held breath softly. Mae held the big sticks out.

"Take 'em," said the man.

25   They reached timidly; each took a stick, and they held them down at their sides and did not look at them. But they looked at each other, and their mouth corners smiled rigidly with embarrassment.

"Thank you ma'am." The man picked up the bread and went out the door, and the little boys marched stiffly behind him, the red-striped sticks held tightly against

30   their legs. They leaped like chipmunks over the front seat and onto the top of the load, and they burrowed back out of sight like chipmunks . . .

From inside the restaurant, the truck drivers and Mae and Al stared after them. Big Bill wheeled back. "Them wasn't two-for-a-cent candy," he said.

"What's that to you?" Mae said fiercely.

35   "Them was nickel apiece candy," said Bill.

—From *The Grapes of Wrath* by John Steinbeck

35. From this passage, we can conclude that the typical migrant family

    (1) wanted to live a better life.
    (2) begged for what they needed as they traveled.
    (3) burdened local governments' welfare systems.
    (4) spent the little money they had with great care.
    (5) was very indulgent toward the children in the family.

36. What makes Mae's lie about the price of candy ironic?

    (1) She reduced the price of a loaf of bread only because Al said she could.
    (2) She probably doesn't have much money.
    (3) The truck drivers know that she lied about the candy's price.
    (4) The man doesn't know she lied to him about the price.
    (5) The boys were delighted to have the candy.

37. The comparison of the boys to chipmunks suggests that they

    (1) are like hungry little animals.
    (2) became playful when they received the candy.
    (3) had squeaky little voices.
    (4) loved their father very much.
    (5) had probably not eaten peppermint sticks before.

38. Mae's question, "What's that to you?" is described as fierce in tone. The best choice for another word to describe that tone would be

    (1) self-defensive.
    (2) angry.
    (3) unhappy.
    (4) sympathetic.
    (5) humorous.

39. Later in the chapter from which this excerpt is taken, the truck drivers leave Mae a 50 cent tip for a cup of coffee that costs a nickel. You can conclude they do this for the following reason:

    (1) Mae is Big Bill's girlfriend.
    (2) They are annoyed by the migrants traveling the roads.
    (3) They are rewarding her for her actions.
    (4) Rich people always leave large tips.
    (5) Al makes excellent coffee.

40. The action most similar to what Mae does about the price of the candy would be

    (1) leaving a very large tip in a restaurant.
    (2) paying for a friend's meal.
    (3) making a donation to the American Red Cross.
    (4) giving money to a homeless person on the street.
    (5) bargaining with a salesperson about the price of an item.

ANALYSIS CHART

Use this table to determine your areas of strength and areas in which more work is needed. The numbers in the boxes refer to the multiple-choice questions in the practice test.

Content Area	Comprehension	Application	Analysis	Synthesis
Unit 1: **Fiction**	13, 29, 32	15, 17, 40	16, 34, 36, 37, 38	12, 14, 30, 31, 33, 35, 39
Unit 2: **Poetry**	23	28	25, 26	24, 27
Unit 3: **Drama**	2		4, 5	1, 3, 6
Unit 4: **Nonfiction**	8, 10, 20	9	7, 18, 22	11, 19, 21

ANSWERS AND EXPLANATIONS

What Does This Conversation Reveal? *(page 159)*

1. **The correct answer is (2). (Synthesis)** In contrast to Tom, who becomes impatient, Laura responds kindly to Amanda's question and is willing to let her repeat a story she has often told before. She is not cruel, mocking, or impatient with her mother, so choices (1), (4), and (5) are incorrect. It is Amanda, not Laura, who is described as flirtatious, so choice (3) can be eliminated.

2. **The correct answer is (4). (Comprehension)** Amanda says, "I want you to stay fresh and pretty for—gentleman callers," and, "It's almost time for our gentleman callers to start arriving." Choice (1) is incorrect because they are finishing their dinner. Amanda suggests that Laura practice shorthand, but this is not the focus of the passage, so choice (2) is not the best answer. There is no evidence to support choices (3) and (5).

3. **The correct answer is (5). (Synthesis)** Tom throws down his paper and groans in response to things his mother says or in response to what Laura says about her. The other choices could be true, but they are not suggested by these stage directions.

4. **The correct answer is (1). (Analysis)** The most likely reason the playwright wants a "very clear light" on Laura's face is because it is important to see her face and its expression at this moment. The light could be coming from a lamp, so choice (2) is incorrect. Laura may be evading her mother, but she has no reason to hide from Tom, so choice (3) can be eliminated. The light shines on Laura's face, not Tom's, so choice (4) can be eliminated. The "faded tapestry' may be related to the family's lack of money, choice (5), but Laura's expression is more important.

5. **The correct answer is (2). (Analysis)** Amanda has just expressed astonishment that Laura doesn't think there will be a gentleman caller, and this figure of speech reinforces her insistence that callers will arrive. While the statement is an exaggeration, she is not talking about her own callers, so choice (3) is not correct. Nothing in the passage suggests the conversation is about the weather, so (1) is not a good choice. Choices (4) and (5) don't fit the context of Amanda's speech.

6. **The correct answer is (4). (Synthesis)** Amanda wants Laura to stay "fresh and pretty," and a blouse and skirt best fits that description. Choice (1), a bathing suit, is obviously not appropriate to receive company. While Laura might look pretty in pants and a T-shirt, choice (2), or a housedress and an apron, choice (3), these outfits are usually worn for casual occasions or doing chores, rather than a potential date. Choice (5) might be elegant, but an evening gown would not be appropriate to wear at home.

What Warranties Does the Manufacturer Offer on its Washing Machine? *(page 179)*

7. **The correct answer is (4). (Analysis)** The information about what is covered is arranged by the amount of time from the date of purchase. While different items are covered at different periods, the contrast is within the material rather than its overall organization, so choice (2) is not a good answer. The warranty discusses the customer's rights, choice (3), and the parts of the washer that are covered, choice (1), but these are subjects, not organizing principles. All of the information is specific, and there is no general conclusion, so choice (5) is incorrect.

8. **The correct answer is (1). (Comprehension)** For all the other time periods, the warranty states "you will be responsible for any labor or in-home service costs."

9. **The correct answer is (2). (Application)** The next-to-last sentence states the warranty extends to "any succeeding owner," which shows choice (2) is correct and choice (1) is not. Choice (3) is incorrect because after one year, the owner pays for labor. The warranty has an exclusion for residents of Alaska, so choice (4) could not apply. Nothing in the warranty discusses your rights towards your neighbor, so (5) can be eliminated.

10. **The correct answer is (5). (Comprehension)** The opening sentence indicates warranty service is provided by Factory Service Centers or authorized Customer Care technicians. Therefore, all of the other choices are incorrect, and the provisions of the warranty would not protect you.

11. **The correct answer is (2). (Synthesis)** While all the other sentences may be true, none of them can be inferred from the terms of the warranty. Since the warranty continues to pay for parts although restricting what parts are covered as time goes on but does not cover labor beyond the first year, one can infer that labor would cost GE more than the parts.

Why Is the Word *No* Important to This Speaker? *(page 163)*

12. **The correct answer is (2). (Inferential comprehension)** In lines 5 and 12–14, the speaker says that "We" do not know how to say "no" and that "Puerto Ricans" do not know how to say "no." By identifying himself with those who do not know how to say "no," he is also identifying himself with Puerto Ricans. Based on this association, the other choices are incorrect.

13. **The correct answer is (4). (Literal comprehension)** According to the speaker, Puerto Ricans may say, "We'll see," but mean "no." To many people, this expression may sound like "yes." Because this confusion exists, choices (1) and (5) are incorrect. The tone of voice described is accommodating, not offensive, so choice (3) is incorrect. There is no evidence for choice (2).

14. **The correct answer is (4). (Inferential comprehension)** In lines 1–5, the speaker explains that the word "no" is necessary to end "anachronistic imperialism," or an outdated system in which a country is ruled by outsiders. Though the speaker might want his people to find better jobs, save the environment, or increase exports, these goals are not the most direct result of the powerful word "no." The other choices are not discussed in this passage.

15. **The correct answer is (3). (Inferential comprehension)** The speaker describes his homeland as full of beauty and generosity. Of the choices, nurturing is closest to this description. Choices (1), (2), and (5) are negative descriptions, and the speaker's devotion to Puerto Rico means that the land is not forgotten, as choice (4) suggests.

16. **The correct answer is (5). (Analysis)** To the speaker, the sound of the *o* in *no* is as sharp and powerful as gunfire. He is referring figuratively to gunfire, so choices (1), (2), and (3) are incorrect. He is trying to motivate his people, not prove that he is brave; therefore, choice (4) can be eliminated.

17. **The correct answer is (3). (Inferential comprehension)** The speaker says that "si" is so prevalent in their thoughts that the word "no" never comes to mind. The speaker uses Choices (1), (2), (4), and (5) to further solidify his point.

What Were the Qualities of Greek Art? *(page 182)*

18. **The correct answer is (4). (Analysis)** The authors write that the building was "not nearly so simple as it appeared to be" and then provide examples of the complications used to create the appearance of perfection. While this is an implied contrast, choice (3) is not the best answer because most of the material in the paragraph is in the form of examples. Choice (5) is the opposite of the way the paragraph works: it begins with the whole and then describes the parts. There is nothing to support choice (1), spatial, or choice (2), chronological.

19. **The correct answer is (3). (Synthesis)** The examples in the first paragraph describe the "subtle distortions" that create the "illusion of perfection." Choice (2) describes the effect of the building rather than how it was created. Choice (1) is a true statement, but it does not explain the total effect of the building. The Parthenon was part of the rebuilt Acropolis, choice (4), but that is not its effect, and choice (5) is not necessarily implied by the fact that the columns were built to look more stable.

20. **The correct answer is (5). (Comprehension)** The passage describes the colors of the Parthenon friezes and "most" Greek statues. While choices (1), (2), and (3) are true of some Greek art, according to the passage, only the statues' coloring is described as true of most of them. Choice (4) is incorrect; although the statues were made of white marble, they were then colored.

21. **The correct answer is (1). (Synthesis)** The words "extraordinarily lifelike" and "wonderfully striking" indicate their admiration. They may regret the destruction of Greek art, but regret, choice (3), is not the prevailing tone of the passage. They do not seem surprised or confused by the art, as they are able to analyze and describe it, so choices (2) and (4) are not good answers. While they are being "truthful," choice (5), that word does not reflect their feelings.

22. **The correct answer is (5). (Analysis)** The correct name also uses the Greek name of the goddess, Aphrodite, while the more common name uses Venus, which was the Roman name of the goddess. Choices (1) and (2) are true statements according to the passage, but they don't explain the function of giving the correct name. Choice (3) is based on the authors' conjecture about the Greek statues, and it is not related to the name of this statue. Choice (4) is not related to the name of this statue and can be eliminated.

How Does This Man Remember His Father? *(page 184)*

23. **The correct answer is (3). (Comprehension)** The mother is unable to stop frowning. The frown suggests disapproval rather than sadness, choice (5), because there is no other indication of unhappiness in the poem. Since she is frowning, choice (4), enjoyment, and choice (2), amusement, are clearly incorrect. Choice (1), hatred, is too strong an emotion to be indicated by a mere frown, so it is not a correct answer.

24. **The correct answer is (3). (Synthesis)** The "battered" knuckle and caked dirt could result from working with plants. There is nothing in the poem to indicate the father is lazy, choice (4). And while his dancing is clumsy, choice (5), that is not related to the condition of his hands. Choices (1) and (2) are exaggerations: while the father has been drinking, there is nothing in the poem that states he is an alcoholic, and he "beats time" of the waltz on the speaker's head, which is not the same as striking him hard enough to cause injury.

25. **The best answer is (4). (Analysis)** Words like *romped, waltz,* and *waltzing* suggest fun rather than anything negative. While the father's dance with the son is noisy and rough, the noise, choice (3), is not the main quality of their dance. The boy seems to enjoy the waltz, so "fear," choice (1), and "shyness," choice (2), are not correct answers. Choice (5) is not a correct answer because it is not unusual for a father to roughhouse with his son.

26. **The correct answer is (5). (Analysis)** He did not want to let go of his father, and at the end of the poem he says he was "clinging" to him, continuing the idea he didn't want to let go. There is no evidence in the poem for choices (2), (3), or (4). While the father played with the boy roughly, the figure of speech does not suggest the father was like death, but that the speaker was, so choice (1) can be eliminated.

27. **The correct answer is (4). (Synthesis)** No one, including the speaker, thanked the father for his efforts. Thus there is a distance between the father and son. In neither poem do we know if the father's work was indoors or outdoors, so choice (1) is incorrect. The day on which "My Papa's Waltz" occurs is not mentioned, so it could be on Sunday, and this would not be a contrast with Hayden's poem; therefore, choice (2) is incorrect. Although the speaker in "My Papa's Waltz" indicates he appreciated his father, and we might guess that choice (4) is something the son feels in Hayden's poem, the quoted lines do not state that he regrets his lack of appreciation of his father, so choice (4) is not a good option. The lines say nothing about the mother, so choice (5) can be eliminated.

28. **The correct answer is (1). (Application)** The poem is about a father and son enjoying each other's company as they play, and people who had similar experiences could easily identify with this. Girls are less likely than boys to roughhouse with their fathers, so choice (2) is not a good answer. Children under the age of ten probably could not appreciate an adult remembering his childhood, so choice (3) is not a good choice. Both choices (4) and (5) mention people who would have unpleasant emotions about anything connected with drinking alcohol or physical roughness, and they would probably not find anything appealing about this poem.

How Is This Woman Spending Her Life? *(page 9)*

29. **The correct answer is (1). (Comprehension)** Christie is described as "grateful and cheerful." Choice (2) implies a negative mood. Choices (3) and (4) are incorrect since she describes herself as already feeling useful. Though Christie shows sympathy to other working women, this trait does not describe her general mood in this passage, so choice (5) is incorrect.

30. **The correct answer is (3). (Synthesis)** Since Christie "set out to seek [her] fortune," and "found it," considers herself "useful," and went to meetings for working women, she is most likely a worker too. Christie may be wealthy and happily married, but there is not enough information in this passage to draw these conclusions; thus, choices (1), (2), and (5) can be eliminated. There is no evidence for choice (4).

31. **The correct answer is (2). (Synthesis)** Christie's sadness results from looking at a "faded cap" and "sheathed sword," which probably belonged to a loved one who died. Choices (1) and (5) are incorrect, because there is no mention of a first marriage and she is not thinking of the workers, respectively. Although Christie has suffered losses and is now 40 years old, she is at peace with both facts and states that she has found her fortune; thus choices (3) and (4) can be eliminated.

32. **The correct answer is (4). (Comprehension)** The theme of middle age as a turning point is described in paragraph two. Choice (1) is contradicted by the statement, "no woman need lament loss of youth or fear approaching age." Choice (5) is too narrow a statement to be called a theme. The passage mentions only certain workers, not all workers as choice (3) suggests. There is no reference to Christie's hard work on behalf of her family, so choice (2) is incorrect.

33. **The correct answer is (5). (Synthesis)** There is no foreshadowing of a bad turn of events in Christie's life, so choices (1), (3), and (4) are unlikely. Choice (2) is possible, but choice (5) is even more likely.

34. **The correct answer is (4). (Analysis)** The metaphor, "half way house," suggests a stopping point or resting spot. Since the statement is figurative, choice (1) can be eliminated. Choices (2) and (3) are incorrect because Christie is content with her age and her life. There is no evidence to support choice (5).

What Does the Passage Show about These Families and the People They Encounter? *(page 11)*

35. **The correct answer is (4). (Synthesis)** The man can only afford to pay 10 cents for a loaf of bread and intends to put the extra penny he takes out with the dime back into his money pouch. Choices (2) and (3) can be eliminated because the man clearly intends to pay for what he needs with whatever money he has. Choice (1) may be a true statement, but it is not suggested by this passage. Choice (5) is contradicted because the man clearly has to consider the price before paying for a treat for his sons.

36. **The correct answer is (1). (Analysis)** Although she did not reduce the price of bread until Al said she could, it is her own decision to lie about the price of the candy. Choices (3), (4), and (5) are correct statements about the passage, but they do not cast an ironic light on Mae's lie. While choice (2) is probably true, since Mae is a waitress in a diner, that does not make her lie ironic, therefore it is not a correct answer.

37. **The correct answer is (2). (Analysis)** The boys carefully hold the candy and do not eat it immediately; nothing suggests they are hungry, so choice (1) is not a good answer. While chipmunks may "squeak," the boys do not talk after they are given the candy, so choice (3) is incorrect. Choices (4) and (5) may be correct statements, but they are unrelated to a comparison of the boys to chipmunks, so they can be eliminated.

38. **The correct answer is (1). (Analysis)** Apparently Mae does not want the truck drivers to comment on her action; she is defending herself from anything they would say, even a compliment. "Fierce" may suggest anger, but there is no reason to assume she is angry with the truck drivers, choice (2), or unhappy about what she has done, choice (3). She is not sympathetic to them, so choice (4) is incorrect. There is nothing funny about her statement, so choice (5) can be eliminated.

39. **The correct answer is (3). (Synthesis)** Just as Mae did something kind by lying about the price of the candy, the truck drivers are kind to leave a large tip. There is no evidence for choices (2) or (5), nor for the idea that Mae is Big Bill's girlfriend, choice (1), so they can be eliminated. Choice (4) may or may not be an accurate generalization, but since truck drivers are not usually rich, it is an incorrect answer anyway.

40. **The correct answer is (4). (Application)** Mae doesn't know the man or his children. Choices (1), (2), and (3) are all acts of generosity, but they are directed to a known person or organization. Choice (5) suggests gaining an advantage rather than being generous, so it can be eliminated.

The New World of Work: Are You Ready for the Twenty-first Century?

MAJOR CHANGES IN THE NEW WORLD OF WORK

Remember the good old days of job stability and company loyalty? Maybe you don't. If you haven't had a career talk with your parents or grandparents yet, you should. Your grandfather or grandmother can tell you that in the good old days, people stayed in the same career field and were loyal to their company. Most workers back then climbed the corporate ladder to success by moving up within the same company. Work was work; it wasn't something they expected to enjoy. If you happened to like your job, it was a bonus. Work was also very streamlined and task oriented. People, for the most part, specialized in carrying out one job and using one main skill.

Times have changed. Before you get started looking for that perfect job, it's important for you to know the work environment that exists today. You must understand the new workforce culture and develop the skills and qualities needed to be successful in it. The major changes in the current and future workforce are outlined later.

DOWNSIZING AND THE EMERGENCE OF SMALLER COMPANIES

As we all are too well aware, companies have been laying off many employees and eliminating numerous jobs, especially middle management jobs. In Fortune 500 companies alone, approximately 15 million jobs have been eliminated over the last twenty years. The elimination of jobs takes place due to market demand, organizational restructuring, building new business processes, incorporating new technology, and relocation of work. In the 1990s, close to 48 percent of companies eliminated jobs. Downsizing occurs when the number of jobs eliminated is greater than the number of jobs created. According to the American Management Association, in the 1990s approximately 30 percent of companies downsized. (Source: Reprinted by permission from *1997 AMA Survey on Corporate Job Creation, Job Elimination, and Downsizing.* Copyright © 1997 American Management Association International, New York, NY. All rights reserved. http:www.amanet.org.)

At the same time, the number of small companies joining the workforce has grown considerably. In fact, almost all of last year's job growth occurred in small and medium-sized companies (under 500 employees). Look at the pie chart and the figures that follow reported by the American Business Information, a division of Info USA Inc., in February, 1998.

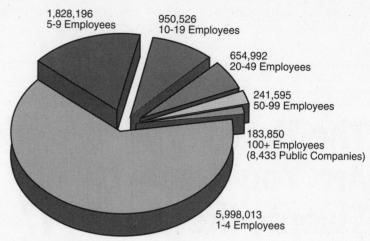

Total U.S. Business Counts by Employee Size

A SERVICE-DOMINATED JOB SECTOR

In the 1970s, approximately 54 percent of the jobs were in the service sector, and 46 percent were in the manufacturing sector. Today, these percentages are closer to 80 percent and 20 percent, respectively. New jobs over the next five years are expected to be dominated even more by the service sector. The U.S. Bureau of Labor Statistics (BLS) estimates that by 2005, almost 93 percent of new jobs created will be in service-producing industries.

JOB- AND COMPANY-HOPPING AND JOB SECURITY

Spending your entire career with one company is a thing of the past. Due to the downsizing and increase in small companies, there's less room to move up within the same company. Therefore, in order to move up, many times you'll need to move out. The average worker in the twenty-first century is projected to change jobs at least seven times in their lifetime.

EMPLOYEES ARE TAKING CONTROL OF THEIR OWN CAREERS

With all this job-hopping and downsizing, employees are no longer expecting their company to take care of them for life. It's very important for today's workers to constantly be thinking and planning ahead, even when things at work seem great. In a recent Towers Perrin survey, 9 out of 10 people reported that they are taking personal responsibility for their career development. Specifically, 94 percent of the respondents reported that *they* are responsible for their careers, not their employers. (Source: Towers Perrin Workplace Index)

GLOBALIZATION OF THE WORLD OF WORK

With the Internet, air travel, and satellite communication, the economies of countries throughout the world are meshing. Just by looking at the cars on the road, it's obvious that other countries are affecting the workplace here in the states. Cars such as Hondas are made both in Japan and here in the U.S. Volkswagens are made in Germany and the U.S. The former Chrysler Corporation is now owned by Daimler/Chrysler, with headquarters in Germany.

Think of some of the products you recently bought. Toys sold in the states are manufactured in China, Korea, and elsewhere. McDonald's hamburgers, Coke, and Pepsi are sold in countries all over the world.

Because of this globalization of economies, employers have greater expectations that their employees will be able to think and communicate with a global perspective. Geographical, cultural, and language proficiencies allow employees and job seekers to be more marketable in the new world of work.

DIVERSITY IN THE WORKPLACE

The workplace is becoming increasingly more diverse. Dominance by the white male in the workforce is gradually coming to an end. Women and racial and ethnic minorities are joining the work force at a much higher rate than white males. Take a look at the following information produced by the Bureau of Labor Statistics.

By the year 2006, women are expected to make up 47 percent of the labor force. From 1996 to 2006, Asian Americans and Hispanics are projected to have the largest net increases of employment growth, 41 and 36 percent, respectively. The rate of growth for African Americans is expected to be 14 percent.

THE EMERGENCE OF PROJECTS AND TEAMS

In the past, when you were hired by a company, you were given a detailed job description that laid out all your daily responsibilities and duties in very specific terms. You were evaluated yearly on the basis of how well *you* completed *your* responsibilities, and, with the exception of a few added responsibilities every year, your job stayed the same. Well, times have changed. In a service-dominated and technology-driven global market, organizational clients have many different needs that frequently change. Therefore, many companies must work with their clients on a project-to-project basis to most effectively fulfill their unique needs.

Since each project is different, a different number of people with different skill sets are required to successfully complete each project. Some projects are larger and require more people to complete them. Some projects are more technical in nature and require people with technical skills. Today, companies are trying to hire people with a wide variety of skills who can move from one team or project to another.

The consulting industry is the most obvious example of project-oriented work. In order to help a company become more efficient and productive, a consulting firm must assess existing technological systems, organizational procedures, personnel, and lines of communication. A team made up of only those members with technical skills lacks the expertise in organizational processes and staffing needed to make a complete evaluation.

To be successful in today's world of work, you must be able to adapt to new situations and projects and work on teams.

THE COMPUTER AGE: HIGH TECH, LOW TOUCH

Perhaps the greatest influential force affecting the workplace today is technology. Computers are taking over the world—at least the world of work. Moving from face-to-face meetings to teleconferencing, to faxing proposals, and to e-mailing and virtual chat sessions, the work world is increasingly moving to a high-tech, low-touch environment. Few would disagree that the incorporation of the computer and the Internet has saved companies lots of time and money. In addition, few would disagree that computers have changed the way we do business. For example, in the human resources industry, technology used to recruit job candidates has recently increased dramatically. In 1995, 40 percent of employers used electronic job sources to find job candidates. By 1997, this figure had more than doubled, reaching 88 percent (Source: Lee Hecht Harrison). Regardless of what industry or career field you want to enter, the demand for computer skills among all workers and job seekers is at an all-time high.

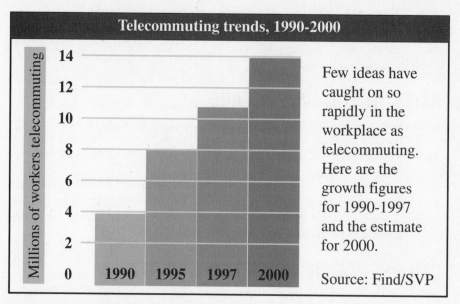

Source: Graph presented in *Career Opportunities News,* Ferguson Publishing, Chicago.

More and More People are Working from Home

These emerging technologies have also led to the emergence of a new type of worker: the telecommuter. The widespread use of e-mail, fax machines, teleconferencing, and other technologies have made it possible for people to do their jobs as effectively at home as in the office. Approximately 10 million employees now work out of their homes, and the number is on the rise. Notice (in the graph above) how this trend has consistently increased since 1990.

Telecommuting is very popular among high-tech companies. Close to 20 percent of employees working for IBM worldwide currently spend a minimum of two days out of the office. Take a look at some of the telecommuting-friendly employers in Table 1.

TABLE 1. TELECOMMUTING-FRIENDLY EMPLOYERS

Employer	Percent of Work Force Telecommuting
Arthur Andersen	20
AT&T	55
Cisco Systems	66
Hewlett-Packard	8
IBM	20
Leisure Company/America West	16
Merrill Lynch	5

Source: Reprinted from the October 12, 1998, issue of *Business Week* by special permission. © 1998 by McGraw-Hill Companies.

TABLE 2. NEW TYPE OF EMERGING WORKERS

Traditional	Emerging
Demand long-term job security	Job security not a driver of commitment
Are less satisfied with their jobs	Are more satisfied with their jobs
Changing jobs damaging to careers	Changing jobs often part of growth
Defines loyalty as tenure	Defines loyalty as accomplishment
Work is opportunity for income	Work provides a chance to grow
Employer responsible for career	Individual responsible for career

A NEW TYPE OF WORKER IS EMERGING

All of these changes—downsizing, service-domination, diversity in the workplace, job-hopping, and globalization— have affected the workforce, and, as a result, a new type of worker is emerging. Not only are the skills of the emerging worker different, but their needs, expectations, and attitudes are different as well. In a recent study from Interim Services, Inc., six major differences between the "Traditional" worker and the "Emerging" worker were found. Take a look at these differences in Table 2.

WHAT EMPLOYERS ARE LOOKING FOR

These changes in the world of work drive the need for new skills and personal characteristics among employees and job candidates. Companies want people who can thrive in this type of work environment, and they know that to do so, employees need certain skills. Table 3 lists the top ten skills as well as the top ten personal characteristics that employers want, based on a survey conducted by the National Association of Colleges and Employers (NACE).

Why These Skills and Qualities are Important

Notice that interpersonal, teamwork, communication, flexibility, and leadership were areas included in both skills and personal characteristics lists. Each of these are qualities that can be developed into useful skills in the workplace. It's important that you clearly understand why these skills and personal characteristics are valued in the new workplace. The best way to convince you of their importance is to show you how dependent they are on changes in

TABLE 3. TOP 10

Skills and Qualities Employers Want	Personal Characteristics Employers Seek in Job Candidates
1. Interpersonal	1. Honesty/Integrity
2. Teamwork	2. Motivation/Initiative
3. Analytical	3. Communication skills
4. Oral communication	4. Self-confidence
5. Flexibility	5. Flexibility
6. Computer	6. Interpersonal skills
7. Written communication	7. Strong work ethic
8. Leadership	8. Teamwork skills
9. Work experience	9. Leadership skills
10. Internship/Co-op experience	10. Enthusiasm

Source: *Job Outlook, 1998.* National Association of Colleges and Employers

the new world of work. These skills are closely related to and, in fact, have emerged because of how much the world of work has changed.

Interpersonal and Teamwork Skills

Notice that the top 2 skills employers want are *people skills:* interpersonal and teamwork. The increase of project work and diversity in the workplace have made these skills extremely valuable to companies. To be successful working in teams and with a wide variety of people from different cultures, you must have strong interpersonal and teamwork skills. Maintaining a positive attitude, handling conflicts tactfully, and having a sense of humor are just a few of the interpersonal skills needed to work well in teams and relate well with a wide variety of people.

Analytical Skills

You must have strong analytical skills to keep up with the ever-changing workplace and computer systems. New problems and situations arise daily and must be assessed and solved. Clients come from different backgrounds and have different perspectives. In order to meet their varying needs and values, workers must be able to think "outside the box."

Oral and Written Communication Skills

With a service-dominated economy and emphasis on teams, you must be able to communicate well with clients and colleagues. Writing skills continue to be important. Today's worker is responsible for writing and producing memos, reports, business letters, and many other documents.

Technology has greatly impacted the way we communicate. Clients, coworkers, and supervisors expect to receive information immediately. Time is money! Faxing and e-mailing have become the preferred methods of communicating to someone in writing because they save so much time. Being able to send information quickly means you'll have to prepare it quickly. You must be able to write quickly without sacrificing quality or clarity. Strong oral and written communication skills are also important in developing and maintaining relationships with clients in foreign markets. Communicating in more than one language is becoming increasingly important in order to do business in the global workforce.

Flexibility

The rise of small businesses and downsizing of larger corporations causes current professionals to wear more hats than ever before. One week you may find yourself minimally assisting a project team that's consulting with a small domestic company, while the next week you may be leading a large project team while working with a Fortune 500 international giant.

As the new workplace becomes more and more transient, the ability to adapt to new working relationships, new jobs, and different companies is more crucial than ever before.

Computer Skills

The importance of computer skills in high-tech occupations such as programming and information systems is obvious. But in our high-tech, low-touch environment, computer skills are important in almost *all* jobs. At the minimum, most jobs today require proficiency in word processing and using the Internet, especially e-mail. Many other jobs require knowledge and efficiency in using a field-specific or company-specific computer application. It could be a special type of database, spreadsheet, or custom-made application that you must learn.

Leadership Skills and Self-Confidence

Companies are looking for candidates who are self-confident, outgoing, and self-starters, all of which are characteristics of a good leader. Organizations need to find people who are not afraid to lead others on various project teams and new initiatives. With fewer people doing more work, job seekers with the ability to take the initiative and lead are highly sought after.

Work Experience, Internships, and Co-op Experience

Because companies have become leaner, they have less time and personnel to devote to training and hand-holding for new employees. They're looking for candidates who have prior experience using the skills needed to perform the job at hand. For high school and college students, completing an internship is more important than ever.

Honesty/Integrity and Strong Work Ethic

There's no substitute for old-fashioned honesty and hard work. Regardless of how skilled and competent you are, the factor that separates most professionals is hard work. Putting in the extra hours, concentrating on tasks, and staying organized are not necessarily fun or exciting, but they add up to success. Being honest with coworkers and clients is the best way to maintain positive, long-lasting working relationships.

Motivation/Initiative and Enthusiasm

Recruiters know that a candidate's motivation and enthusiasm toward the job and company are critical factors of success and retention. If you can't prove to prospective employers that your heart is in the job and that you genuinely want to work for their company, then they'll find someone who can. Typically, the more enthusiastic you are about your job, the more productive you will be. The characteristics of the job and company that you choose should ideally be consistent with your personal interests and values.

HOT OCCUPATIONS AND CITIES

There are many factors to consider when deciding on the right career to pursue. In the next chapter, you'll learn about the importance of assessing your interests, skills, values, and personal qualities and determining how they relate to career options. It's also important to keep in mind those jobs and career fields that are currently in demand and those that are projected to be in demand in the future. As the workforce changes, different jobs become more or less in demand.

The types of occupations that are in demand in the twenty-first century world of work are presented later. The cities that will have the greatest employment growth are also presented. It's a good idea to keep an eye on these hot occupations and cities as you explore various career options.

FASTEST-GROWING OCCUPATIONS

The fastest-growing occupations are occupations projected to add the highest percentage of jobs from 1996 to 2006. For example, in Table 4, a 109 percent change for computer engineers means that the number of computer engineers needed in 2006 (451,000) is more than double the number needed ten years previously (215,700).

TABLE 4. TOP 25 FASTEST-GROWING OCCUPATIONS
(From 1996 to 2006)

Occupation	Employment		Percent Change*
	1996	2006	
Computer engineers	215,700	451,000	109
Systems analysts, electronic data processing	505,500	1,025,100	103
Personal and home-care aides	202,500	373,900	85
Physical and corrective	84,500	150,900	79
Therapy assistants and aides; Home-health aides	94,700	872,900	77
Electronic pagination	30,400	52,800	74
Medical assistants	224,800	391,200	74
Physical therapists	114,500	195,600	71
Occupational therapy assistants and aides	15,700	26,400	69
Paralegal personnel	112,900	189,300	68
Occupational therapists	57,400	95,300	66
Teachers, special education	407,000	647,700	59
Human services workers	177,800	276,300	55
Data-processing equipment repairers	79,700	121,500	52
Medical records technicians	87,300	131,800	51
Speech-language pathologists and audiologists	87,300	131,500	51
Amusement and recreation attendants	288,100	426,100	48
Dental hygienists	132,800	196,800	48
Physician's assistants	63,800	93,500	47
Adjustment clerks	401,300	583,900	46
Respiratory therapists	81,800	119,300	46
Emergency medical technicians	149,700	217,100	45
Engineering, mathematical, and natural sciences managers	342,900	498,000	45
Manicurists	43,100	62,400	45
Bill and account collectors	268,600	381,100	42

* The national average percent change is between 10 and 20. Source: Bureau of Labor Statistics, 1996

HOT OCCUPATIONS BY EDUCATIONAL LEVEL

The following list identifies occupations projected to have the fastest rate of job growth in ten years, broken down by educational level. Find your appropriate educational level, and see what types of jobs that will be in demand.

High School Diploma Plus Up to One Year of Job Experience

- Home-care aides
- Retail salespersons
- Amusement attendants
- Truck drivers
- Cashiers
- Teacher's aides and educational assistants
- Medical assistants
- Dental assistants

Educational Level Open but Long-Term Work or Training Required

- Desktop-publishing specialists
- Musicians
- Flight attendants
- Police patrol officers
- Food service and lodging managers
- Carpenters
- Clerical supervisors
- Cooks, restaurant

Career School or Other Vocational Training

- Data-processing equipment repairers
- Manicurists
- Licensed Practical Nurses
- Surgical technologists
- Cosmetologists or barbers
- Medical secretaries
- Emergency Medical Technicians
- Automotive mechanics

Associate (Two-Year College) Degree

- Dental hygienists
- Registered Nurses
- Paralegals
- Radiologic technologists
- Respiratory therapists
- Health information technicians
- Cardiology technologists

Bachelor's Degree

- Database administrators
- Computer engineers
- Special education teachers
- Systems analysts
- Physical and corrective therapy assistants and aides

Master's Degree

- Physical and occupational therapists
- Speech pathologists
- Operations research analysts
- Librarians
- Psychologists
- Counselors
- Curators and archivists

Doctorate

- Biological scientists
- Mathematicians and related fields
- College faculty member
- Medical scientists

Professional Degree

- Lawyers
- Veterinarians
- Physicians
- Chiropractors
- Clergy
- Dentists

Minichart developed by the Career Opportunity News, Ferguson Publishing, Chicago, based on data from the *Occupational Outlook Handbook*, 1998–99.

WHAT IT ALL MEANS TO YOU

The days when the company took care of the career development of its workers are over. You must become self-sufficient when it comes to progressing through your career and job searching. Keep your resume updated and references current. Anticipate next steps by examining prospective jobs and companies, even when you are content in your current position. Remember that you're likely to change jobs close to seven times in your lifetime.

It's important to realize that most skills are transferable from one job to another and from one career field to another. It's critical that you constantly and consistently assess the skills that you enjoy utilizing and the parts of the job that are most rewarding. In doing this, you will have the capability of identifying that next perfect job and the one after that.

THE WHOLE IN ONE

- Smaller companies, diversity in the workplace, job-hopping employees, new technologies, global markets, and projects replacing jobs are some of the major concepts changing the way we do business.

- Interpersonal, analytical, computer, and communication skills, combined with teamwork, flexibility, leadership, motivation, self-confidence, honesty, and enthusiasm, are some of the top skills and qualities that current and future employers will be looking for in candidates.

- To succeed in the new world of work, you must be in control of your own destiny and examine your transferable skills on an ongoing basis.

Sample Word List

USE THE WORDS YOU LEARN

Make a deliberate effort to include the new words you're learning in your daily speech and writing. It will impress people (teachers, bosses, friends, and enemies), and it will help solidify your memory of the words and their meanings. Maybe you've heard this tip about meeting new people: if you use a new acquaintance's name several times, you're unlikely to forget it. The same is true with new words: use them, and you won't lose them.

CREATE YOUR OWN WORD LIST

Get into the habit of reading a little every day with your dictionary nearby. When you encounter a new word in a newspaper, magazine, or book, look it up. Then jot down the new word, its definition, and the sentence in which you encountered it in a notebook set aside for this purpose. Review your vocabulary notebook periodically—say, once a week. Your notebook will reflect the kinds of things you read and the words you find most difficult. The fact that you've taken the time and made the effort to write down the words and their meanings will help to fix them in your memory. Chances are good that you'll encounter a few words from your vocabulary notebook on the Language Arts, Reading test..

A SAMPLE WORD LIST

A

abbreviate (verb)   to make briefer, to shorten. *Because time was running out, the speaker had to abbreviate his remarks.* **abbreviation** (noun).

abrasive (adjective)   irritating, grinding, rough. *The manager's rude, abrasive way of criticizing the workers was bad for morale.* **abrasion** (noun).

abridge (verb)   to shorten, to reduce. *The Bill of Rights is designed to prevent Congress from abridging the rights of Americans.* **abridgment** (noun).

absolve (verb)   to free from guilt, to exonerate. *The criminal jury absolved O. J. Simpson of the murder of his ex-wife and her friend.* **absolution** (noun).

abstain (verb)   to refrain, to hold back. *After his heart attack, he was warned by the doctor to abstain from smoking, drinking, and overeating.* **abstinence** (noun), **abstemious** (adjective).

accentuate (verb)   to emphasize, to stress. *The overcast skies and chill winds accentuated our gloomy mood.*

acrimonious (adjective)   biting, harsh, caustic. *The election campaign became acrimonious, as the candidates traded insults and accusations.* **acrimony** (noun).

adaptable (adjective)   able to be changed to be suitable for a new purpose. *Some scientists say that the mammals outlived the dinosaurs because they were more adaptable to a changing climate.* **adapt** (verb), **adaptation** (noun).

adulation (noun)   extreme admiration. *Few young actors have received greater adulation than did Marlon Brando after his performance in* A Streetcar Named Desire. **adulate** (verb), **adulatory** (adjective).

adversary (noun)   an enemy or opponent. *When the former Soviet Union became an American ally, the United States lost its last major adversary.*

adversity (noun)   misfortune. *It's easy to be patient and generous when things are going well; a person's true character is revealed under adversity.* **adverse** (adjective).

aesthetic (adjective)   relating to art or beauty. *Mapplethorpe's photos may be attacked on moral grounds, but no one questions their aesthetic value—they are beautiful.* **aestheticism** (noun).

affected (adjective)   false, artificial. *At one time, Japanese women were taught to speak in an affected high-pitched voice, which was thought girlishly attractive.* **affect** (verb), **affectation** (noun).

aggressive (adjective)   forceful, energetic, and attacking. *A football player needs a more aggressive style of play than a soccer player.* **aggression** (noun).

alacrity (noun)   promptness, speed. *Thrilled with the job offer, he accepted with alacrity—"Before they can change their minds!" he thought.*

allege (verb)   to state without proof. *Some have alleged that Foster was murdered, but all the evidence points to suicide.* **allegation** (noun).

alleviate (verb)   to make lighter or more bearable. *Although no cure for AIDS has been found, doctors are able to alleviate the suffering of those with the disease.* **alleviation** (noun).

ambiguous (adjective)   having two or more possible meanings. *The phrase, "Let's table that discussion" is ambiguous; some think it means, "Let's discuss it now," while others think it means, "Let's save it for later."* **ambiguity** (noun).

ambivalent (adjective)   having two or more contradictory feelings or attitudes; uncertain. *She was ambivalent toward her impending marriage; at times she was eager to go ahead, while at other times she wanted to call it off.* **ambivalence** (noun).

amiable (adjective)   likable, agreeable, friendly. *He was an amiable lab partner, always smiling, on time, and ready to work.* **amiability** (verb).

amicable (adjective)   friendly, peaceable. *Although they agreed to divorce, their settlement was amicable and they remained friends afterward.*

amplify (verb)   to enlarge, expand, or increase. *Uncertain as to whether they understood, the students asked the teacher to amplify his explanation.* **amplification** (noun).

anachronistic (adjective)   out of the proper time. *The reference, in Shakespeare's* Julius Caesar, *to "the clock striking twelve" is anachronistic, since there were no striking timepieces in ancient Rome.* **anachronism** (noun).

anarchy (noun)   absence of law or order. *For several months after the Nazi government was destroyed, there was no effective government in parts of Germany, and anarchy ruled.* **anarchic** (adjective).

anomaly (noun)   something different or irregular. *The tiny planet Pluto, orbiting next to the giants Jupiter, Saturn, and Neptune, has long appeared to be an anomaly.* **anomalous** (adjective).

antagonism (noun) hostility, conflict, opposition. *As more and more reporters investigated the Watergate scandal, antagonism between Nixon and the press increased.* **antagonistic** (adjective), **antagonize** (verb).

antiseptic (adjective) fighting infection; extremely clean. *A wound should be washed with an antiseptic solution. The all-white offices were bare and almost antiseptic in their starkness.*

apathy (noun) lack of interest, concern, or emotion. *American voters are showing increasing apathy over politics; fewer than half voted in the last election.* **apathetic** (adjective).

arable (adjective) able to be cultivated for growing crops. *Rocky New England has relatively little arable farmland.*

arbiter (noun) someone able to settle dispute; a judge or referee. *The public is the ultimate arbiter of commercial value: It decides what sells and what doesn't.*

arbitrary (adjective) based on random or merely personal preference. *Both computers cost the same and had the same features, so in the end I made an arbitrary decision about which to buy.*

arcane (adjective) little-known, mysterious, obscure. *Eliot's* Waste Land *is filled with arcane lore, including quotations in Latin, Greek, French, German, and Sanskrit.* **arcana** (noun, plural).

ardor (noun) a strong feeling of passion, energy, or zeal. *The young revolutionary proclaimed his convictions with an ardor that excited the crowd.* **ardent** (adjective).

arid (adjective) very dry; boring and meaningless. *The arid climate of Arizona makes farming difficult. Some find the law a fascinating topic, but for me it is an arid discipline.* **aridity** (noun).

ascetic (adjective) practicing strict self-discipline for moral or spiritual reasons. *The so-called Desert Fathers were hermits who lived an ascetic life of fasting, study, and prayer.* **asceticism** (verb).

assiduous (verb) working with care, attention, and diligence. *Although Karen is not a naturally gifted math student, by assiduous study she managed to earn an A in trigonometry.* **assiduity** (noun).

astute (adjective) observant, intelligent, and shrewd. *Safire's years of experience in Washington and his personal acquaintance with many political insiders make him an astute commentator on politics.*

atypical (adjective) not typical; unusual. *In* The Razor's Edge, *Bill Murray, best known as a comic actor, gave an atypical dramatic performance.*

audacious (adjective) bold, daring, adventurous. *Her plan to cross the Atlantic single-handed in a 12-foot sailboat was audacious, if not reckless.* **audacity** (noun).

audible (adjective) able to be heard. *Although she whispered, her voice was picked up by the microphone, and her words were audible throughout the theater.* **audibility** (noun).

auspicious (adjective) promising good fortune; propitious. *The news that a team of British climbers had reached the summit of Everest seemed an auspicious sign for the reign of newly crowned Queen Elizabeth II.*

authoritarian (adjective) favoring or demanding blind obedience to leaders. *Despite Americans' belief in democracy, the American government has supported authoritarian regimes in other countries.* **authoritarianism** (noun)

B

belated (adjective)   delayed past the proper time. *She called her mother on January 5th to offer her a belated "Happy New Year."*

belie (verb)   to present a false or contradictory appearance. *Lena Horne's youthful appearance belies her long, distinguished career in show business.*

benevolent (adjective)   wishing or doing good. *In old age, Carnegie used his wealth for benevolent purposes, donating large sums to found libraries and schools.* **benevolence** (noun).

berate (verb)   to scold or criticize harshly. *The judge angrily berated the two lawyers for their unprofessional behavior.*

bereft (adjective)   lacking or deprived of something. *Bereft of parental love, orphans sometimes grow up to be insecure.*

bombastic (adjective)   inflated or pompous in style. *Old-fashioned bombastic political speeches don't work on television, which demands a more intimate style of communication.* **bombast** (noun).

bourgeois (adjective)   middle-class or reflecting middle-class values. *The Dadaists of the 1920s produced art deliberately designed to offend bourgeois art collectors, with their taste for respectable, refined, uncontroversial pictures.* **bourgeois** (noun).

buttress (noun)   something that supports or strengthens. *The endorsement of the American Medical Association is a powerful buttress for the claims made about this new medicine.* **buttress** (verb).

C

camaraderie (noun)   a spirit of friendship. *Spending long days and nights together on the road, the members of a traveling theater group develop a strong sense of camaraderie.*

candor (noun)   openness, honesty, frankness. *In his memoir about the Vietnam War, former defense secretary McNamara describes his mistakes with remarkable candor.* **candid** (adjective).

capricious (adjective)   unpredictable, willful, whimsical. *The pop star Madonna has changed her image so many times that each new transformation now appears capricious rather than purposeful.* **caprice** (noun).

carnivorous (adjective)   meat-eating. *The long, dagger-like teeth of the Tyrannosaurus make it obvious that this was a carnivorous dinosaur.* **carnivore** (noun).

carping (adjective)   unfairly or excessively critical; querulous. *New York is famous for its demanding critics, but none is harder to please than the carping John Simon, said to have single-handedly destroyed many acting careers.* **carp** (verb).

catalytic (adjective)   bringing about, causing, or producing some result. *The conditions for revolution existed in America by 1765; the disputes about taxation that arose later were the catalytic events that sparked the rebellion.* **catalyze** (verb).

caustic (adjective)   burning, corrosive. *No one was safe when the satirist H. L. Mencken unleashed his caustic wit.*

censure (noun)   blame, condemnation. *The news that Senator Packwood had harassed several women brought censure from many feminists.* **censure** (verb).

chaos (noun)   disorder, confusion, chance. *The first few moments after the explosion were pure chaos: no one was sure what had happened, and the area was filled with people running and yelling.* **chaotic** (adjective).

circuitous (adjective)   winding or indirect. *We drove to the cottage by a circuitous route so we could see as much of the surrounding countryside as possible.*

circumlocution (noun)   speaking in a roundabout way; wordiness. *Legal documents often contain circumlocutions that make them difficult to understand.*

circumscribe (verb)   to define by a limit or boundary. *Originally, the role of the executive branch of government was clearly circumscribed, but that role has greatly expanded over time.* **circumscription** (noun).

circumvent (verb)   to get around. *When Jerry was caught speeding, he tried to circumvent the law by offering the police officer a bribe.*

clandestine (adjective)   secret, surreptitious. *As a member of the underground, Balas took part in clandestine meetings to discuss ways of sabotaging the Nazi forces.*

cloying (adjective)   overly sweet or sentimental. *The deathbed scenes in the novels of Dickens are famously cloying: as Oscar Wilde said, "One would need a heart of stone to read the death of Little Nell without laughing."*

cogent (adjective)   forceful and convincing. *The committee members were won over to the project by the cogent arguments of the chairman.* **cogency** (noun).

cognizant (adjective)   aware, mindful. *Cognizant of the fact that it was getting late, the master of ceremonies cut short the last speech.* **cognizance** (noun).

cohesive (adjective)   sticking together, unified. *An effective military unit must be a cohesive team, all its members working together for a common goal.* **cohere** (verb), **cohesion** (noun).

collaborate (verb)   to work together. *To create a truly successful movie, the director, writers, actors, and many others must collaborate closely.* **collaboration** (noun), **collaborative** (adjective).

colloquial (adjective)   informal in language; conversational. *Some expressions from Shakespeare, such as the use of thou and thee, sound formal today but were colloquial English in Shakespeare's time.*

competent (adjective)   having the skill and knowledge needed for a particular task; capable. *Any competent lawyer can draw up a will.* **competence** (noun).

complacent (adjective)   smug, self-satisfied. *During the 1970s, American auto makers became complacent, believing that they would continue to be successful with little effort.* **complacency** (noun).

composure (noun)   calm, self-assurance. *The president managed to keep his composure during his speech even when the TelePrompTer broke down, leaving him without a script.* **composed** (adjective).

conciliatory (adjective)   seeking agreement, compromise, or reconciliation. *As a conciliatory gesture, the union leaders agreed to postpone a strike and to continue negotiations with management.* **conciliate** (verb), **conciliation** (noun).

concise (adjective)   expressed briefly and simply; succinct. *Less than a page long, the Bill of Rights is a concise statement of the freedoms enjoyed by all Americans.* **concision** (noun).

condescending (adjective)   having an attitude of superiority toward another; patronizing. *"What a cute little car!" she remarked in a condescending style. "I suppose it's the nicest one someone like you could afford!"* **condescension** (noun).

condolence (noun)   pity for someone else's sorrow or loss; sympathy. *After the sudden death of Princess Diana, thousands of messages of condolence were sent to her family.* **condole** (verb).

confidant (noun)   someone entrusted with another's secrets. *No one knew about Janee's engagement except Sarah, her confidant.* **confide** (verb), **confidential** (adjective).

conformity (noun)   agreement with or adherence to custom or rule. *In my high school, conformity was the rule: everyone dressed the same, talked the same, and listened to the same music.* **conform** (verb), **conformist** (adjective).

consensus (noun)   general agreement among a group. *Among Quakers, voting traditionally is not used; instead, discussion continues until the entire group forms a consensus.*

consolation (noun)   relief or comfort in sorrow or suffering. *Although we miss our dog very much, it is a consolation to know that she died quickly, without suffering.* **console** (verb).

consternation (noun)   shock, amazement, dismay. *When a voice in the back of the church shouted out, "I know why they should not be married!" the entire gathering was thrown into consternation.*

consummate (verb)   to complete, finish, or perfect. *The deal was consummated with a handshake and the payment of the agreed-upon fee.* **consummate** (adjective), **consummation** (noun).

contaminate (verb)   to make impure. *Chemicals dumped in a nearby forest had seeped into the soil and contaminated the local water supply.* **contamination** (noun).

contemporary (adjective)   modern, current; from the same time. *I prefer old-fashioned furniture rather than contemporary styles. The composer Vivaldi was roughly contemporary with Bach.* **contemporary** (noun).

contrite (adjective)   sorry for past misdeeds. *The public is often willing to forgive celebrities who are involved in some scandal, as long as they appear contrite.* **contrition** (noun).

conundrum (noun)   a riddle, puzzle, or problem. *The question of why an all-powerful, all-loving God allows evil to exist is a conundrum many philosophers have pondered.*

convergence (noun)   the act of coming together in unity or similarity. *A remarkable example of evolutionary convergence can be seen in the shark and the dolphin, two sea creatures that developed from different origins to become very similar in form.* **converge** (verb).

convoluted (adjective)   twisting, complicated, intricate. *Tax law has become so convoluted that it's easy for people to accidentally violate it.* **convolute** (verb), **convolution** (noun).

corroborating (adjective)   supporting with evidence; confirming. *A passerby who had witnessed the crime gave corroborating testimony about the presence of the accused person.* **corroborate** (verb), **corroboration** (noun).

corrosive (adjective)   eating away, gnawing, or destroying. *Years of poverty and hard work had a corrosive effect on her beauty.* **corrode** (verb), **corrosion** (noun).

credulity (noun)   willingness to believe, even with little evidence. *Con artists fool people by taking advantage of their credulity.* **credulous** (adjective).

criterion (noun)   a standard of measurement or judgment. (The plural is criteria.) *In choosing a design for the new taxicabs, reliability will be our main criterion.*

critique (noun)   a critical evaluation. *The editor gave a detailed critique of the manuscript, explaining its strengths and its weaknesses.* **critique** (verb).

culpable (adjective)   deserving blame, guilty. *Although he committed the crime, because he was mentally ill he should not be considered culpable for his actions.* **culpability** (noun).

cumulative (adjective)   made up of successive additions. *Smallpox was eliminated only through the cumulative efforts of several generations of doctors and scientists.* **accumulation** (noun), **accumulate** (verb).

curtail (verb)   to shorten. *Because of the military emergency, all soldiers on leave were ordered to curtail their absences and return to duty.*

D

debased (adjective)   lowered in quality, character, or esteem. *The quality of TV journalism has been debased by the many new tabloid-style talk shows.* **debase** (verb).

debunk (verb)   to expose as false or worthless. *Magician James Randi loves to debunk psychics, mediums, clairvoyants, and others who claim supernatural powers.*

decorous (adjective)   having good taste; proper, appropriate. *The once reserved and decorous style of the British monarchy began to change when the chic, flamboyant young Diana Spencer joined the family.* **decorum** (noun).

decry (verb)   to criticize or condemn. *Cigarette ads aimed at youngsters have led many to decry the marketing tactics of the tobacco industry.*

deduction (noun)   a logical conclusion, especially a specific conclusion based on general principles. *Based on what is known about the effects of greenhouse gases on atmospheric temperature, scientists have made several deductions about the likelihood of global warming.* **deduce** (verb).

delegate (verb)   to give authority or responsibility. *The president delegated the vice president to represent the administration at the peace talks.* **delegate** (noun).

deleterious (adjective)   harmful. *About thirty years ago, scientists proved that working with asbestos could be deleterious to one's health, producing cancer and other diseases.*

delineate (verb)   to outline or describe. *Naturalists had long suspected the fact of evolution, but Darwin was the first to delineate a process—natural selection—through which evolution could occur.*

demagogue (noun)   a leader who plays dishonestly on the prejudices and emotions of his followers. *Senator Joseph McCarthy was a demagogue who used the paranoia of the anti-Communist 1950s as a way of seizing fame and power in Washington.* **demagoguery** (noun).

demure (adjective)   modest or shy. *The demure heroines of Victorian fiction have given way to today's stronger, more opinionated, and more independent female characters.*

denigrate (verb)   to criticize or belittle. *The firm's new president tried to explain his plans for improving the company without seeming to denigrate the work of his predecessor.* **denigration** (noun).

depose (verb)   to remove from office, especially from a throne. *Iran was formerly ruled by a monarch called the Shah, who was deposed in 1976.*

derelict (adjective)   neglecting one's duty. *The train crash was blamed on a switchman who was derelict, having fallen asleep while on duty.* **dereliction** (noun).

derivative (adjective)   taken from a particular source. *When a person first writes poetry, her poems are apt to be derivative of whatever poetry she most enjoys reading.* **derivation** (noun), **derive** (verb).

desolate (adjective)   empty, lifeless, and deserted; hopeless, gloomy. *Robinson Crusoe was shipwrecked and had to learn to survive alone on a desolate island. The murder of her husband left Mary Lincoln desolate.* **desolation** (noun).

destitute (adjective)   very poor. *Years of rule by a dictator who stole the wealth of the country had left the people of the Philippines destitute.* **destitution** (noun).

deter (verb)   to discourage from acting. *The best way to deter crime is to insure that criminals will receive swift and certain punishment.* **deterrence** (noun), **deterrent** (adjective).

detractor (noun) someone who belittles or disparages. *Neil Diamond has many detractors who consider his music boring, inane, and sentimental.* **detract** (verb).

deviate (verb)   to depart from a standard or norm. *Having agreed upon a spending budget for the company, we mustn't deviate from it; if we do, we may run out of money soon.* **deviation** (noun).

devious (adjective)   tricky, deceptive. *Milken's devious financial tactics were designed to enrich his firm while confusing or misleading government regulators.*

didactic (adjective)   intended to teach, instructive. *The children's TV show* Sesame Street *is designed to be both entertaining and didactic.*

diffident (adjective)   hesitant, reserved, shy. *Someone with a diffident personality should pursue a career that involves little public contact.* **diffidence** (noun).

diffuse (verb)   to spread out, to scatter. *The red dye quickly became diffused through the water, turning it a very pale pink.* **diffusion** (noun).

digress (verb)   to wander from the main path or the main topic. *My high school biology teacher loved to digress from science into personal anecdotes about his college adventures.* **digression** (noun), **digressive** (adjective).

dilatory (adjective)   delaying, procrastinating. *The lawyer used various dilatory tactics, hoping that his opponent would get tired of waiting for a trial and drop the case.*

diligent (adjective)   working hard and steadily. *Through diligent efforts, the townspeople were able to clear away the debris from the flood in a matter of days.* **diligence** (noun).

diminutive (adjective)   unusually small, tiny. *Children are fond of Shetland ponies because their diminutive size makes them easy to ride.* **diminution** (noun).

discern (verb)   to detect, notice, or observe. *I could discern the shape of a whale off the starboard bow, but it was too far away to determine its size or species.* **discernment** (noun).

disclose (verb)   to make known; to reveal. *Election laws require candidates to disclose the names of those who contribute money to their campaigns.* **disclosure** (noun).

discomfit (verb)   to frustrate, thwart, or embarrass. *Discomfited by the interviewer's unexpected question, Peter could only stammer in reply.* **discomfiture** (noun).

disconcert (verb)   to confuse or embarrass. *When the hallway bells began to ring halfway through her lecture, the speaker was disconcerted and didn't know what to do.*

discredit (verb)   to cause disbelief in the accuracy of some statement or the reliability of a person. *Although many people still believe in UFOs, among scientists the reports of "alien encounters" have been thoroughly discredited.*

discreet (adjective)   showing good judgment in speech and behavior. *Be discreet when discussing confidential business matters—don't talk among strangers on the elevator, for example.* **discretion** (noun).

discrepancy (noun)   a difference or variance between two or more things. *The discrepancies between the two witnesses' stories show that one of them must be lying.* **discrepant** (adjective).

disdain (noun)   contempt, scorn. *Millionaire Leona Helmsley was disliked by many people because she treated "little people" with such disdain.* **disdain** (verb), **disdainful** (adjective).

disingenuous (adjective)   pretending to be candid, simple, and frank. *When Texas billionaire H. Ross Perot ran for president, many considered his "jest plain folks" style disingenuous.*

disparage (verb)   to speak disrespectfully about, to belittle. *Many political ads today both praise their own candidate and disparage his or her opponent.* **disparagement** (noun), **disparaging** (adjective).

disparity (noun)   difference in quality or kind. *There is often a disparity between the kind of high-quality television people say they want and the low-brow programs they actually watch.* **disparate** (adjective).

disregard (verb)   to ignore, to neglect. *If you don't write a will, when you die, your survivors may disregard your wishes about how your property should be handled.* **disregard** (noun).

disruptive (adjective)   causing disorder, interrupting. *When the senator spoke at our college, angry demonstrators picketed, heckled, and engaged in other disruptive activities.* **disrupt** (verb), **disruption** (noun).

dissemble (verb)   to pretend, to simulate. *When the police questioned her about the crime, she dissembled innocence.*

dissipate (verb)   to spread out or scatter. *The windows and doors were opened, allowing the smoke that had filled the room to dissipate.* **dissipation** (noun).

dissonance (noun)   lack of music harmony; lack of agreement between ideas. *Most modern music is characterized by dissonance, which many listeners find hard to enjoy. There is a noticeable dissonance between two common beliefs of most conservatives: their faith in unfettered free markets and their preference for traditional social values.* **dissonant** (adjective).

diverge (verb)   to move in different directions. *Frost's poem* The Road Less Traveled *tells of the choice he made when "Two roads diverged in a yellow wood."* **divergence** (noun), **divergent** (adjective).

diversion (noun)   a distraction or pastime. *During the two hours he spent in the doctor's waiting room, his hand-held computer game was a welcome diversion.* **divert** (verb).

divination (noun)   the art of predicting the future. *In ancient Greece, people wanting to know their fate would visit the priests at Delphi, supposedly skilled at divination.* **divine** (verb).

divisive (adjective)   causing disagreement or disunity. *Throughout history, race has been the most divisive issue in American society.*

divulge (verb)   to reveal. *The people who count the votes for the Oscar awards are under strict orders not to divulge the names of the winners.*

dogmatic (adjective)   holding firmly to a particular set of beliefs with little or no basis. *Believers in Marxist doctrine tend to be dogmatic, ignoring evidence that contradicts their beliefs.* **dogmatism** (noun).

dominant (adjective)   greatest in importance or power. *Turner's* Frontier Thesis *suggests that the existence of the frontier had a dominant influence on American culture.* **dominate** (verb), **domination** (noun).

dubious (adjective)   doubtful, uncertain. *Despite the chairman's attempts to convince the committee members that his plan would succeed, most of them remained dubious.* **dubiety** (noun).

durable (adjective)   longlasting. *Denim is a popular material for work clothes because it is strong and durable.*

duress (noun)   compulsion or restraint. *Fearing that the police might beat him, he confessed to the crime, not willingly but under duress.*

E

eclectic (adjective)   drawn from many sources; varied, heterogeneous. *The Mellon family art collection is an eclectic one, including works ranging from ancient Greek sculptures to modern paintings.* **eclecticism** (noun).

efficacious (adjective)   able to produce a desired effect. *Though thousands of people today are taking herbal supplements to treat depression, researchers have not yet proved them efficacious.* **efficacy** (noun).

effrontery (noun)   shameless boldness. *The sports world was shocked when a pro basketball player had the effrontery to choke his head coach during a practice session.*

effusive (adjective)   pouring forth one's emotions very freely. *Having won the Oscar for Best Actress, Sally Field gave an effusive acceptance speech in which she marveled, "You like me! You really like me!"* **effusion** (noun).

egoism (noun)   excessive concern with oneself; conceit. *Robert's egoism was so great that all he could talk about was the importance—and the brilliance—of his own opinions.* **egoistic** (adjective).

egregious (adjective)   obvious, conspicuous, flagrant. *It's hard to imagine how the editor could allow such an egregious error to appear.*

elated (adjective)   excited and happy; exultant. *When the Green Bay Packers' last, desperate pass was dropped, the elated fans of the Denver Broncos began to celebrate.* **elate** (verb), **elation** (noun).

elliptical (adjective)   very terse or concise in writing or speech; difficult to understand. *Rather than speak plainly, she hinted at her meaning through a series of nods, gestures, and elliptical half sentences.*

elusive (adjective)   hard to capture, grasp, or understand. *Though everyone thinks they know what "justice" is, when you try to define the concept precisely, it proves to be quite elusive.*

embezzle (verb)   to steal money or property that has been entrusted to your care. *The church treasurer was found to have embezzled thousands of dollars by writing phony checks on the church bank account.* **embezzlement** (noun).

emend (verb)   to correct. *Before the letter is mailed, please emend the two spelling errors.* **emendation** (noun).

emigrate (verb)   to leave one place or country to settle elsewhere. *Millions of Irish emigrated to the New World in the wake of the great Irish famines of the 1840s.* **emigrant** (noun), **emigration** (noun).

eminent (adjective)   noteworthy, famous. *Vaclav Havel was an eminent author before being elected president of the Czech Republic.* **eminence** (noun).

emissary (noun)   someone who represents another. *In an effort to avoid a military showdown, Carter was sent as an emissary to Korea to negotiate a settlement.*

emollient (noun)   something that softens or soothes. *She used a hand cream as an emollient on her dry, work-roughened hands.* **emollient** (adjective).

empathy (noun)   imaginative sharing of the feelings, thoughts, or experiences of another. *It's easy for a parent to have empathy for the sorrow of another parent whose child has died.* **empathetic** (adjective).

empirical (adjective)   based on experience or personal observation. *Although many people believe in ESP, scientists have found no empirical evidence of its existence.* **empiricism** (noun).

emulate (verb)   to imitate or copy. *The British band Oasis admitted their desire to emulate their idols, the Beatles.* **emulation** (noun).

encroach (verb)   to go beyond acceptable limits; to trespass. *By quietly seizing more and more authority, Robert Moses continually encroached on the powers of other government leaders.* **encroachment** (noun).

enervate (verb)   to reduce the energy or strength of someone or something. *The stress of the operation left her feeling enervated for about two weeks.*

engender (verb)   to produce, to cause. *Countless disagreements over the proper use of national forests have engendered feelings of hostility between ranchers and environmentalists.*

enhance (verb)   to improve in value or quality. *New kitchen appliances will enhance your house and increase the amount of money you'll make when you sell it.* **enhancement** (noun).

enmity (noun)   hatred, hostility, ill will. *Long-standing enmity, like that between the Protestants and Catholics in Northern Ireland, is difficult to overcome.*

enthrall (verb)   to enchant or charm. *When the Swedish singer Jenny Lind toured America in the nineteenth century, audiences were enthralled by her beauty and talent.*

ephemeral (adjective)   quickly disappearing; transient. *Stardom in pop music is ephemeral; most of the top acts of ten years ago are forgotten today.*

equanimity (noun)   calmness of mind, especially under stress. *Roosevelt had the gift of facing the great crises of his presidency—the Depression and the Second World War—with equanimity and even humor.*

eradicate (verb)   to destroy completely. *American society has failed to eradicate racism, although some of its worst effects have been reduced.*

espouse (verb)   to take up as a cause; to adopt. *No politician in American today will openly espouse racism, although some behave and speak in racially prejudiced ways.*

euphoric (adjective)   a feeling of extreme happiness and well-being; elation. *One often feels euphoric during the earliest days of a new love affair.* **euphoria** (noun).

evanescent (adjective)   vanishing like a vapor; fragile and transient. *As she walked by, the evanescent fragrance of her perfume reached me for just an instant.*

exacerbate (verb)   to make worse or more severe. *The roads in our town already have too much traffic; building a new shopping mall will exacerbate the problem.*

exasperate (verb)   to irritate or annoy. *Because she was trying to study, Sharon was exasperated by the yelling of her neighbors' children.*

exculpate (verb)   to free from blame or guilt. *When someone else confessed to the crime, the previous suspect was exculpated.* **exculpation** (noun), **exculpatory** (adjective).

exemplary (adjective)   worthy to serve as a model. *The Baldrige Award is given to a company with exemplary standards of excellence in products and service.* **exemplar** (noun), **exemplify** (verb).

exonerate (verb)   to free from blame. *Although Jewell was suspected at first of being involved in the bombing, later evidence exonerated him.* **exoneration** (noun), **exonerative** (adjective).

expansive (adjective)   broad and large; speaking openly and freely. *The LBJ Ranch is located on an expansive tract of land in Texas. Over dinner, she became expansive in describing her dreams for the future.*

expedite (verb)   to carry out promptly. *As the flood waters rose, the governor ordered state agencies to expedite their rescue efforts.*

expertise (noun)   skill, mastery. *The software company was eager to hire new graduates with programming expertise.*

expiate (verb)   to atone for. *The president's apology to the survivors of the notorious Tuskegee experiments was his attempt to expiate the nation's guilt over their mistreatment.* **expiation** (noun).

expropriate (verb)   to seize ownership of. *When the Communists came to power in China, they expropriated most businesses and turned them over to government-appointed managers.* **expropriation** (noun).

extant (adjective)   currently in existence. *Of the seven ancient Wonders of the World, only the pyramids of Egypt are still extant.*

extenuate (verb)   to make less serious. *Karen's guilt is extenuated by the fact that she was only twelve when she committed the theft.* **extenuating** (adjective), **extenuation** (noun).

extol (verb)   to greatly praise. *At the party convention, speaker after speaker rose to extol their candidate for the presidency.*

extricate (verb)   to free from a difficult or complicated situation. *Much of the humor in the TV show* I Love Lucy *comes in watching Lucy try to extricate herself from the problems she creates by fibbing or trickery.* **extricable** (adjective).

extrinsic (adjective)   not an innate part or aspect of something; external. *The high price of old baseball cards is due to extrinsic factors, such as the nostalgia felt by baseball fans for the stars of their youth, rather than the inherent beauty or value of the cards themselves.*

exuberant (adjective)   wildly joyous and enthusiastic. *As the final seconds of the game ticked away, the fans of the winning team began an exuberant celebration.* **exuberance** (noun).

F

facile (adjective)   easy; shallow or superficial. *The one-minute political commercial favors a candidate with facile opinions rather than serious, thoughtful solutions.* **facilitate** (verb), **facility** (noun).

fallacy (noun)   an error in fact or logic. *It's a fallacy to think that "natural" means "healthful"; after all, the deadly poison arsenic is completely natural.* **fallacious** (adjective).

felicitous (adjective)   pleasing, fortunate, apt. *The sudden blossoming of the dogwood trees on the morning of Matt's wedding seemed a felicitous sign of good luck.* **felicity** (noun).

feral (adjective)   wild. *The garbage dump was inhabited by a pack of feral dogs, that had escaped from their owners and become completely wild.*

fervent (adjective)   full of intense feeling; ardent, zealous. *In the days just after his religious conversion, his piety was at its most fervent.* **fervid** (adjective), **fervor** (noun).

flagrant (adjective)   obviously wrong; offensive. *Nixon was forced to resign the presidency after a series of flagrant crimes against the U.S. Constitution.* **flagrancy** (noun).

flamboyant (adjective)   very colorful, showy, or elaborate. *At Mardi Gras, partygoers compete to show off the most wild and flamboyant outfits.*

florid (adjective)   flowery, fancy; reddish. *The grand ballroom was decorated in a florid style. Years of heavy drinking had given him a florid complexion.*

foppish (adjective)   describing a man who is foolishly vain about his dress or appearance. *The foppish character of the 1890s wore bright-colored spats and a top hat; in the 1980s, he wore fancy suspenders and a shirt with a contrasting collar.* **fop** (noun).

formidable (adjective)   awesome, impressive, or frightening. *According to his plaque in the Baseball Hall of Fame, pitcher Tom Seaver turned the New York Mets "from lovable losers into formidable foes."*

fortuitous (adjective)   lucky, fortunate. *Although the mayor claimed credit for the falling crime rate, it was really caused by several fortuitous trends.*

fractious (adjective)   troublesome, unruly. *Members of the British Parliament are often fractious, shouting insults and sarcastic questions during debates.*

fragility (noun)   the quality of being easy to break; delicacy, weakness. *Because of their fragility, few stained glass windows from the early Middle Ages have survived.* **fragile** (adjective).

fraternize (verb)   to associate with on friendly terms. *Although baseball players aren't supposed to fraternize with their opponents, players from opposing teams often chat before games.* **fraternization** (noun).

frenetic (adjective)   chaotic, frantic. *The floor of the stock exchange, filled with traders shouting and gesturing, is a scene of frenetic activity.*

frivolity (noun)   lack of seriousness; levity. *The frivolity of the Mardi Gras carnival is in contrast to the seriousness of the religious season of Lent that follows.* **frivolous** (adjective).

frugal (adjective)   spending little. *With our last few dollars, we bought a frugal dinner: a loaf of bread and a piece of cheese.* **frugality** (noun).

fugitive (noun)   someone trying to escape. *When two prisoners broke out of the local jail, police were warned to keep an eye out for the fugitives.* **fugitive** (adjective).

G

gargantuan (adjective)   huge, colossal. *The building of the Great Wall of China was one of the most gargantuan projects ever undertaken.*

genial (adjective)   friendly, gracious. *A good host welcomes all visitors in a warm and genial fashion.*

grandiose (adjective)   overly large, pretentious, or showy. *Among Hitler's grandiose plans for Berlin was a gigantic building with a dome several times larger than any ever built.* **grandiosity** (noun).

gratuitous (adjective)   given freely or without cause. *Since her opinion was not requested, her harsh criticism of his singing seemed a gratuitous insult.*

gregarious (adjective)   enjoying the company of others; sociable. *Marty is naturally gregarious, a popular member of several clubs and a sought-after lunch companion.*

guileless (adjective)   without cunning; innocent. *Deborah's guileless personality and complete honesty make it hard for her to survive in the harsh world of politics.*

gullible (adjective)   easily fooled. *When the sweepstakes entry form arrived bearing the message, "You may be a winner!" my gullible neighbor tried to claim a prize.* **gullibility** (noun).

H

hackneyed (adjective)   without originality, trite. *When someone invented the phrase, "No pain, no gain," it was clever, but now it is so commonly heard that it seems hackneyed.*

haughty (adjective)   overly proud. *The fashion model strode down the runway, her hips thrust forward and a haughty expression, like a sneer, on her face.* **haughtiness** (noun).

hedonist (noun)   someone who lives mainly to pursue pleasure. *Having inherited great wealth, he chose to live the life of a hedonist, traveling the world in luxury.* **hedonism** (noun), **hedonistic** (adjective).

heinous (adjective)   very evil, hateful. *The massacre by Pol Pot of more than a million Cambodians is one of the twentieth century's most heinous crimes.*

hierarchy (noun)   a ranking of people, things, or ideas from highest to lowest. *A cabinet secretary ranks just below the president and vice president in the hierarchy of the executive branch.* **hierarchical** (adjective).

hypocrisy (noun)   a false pretense of virtue. *When the sexual misconduct of the television preacher was exposed, his followers were shocked at his hypocrisy.* **hypocritical** (adjective).

I

iconoclast (noun)   someone who attacks traditional beliefs or institutions. *Comedian Dennis Miller enjoys his reputation as an iconoclast, though people in power often resent his satirical jabs.* **iconoclasm** (noun), **iconoclastic** (adjective).

idiosyncratic (adjective)   peculiar to an individual; eccentric. *Cyndi Lauper sings pop music in an idiosyncratic style, mingling high-pitched whoops and squeals with throaty gurgles.* **idiosyncrasy** (noun).

idolatry (noun)   the worship of a person, thing, or institution as a god. *In Communist China, Chairman Mao was the subject of idolatry; his picture was displayed everywhere, and millions of Chinese memorized his sayings.* **idolatrous** (adjective).

impartial (adjective)   fair, equal, unbiased. *If a judge is not impartial, then all of her rulings are questionable.* **impartiality** (noun).

impeccable (adjective)   flawless. *The crooks printed impeccable copies of the Super Bowl tickets, making it impossible to distinguish them from the real ones.*

impetuous (adjective)   acting hastily or impulsively. *Ben's resignation was an impetuous act; he did it without thinking, and he soon regretted it.* **impetuosity** (noun).

impinge (verb)   to encroach upon, touch, or affect. *You have a right to do whatever you want, so long as your actions don't impinge on the rights of others.*

implicit (adjective)   understood without being openly expressed; implied. *Although most clubs had no rules excluding blacks and Jews, many had an implicit understanding that no blacks or Jews would be allowed to join.*

impute (verb)   to credit or give responsibility to; to attribute. *Although Sarah's comments embarrassed me, I don't impute any ill will to her; I think she didn't realize what she was saying.* **imputation** (noun).

inarticulate (adjective)   unable to speak or express oneself clearly and understandably. *A skilled athlete may be an inarticulate public speaker, as demonstrated by many post-game interviews.*

incisive (adjective)   expressed clearly and directly. *Franklin settled the debate with a few incisive remarks that summed up the issue perfectly.*

incompatible (adjective)   unable to exist together; conflicting. *Many people hold seemingly incompatible beliefs: for example, supporting the death penalty while believing in the sacredness of human life.* **incompatibility** (noun).

inconsequential (adjective)   of little importance. *When the stereo was delivered, it was a different shade of gray than I expected, but the difference was inconsequential.*

incontrovertible (adjective)   impossible to question. *The fact that Sheila's fingerprints were the only ones on the murder weapon made her guilt seem incontrovertible.*

incorrigible (adjective)   impossible to manage or reform. *Lou is an incorrigible trickster, constantly playing practical jokes no matter how much his friends complain.*

incremental (adjective)   increasing gradually by small amounts. *Although the initial cost of the Medicare program was small, the incremental expenses have grown to be very large.* **increment** (noun).

incriminate (adjective)   to give evidence of guilt. *The fifth amendment to the Constitution says that no one is required to reveal information that would incriminate him in a crime.* **incriminating** (adjective).

incumbent (noun)   someone who occupies an office or position. *It is often difficult for a challenger to win a seat in Congress from the incumbent.* **incumbency** (noun), **incumbent** (adjective).

indeterminate (adjective)   not definitely known. *The college plans to enroll an indeterminate number of students; the size of the class will depend on the number of applicants and how many accept offers of admission.* **determine** (verb).

indifferent (adjective)   unconcerned, apathetic. *The mayor's small proposed budget for education suggests that he is indifferent to the needs of our schools.* **indifference** (noun).

indistinct (adjective)   unclear, uncertain. *We could see boats on the water, but in the thick morning fog their shapes were indistinct.*

indomitable (adjective)   unable to be conquered or controlled. *The world admired the indomitable spirit of Nelson Mandela; he remained courageous despite years of imprisonment.*

induce (verb)   to cause. *The doctor prescribed a medicine that was supposed to induce a lowering of the blood pressure.* **induction** (noun).

ineffable (adjective)   difficult to describe or express. *He gazed in silence at the sunrise over the Taj Mahal, his eyes reflecting an ineffable sense of wonder.*

inevitable (adjective)   unable to be avoided. *Once the Japanese attacked Pearl Harbor, American involvement in World War Two was inevitable.* **inevitability** (noun).

inexorable (adjective)   unable to be deterred; relentless. *It's difficult to imagine how the mythic character of Oedipus could have avoided his evil destiny; his fate appears inexorable.*

ingenious (adjective)   showing cleverness and originality. *The Post-It note is an ingenious solution to a common problem—how to mark papers without spoiling them.* **ingenuity** (noun).

inherent (adjective)   naturally part of something. *Compromise is inherent in democracy, since everyone cannot get his way.* **inhere** (verb), **inherence** (noun).

innate (adjective)   inborn, native. *Not everyone who takes piano lessons becomes a fine musician, which shows that music requires innate talent as well as training.*

innocuous (adjective)   harmless, inoffensive. *I was surprised that Andrea took offense at such an innocuous joke.*

inoculate (verb)   to prevent a disease by infusing with a disease-causing organism. *Pasteur found he could prevent rabies by inoculating patients with the virus that causes the disease.* **inoculation** (noun).

insipid (adjective)   flavorless, uninteresting. *Most TV shows are so insipid that you can watch them while reading without missing a thing.* **insipidity** (noun).

insolence (noun)   an attitude or behavior that is bold and disrespectful. *Some feel that news reporters who shout questions at the president are behaving with insolence.* **insolent** (adjective).

insular (adjective)   narrow or isolated in attitude or viewpoint. *Americans are famous for their insular attitudes; they seem to think that nothing important has ever happened outside of their country.* **insularity** (noun).

insurgency (noun)   uprising, rebellion. *The angry townspeople had begun an insurgency bordering on downright revolution; they were collecting arms, holding secret meetings, and refusing to pay certain taxes.* **insurgent** (adjective).

integrity (noun) honesty, uprightness; soundness, completeness. *"Honest Abe" Lincoln is considered a model of political integrity. Inspectors examined the building's support beams and foundation and found no reason to doubt its structural integrity.*

interlocutor (noun) someone taking part in a dialogue or conversation. *Annoyed by the constant questions from someone in the crowd, the speaker challenged his interlocutor to offer a better plan.* **interlocutory** (adjective).

interlude (noun) an interrupting period or performance. *The two most dramatic scenes in King Lear are separated, strangely, by a comic interlude starring the king's jester.*

interminable (adjective) endless or seemingly endless. *Addressing the United Nations, Castro announced, "We will be brief"—then delivered an interminable 4-hour speech.*

intransigent (adjective) unwilling to compromise. *Despite the mediator's attempts to suggest a fair solution, the two parties were intransigent, forcing a showdown.* **intransigence** (noun).

intrepid (adjective) fearless and resolute. *Only an intrepid adventurer is willing to undertake the long and dangerous trip by sled to the South Pole.* **intrepidity** (noun).

intrusive (adjective) forcing a way in without being welcome. *The legal requirement of a search warrant is supposed to protect Americans from intrusive searches by the police.* **intrude** (verb), **intrusion** (noun).

intuitive (adjective) known directly, without apparent thought or effort. *An experienced chess player sometimes has an intuitive sense of the best move to make, even if she can't explain it.* **intuit** (verb), **intuition** (noun).

inundate (verb) to flood; to overwhelm. *As soon as playoff tickets went on sale, eager fans inundated the box office with orders.*

invariable (adjective) unchanging, constant. *When writing a book, it was her invariable habit to rise at 6 and work at her desk from 7 to 12.* **invariability** (noun).

inversion (noun) a turning backwards, inside-out, or upside-down; a reversal. *Latin poetry often features inversion of word order; for example, those in the first line of Vergil's Aeneid: "Arms and the man I sing."* **invert** (verb), **inverted** (adjective).

inveterate (adjective) persistent, habitual. *It's very difficult for an inveterate gambler to give up the pastime.* **inveteracy** (noun).

invigorate (verb) to give energy to, to stimulate. *As her car climbed the mountain road, Lucinda felt invigorated by the clear air and the cool breezes.*

invincible (adjective) impossible to conquer or overcome. *For three years at the height of his career, boxer Mike Tyson seemed invincible.*

inviolable (adjective) impossible to attack or trespass upon. *In the president's remote hideaway at Camp David, guarded by the Secret Service, his privacy is, for once, inviolable.*

irrational (adjective) unreasonable. *Charles knew that his fear of insects was irrational, but he was unable to overcome it.* **irrationality** (noun).

irresolute (adjective) uncertain how to act, indecisive. *When McGovern first said he supported his vice presidential candidate "one thousand percent," then dropped him from the ticket, it made McGovern appear irresolute.* **irresolution** (noun).

J

jeopardize (verb) to put in danger. *Terrorist attacks jeopardize the fragile peace in the Middle East.* **jeopardy** (noun).

juxtapose (verb) to put side by side. *It was strange to see the old-time actor Charlton Heston and rock icon Bob Dylan juxtaposed at the awards ceremony.* **juxtaposition** (noun).

L

languid (adjective)   without energy; slow, sluggish, listless. *The hot, humid weather of late August can make anyone feel languid.* **languish** (verb), **languor** (noun).

latent (adjective)   not currently obvious or active; hidden. *Although he had committed only a single act of violence, the psychiatrist who examined him said he had probably always had a latent tendency toward violence.* **latency** (noun).

laudatory (adjective)   giving praise. *The ads for the movie are filled with laudatory comments from critics.*

lenient (adjective)   mild, soothing, or forgiving. *The judge was known for his lenient disposition; he rarely imposed long jail sentences on criminals.* **leniency** (noun).

lethargic (adjective)   lacking energy; sluggish. *Visitors to the zoo are surprised that the lions appear so lethargic, but, in the wild, lions sleep up to 18 hours a day.* **lethargy** (noun).

liability (noun)   an obligation or debt; a weakness or drawback. *The insurance company had a liability of millions of dollars after the town was destroyed by a tornado. Slowness afoot is a serious liability in an aspiring basketball player.* **liable** (adjective).

lithe (adjective)   flexible and graceful. *The ballet dancer was almost as lithe as a cat.*

longevity (noun)   length of life; durability. *The reduction in early deaths from infectious diseases is responsible for most of the increase in human longevity over the past two centuries.*

lucid (adjective)   clear and understandable. *Hawking's* A Short History of the Universe *is a lucid explanation of modern scientific theories about the origin of the universe.* **lucidity** (noun).

lurid (adjective)   shocking, gruesome. *While the serial killer was on the loose, the newspapers were filled with lurid stories about his crimes.*

M

malediction (noun)   curse. *In the fairy tale "Sleeping Beauty," the princess is trapped in a death-like sleep because of the malediction uttered by an angry witch.*

malevolence (noun)   hatred, ill will. *Critics say that Iago, the villain in Shakespeare's* Othello, *seems to exhibit malevolence with no real cause.* **malevolent** (noun).

malinger (verb)   to pretend incapacity or illness to avoid a duty or work. *During the labor dispute, hundreds of employees malingered, forcing the company to slow production and costing it millions in profits.*

malleable (adjective)   able to be changed, shaped, or formed by outside pressures. *Gold is a very useful metal because it is so malleable. A child's personality is malleable and deeply influenced by the things her parents say and do.* **malleability** (noun).

mandate (noun)   order, command. *The new policy on gays in the military went into effect as soon as the president issued his mandate about it.* **mandate** (verb), **mandatory** (adjective).

maturation (noun)   the process of becoming fully grown or developed. *Free markets in the former Communist nations are likely to operate smoothly only after a long period of maturation.* **mature** (adjective and verb), **maturity** (noun).

mediate (verb)   to act to reconcile differences between two parties. *During the baseball strike, both the players and the club owners were willing to have the president mediate the dispute.* **mediation** (noun).

mediocrity (noun)   the state of being middling or poor in quality. *The New York Mets, who finished in ninth place in 1968, won the world's championship in 1969, going from horrible to great in a single year and skipping mediocrity.* **mediocre** (adjective).

mercurial (adjective)   changing quickly and unpredictably. *The mercurial personality of Robin Williams, with his many voices and styles, made him perfect for the role of the ever-changing genie in* Aladdin.

meticulous (adjective)   very careful with details. *Repairing watches calls for a craftsperson who is patient and meticulous.*

mimicry (noun)   imitation, aping. *The continued popularity of Elvis Presley has given rise to a class of entertainers who make a living through mimicry of "The King."* **mimic** (noun and verb).

misconception (noun)   a mistaken idea. *Columbus sailed west with the misconception that he would reach the shores of Asia.* **misconceive** (verb).

mitigate (verb)   to make less severe; to relieve. *Wallace certainly committed the assault, but the verbal abuse he'd received helps to explain his behavior and somewhat mitigates his guilt.* **mitigation** (noun).

modicum (noun)   a small amount. *The plan for your new business is well designed; with a modicum of luck, you should be successful.*

mollify (verb)   to soothe or calm; to appease. *Carla tried to mollify the angry customer by promising him a full refund.*

morose (adjective)   gloomy, sullen. *After Chuck's girlfriend dumped him, he lay around the house for a couple of days, feeling morose.*

mundane (adjective)   everyday, ordinary, commonplace. *Moviegoers in the 1930s liked the glamorous films of Fred Astaire because they provided an escape from the mundane problems of life during the Great Depression.*

munificent (adjective)   very generous; lavish. *Ted Turner's billion-dollar donation to the United Nations is probably the most munificent act of charity in history.* **munificence** (noun).

mutable (adjective)   likely to change. *A politician's reputation can be highly mutable, as seen in the case of Harry Truman—mocked during his lifetime, revered afterward.*

N

narcissistic (adjective)   showing excessive love for oneself; egoistic. *Andre's room, decorated with photos of himself and the sports trophies he has won, suggests a narcissistic personality.* **narcissism** (noun).

nocturnal (adjective)   of the night; active at night. *Travelers on the Underground Railroad escaped from slavery to the North by a series of nocturnal flights. The eyes of nocturnal animals must be sensitive in dim light.*

nonchalant (adjective)   appearing to be unconcerned. *Unlike the other players on the football team, who pumped their fists when their names were announced, John ran on the field with a nonchalant wave.* **nonchalance** (noun).

nondescript (adjective)   without distinctive qualities; drab. *The bank robber's clothes were nondescript; none of the witnesses could remember their color or style.*

notorious (adjective)   famous, especially for evil actions or qualities. *Warner Brothers produced a series of movies about notorious gangsters such as John Dillinger and Al Capone.* **notoriety** (noun).

novice (noun)   beginner, tyro. *Lifting your head before you finish your swing is a typical mistake committed by the novice at golf.*

nuance (noun)   a subtle difference or quality. *At first glance, Monet's paintings of water lilies all look much alike, but the more you study them, the more you appreciate the nuances of color and shading that distinguish them.*

nurture (verb)   to nourish or help to grow. *The money given by the National Endowment for the Arts helps nurture local arts organizations throughout the country.* **nurture** (noun).

O

obdurate (adjective)   unwilling to change; stubborn, inflexible. *Despite the many pleas he received, the governor was obdurate in his refusal to grant clemency to the convicted murderer.*

objective (adjective)   dealing with observable facts rather than opinions or interpretations. *When a legal case involves a shocking crime, it may be hard for a judge to remain objective in his rulings.*

oblivious (adjective)   unaware, unconscious. *Karen practiced her oboe with complete concentration, oblivious to the noise and activity around her.* **oblivion** (noun), **obliviousness** (noun).

obscure (adjective)   little known; hard to understand. *Mendel was an obscure monk until decades after his death, when his scientific work was finally discovered. Most people find the writings of James Joyce obscure; hence the popularity of books that explain his books.* **obscure** (verb), **obscurity** (noun).

obsessive (adjective)   haunted or preoccupied by an idea or feeling. *His concern with cleanliness became so obsessive that he washed his hands twenty times every day.* **obsess** (verb), **obsession** (noun).

obsolete (adjective)   no longer current; old-fashioned. *W. H. Auden said that his ideal landscape would include water wheels, wooden grain mills, and other forms of obsolete machinery.* **obsolescence** (noun).

obstinate (adjective)   stubborn, unyielding. *Despite years of effort, the problem of drug abuse remains obstinate.* **obstinacy** (noun).

obtrusive (adjective)   overly prominent. *Philip should sing more softly; his bass is so obtrusive that the other singers can barely be heard.* **obtrude** (verb), **obtrusion** (noun).

ominous (adjective)   foretelling evil. *Ominous black clouds gathered on the horizon, for a violent storm was fast approaching.* **omen** (noun).

onerous (adjective)   heavy, burdensome. *The hero Hercules was ordered to clean the Augean Stables, one of several onerous tasks known as "the labors of Hercules."* **onus** (noun).

opportunistic (adjective)   eagerly seizing chances as they arise. *When Princess Diana died suddenly, opportunistic publishers quickly released books about her life and death.* **opportunism** (noun).

opulent (adjective)   rich, lavish. *The mansion of newspaper tycoon Hearst is famous for its opulent decor.* **opulence** (noun).

ornate (adjective)   highly decorated, elaborate. *Baroque architecture is often highly ornate, featuring surfaces covered with carving, sinuous curves, and painted scenes.*

ostentatious (adjective)   overly showy, pretentious. *To show off his wealth, the millionaire threw an ostentatious party featuring a full orchestra, a famous singer, and tens of thousands of dollars worth of food.*

ostracize (verb)   to exclude from a group. *In Biblical times, those who suffered from the disease of leprosy were ostracized and forced to live alone.* **ostracism** (noun).

P

pallid (adjective)   pale; dull. *Working all day in the coal mine had given him a pallid complexion. The new musical offers only pallid entertainment: the music is lifeless, the acting dull, the story absurd.*

parched (adjective)   very dry; thirsty. *After two months without rain, the crops were shriveled and parched by the sun.* **parch** (verb).

pariah (noun)   outcast. *Accused of robbery, he became a pariah; his neighbors stopped talking to him, and people he'd considered friends no longer called.*

partisan (adjective)   reflecting strong allegiance to a particular party or cause. *The vote on the president's budget was strictly partisan: every member of the president's party voted yes, and all others voted no.* **partisan** (noun).

pathology (noun)   disease or the study of disease; extreme abnormality. *Some people believe that high rates of crime are symptoms of an underlying social pathology.* **pathological** (adjective).

pellucid (adjective)   very clear; transparent; easy to understand. *The water in the mountain stream was cold and pellucid. Thanks to the professor's pellucid explanation, I finally understand relativity theory.*

penitent (adjective)   feeling sorry for past crimes or sins. *Having grown penitent, he wrote a long letter of apology, asking forgiveness.*

penurious (adjective)   extremely frugal; stingy. *Haunted by memories of poverty, he lived in penurious fashion, driving a twelve-year-old car and wearing only the cheapest clothes.* **penury** (noun).

perceptive (adjective)   quick to notice, observant. *With his perceptive intelligence, Holmes was the first to notice the importance of this clue.* **perceptible** (adjective), **perception** (noun).

perfidious (adjective)   disloyal, treacherous. *Although he was one of the most talented generals of the American Revolution, Benedict Arnold is remembered today as a perfidious betrayer of his country.* **perfidy** (noun).

perfunctory (adjective)   unenthusiastic, routine, or mechanical. *When the play opened, the actors sparkled, but, by the thousandth night, their performance had become perfunctory.*

permeate (verb)   to spread through or penetrate. *Little by little, the smell of gas from the broken pipe permeated the house.*

persevere (adjective)   to continue despite difficulties. *Although several of her teammates dropped out of the marathon, Laura persevered.* **perseverance** (noun).

perspicacity (noun)   keenness of observation or understanding. *Journalist Murray Kempton was famous for the perspicacity of his comments on social and political issues.* **perspicacious** (adjective).

peruse (verb)   to examine or study. *Mary-Jo perused the contract carefully before she signed it.* **perusal** (noun).

pervasive (adjective)   spreading throughout. *As news of the disaster reached the town, a pervasive sense of gloom could be felt.* **pervade** (verb).

phlegmatic (adjective)   sluggish and unemotional in temperament. *It was surprising to see Tom, who is normally so phlegmatic, acting excited.*

placate (verb)   to soothe or appease. *The waiter tried to placate the angry customer with the offer of a free dessert.* **placatory** (adjective).

plastic (adjective)   able to be molded or reshaped. *Because it is highly plastic, clay is an easy material for beginning sculptors to use.*

plausible (adjective)   apparently believable. *The idea that a widespread conspiracy to kill President Kennedy has been kept secret for over thirty years hardly seems plausible.* **plausibility** (noun).

polarize (adjective)   to separate into opposing groups or forces. *For years, the abortion debate polarized the American people, with many people voicing extreme views and few trying to find a middle ground.* **polarization** (noun).

portend (verb)   to indicate a future event; to forebode. *According to folklore, a red sky at dawn portends a day of stormy weather.*

potentate (noun)   a powerful ruler. *Before the Russian Revolution, the Tsar was one of the last hereditary potentates of Europe.*

pragmatism (noun)   a belief in approaching problems through practical rather than theoretical means. *Roosevelt's approach toward the Great Depression was based on pragmatism: "Try something," he said; "If it doesn't work, try something else."* **pragmatic** (adjective).

preamble (noun)   an introductory statement. *The preamble to the Constitution begins with the famous words, "We the people of the United States of America . . ."*

precocious (adjective)   mature at an unusually early age. *Picasso was so precocious as an artist that, at nine, he is said to have painted far better pictures than his teacher.* **precocity** (noun).

predatory (adjective)   living by killing and eating other animals; exploiting others for personal gain. *The tiger is the largest predatory animal native to Asia. Microsoft has been accused of predatory business practices that prevent other software companies from competing with them.* **predation** (noun), **predator** (noun).

predilection (noun)   a liking or preference. *To relax from his presidential duties, Kennedy had a predilection for spy novels featuring James Bond.*

predominant (adjective)   greatest in numbers or influence. *Although hundreds of religions are practiced in India, the predominant faith is Hinduism.* **predominance** (noun), **predominate** (verb).

prepossessing (adjective)   attractive. *Smart, lovely, and talented, she has all the prepossessing qualities that mark a potential movie star.*

presumptuous (adjective)   going beyond the limits of courtesy or appropriateness. *The senator winced when the presumptuous young staffer addressed him as "Chuck."* **presume** (verb), **presumption** (noun).

pretentious (adjective)   claiming excessive value or importance. *For a shoe salesman to call himself a "Personal Foot Apparel Consultant" seems awfully pretentious.* **pretension** (noun).

procrastinate (verb)   to put off, to delay. *If you habitually procrastinate, try this technique: never touch a piece of paper without either filing it, responding to it, or throwing it out.* **procrastination** (noun).

profane (adjective)   impure, unholy. *It seems inappropriate to have such profane activities as roller blading and disco dancing in a church.* **profane** (verb), **profanity** (noun).

proficient (adjective)   skillful, adept. *A proficient artist, Louise quickly and accurately sketched the scene.* **proficiency** (noun).

proliferate (verb)   to increase or multiply. *Over the past fifteen years, high-tech companies have proliferated in northern California, Massachusetts, and other regions.* **proliferation** (noun).

prolific (adjective)   producing many offspring or creations. *With more than three hundred books to his credit, Isaac Asimov was one of the most prolific writers of all time.*

prominence (noun)   the quality of standing out; fame. *Kennedy's victory in the West Virginia primary gave him a position of prominence among the Democratic candidates for president.* **prominent** (adjective).

promulgate (verb)   to make public, to declare. *Lincoln signed the proclamation that freed the slaves in 1862, but he waited several months to promulgate it.*

propagate (verb)   to cause to grow; to foster. *John Smithson's will left his fortune for the founding of an institution to propagate knowledge, without saying whether that meant a university, a library, or a museum.* **propagation** (noun).

propriety (noun)   appropriateness. *Some people had doubts about the propriety of Clinton's discussing his underwear on MTV.*

prosaic (adjective)   everyday, ordinary, dull. *"Paul's Case" tells the story of a boy who longs to escape from the prosaic life of a clerk into a world of wealth, glamour, and beauty.*

protagonist (noun)   the main character in a story or play; the main supporter of an idea. *Leopold Bloom is the protagonist of James Joyce's great novel* Ulysses.

provocative (adjective)   likely to stimulate emotions, ideas, or controversy. *The demonstrators began chanting obscenities, a provocative act that they hoped would cause the police to lose control.* **provoke** (verb), **provocation** (noun).

proximity (noun)   closeness, nearness. *Neighborhood residents were angry over the proximity of the sewage plant to the local school.* **proximate** (adjective).

prudent (adjective)   wise, cautious, and practical. *A prudent investor will avoid putting all of her money into any single investment.* **prudence** (noun), **prudential** (adjective).

pugnacious (adjective)   combative, bellicose, truculent; ready to fight. *Ty Cobb, the pugnacious outfielder for the Detroit Tigers, got into more than his fair share of brawls, both on and off the field.* **pugnacity** (noun).

punctilious (adjective)   very concerned about proper forms of behavior and manners. *A punctilious dresser like James would rather skip the party altogether than wear the wrong color tie.* **punctilio** (noun).

pundit (noun)   someone who offers opinions in an authoritative style. *The Sunday afternoon talk shows are filled with pundits, each with his or her own theory about the week's political news.*

punitive (adjective)   inflicting punishment. *The jury awarded the plaintiff one million dollars in punitive damages, hoping to teach the defendant a lesson.*

purify (verb)   to make pure, clean, or perfect. *The new plant is supposed to purify the drinking water provided to everyone in the nearby towns.* **purification** (noun).

Q

quell (verb)   to quiet, to suppress. *It took a huge number of police to quell the rioting.*

querulous (adjective)   complaining, whining. *The nursing home attendant needed a lot of patience to care for the three querulous, unpleasant residents on his floor.*

R

rancorous (adjective)   expressing bitter hostility. *Many Americans are disgusted by recent political campaigns, which seem more rancorous than ever before.* **rancor** (noun).

rationale (noun)   an underlying reason or explanation. *At first, it seemed strange that several camera companies would freely share their newest technology; but their rationale was that offering one new style of film would benefit them all.*

raze (verb)   to completely destroy; demolish. *The old Coliseum building will soon be razed to make room for a new hotel.*

reciprocate (verb)   to make a return for something. *If you'll baby-sit for my kids tonight, I'll reciprocate by taking care of yours tomorrow.* **reciprocity** (noun).

reclusive (adjective)   withdrawn from society. *During the last years of her life, actress Greta Garbo led a reclusive existence, rarely appearing in public.* **recluse** (noun).

reconcile (verb)   to make consistent or harmonious. *Roosevelt's greatness as a leader can be seen in his ability to reconcile the demands and values of the varied groups that supported him.* **reconciliation** (noun).

recriminate (verb)   to accuse, often in response to an accusation. *Divorce proceedings sometimes become bitter, as the two parties recriminate each other over the causes of the breakup.* **recrimination** (noun), **recriminatory** (adjective).

recuperate (verb)   to regain health after an illness. *Although she left the hospital two days after her operation, it took her a few weeks to fully recuperate.* **recuperation** (noun), **recuperative** (adjective).

redoubtable (adjective)   inspiring respect, awe, or fear. *Johnson's knowledge, experience, and personal clout made him a redoubtable political opponent.*

refurbish (verb)   to fix up; renovate. *It took three days' work by a team of carpenters, painters, and decorators to completely refurbish the apartment.*

refute (adjective)   to prove false. *The company invited reporters to visit their plant in an effort to refute the charges of unsafe working conditions.* **refutation** (noun).

relevance (noun)   connection to the matter at hand; pertinence. *Testimony in a criminal trial may be admitted only if it has clear relevance to the question of guilt or innocence.* **relevant** (adjective).

remedial (adjective)   serving to remedy, cure, or correct some condition. *Affirmative action can be justified as a remedial step to help minority members overcome the effects of past discrimination.* **remediation** (noun), **remedy** (verb).

remorse (noun)   a painful sense of guilt over wrongdoing. *In Poe's story "The Tell-Tale Heart," a murderer is driven insane by remorse over his crime.* **remorseful** (adjective).

remuneration (noun)   pay. *In a civil lawsuit, the attorney often receives part of the financial settlement as his or her remuneration.* **remunerate** (verb), **remunerative** (adjective).

renovate (verb)   to renew by repairing or rebuilding. *The television program "This Old House" shows how skilled craftspeople renovate houses.* **renovation** (noun).

renunciation (noun)   the act of rejecting or refusing something. *King Edward VII's renunciation of the British throne was caused by his desire to marry an American divorcee, something he couldn't do as king.* **renounce** (verb).

replete (adjective)   filled abundantly. *Graham's book is replete with wonderful stories about the famous people she has known.*

reprehensible (adjective)   deserving criticism or censure. *Although Pete Rose's misdeeds were reprehensible, not all fans agree that he deserves to be excluded from the Baseball Hall of Fame.* **reprehend** (verb), **reprehension** (noun).

repudiate (verb)   to reject, to renounce. *After it became known that Duke had been a leader of the Ku Klux Klan, most Republican leaders repudiated him.* **repudiation** (noun).

reputable (adjective)   having a good reputation; respected. *Find a reputable auto mechanic by asking your friends for recommendations based on their own experiences.* **reputation** (noun), **repute** (noun).

resilient (adjective)   able to recover from difficulty. *A pro athlete must be resilient, able to lose a game one day and come back the next with confidence and enthusiasm.* **resilience** (adjective).

resplendent (adjective)   glowing, shining. *In late December, midtown New York is resplendent with holiday lights and decorations.* **resplendence** (noun).

responsive (adjective)   reacting quickly and appropriately. *The new director of the Internal Revenue Service has promised to make the agency more responsive to public complaints.* **respond** (verb), **response** (noun).

restitution (noun)   return of something to its original owner; repayment. *Some Native American leaders are demanding that the U.S. government make restitution for the lands taken from them by white settlers.*

revere (verb)   to admire deeply, to honor. *Millions of people around the world revered Mother Teresa for her saintly generosity.* **reverence** (noun), **reverent** (adjective).

rhapsodize (verb)   to praise in a wildly emotional way. *That critic is such a huge fan of Toni Morrison that she will surely rhapsodize over the writer's next novel.* **rhapsodic** (adjective).

S

sagacious (adjective)   discerning, wise. *Only a leader as sagacious as Nelson Mandela could have united South Africa so successfully and peacefully.* **sagacity** (noun).

salvage (verb)   to save from wreck or ruin. *After the earthquake destroyed her home, she was able to salvage only a few of her belongings.* **salvage** (noun), **salvageable** (adjective).

sanctimonious (adjective)   showing false or excessive piety. *The sanctimonious prayers of the TV preacher were interspersed with requests that the viewers send him money.* **sanctimony** (noun).

scapegoat (noun)   someone who bears the blame for others' acts; someone hated for no apparent reason. *Although Buckner's error was only one reason the Red Sox lost, many fans made him the scapegoat, booing him mercilessly.*

scrupulous (adjective)   acting with extreme care; painstaking. *Disney theme parks are famous for their scrupulous attention to small details.* **scruple** (noun).

scrutinize (verb)   to study closely. *The lawyer scrutinized the contract, searching for any sentence that could pose a risk for her client.* **scrutiny** (noun).

secrete (verb)   to emit; to hide. *Glands in the mouth secrete saliva, a liquid that helps in digestion. The jewel thieves secreted the necklace in a tin box buried underground.*

sedentary (adjective)   requiring much sitting. *When Officer Samson was given a desk job, she had trouble getting used to sedentary work after years on the street.*

sequential (adjective)   arranged in an order or series. *The courses for the chemistry major are sequential; you must take them in the order, since each course builds on the previous ones.* **sequence** (noun).

serendipity (noun)   the ability to make lucky accidental discoveries. *Great inventions sometimes come about through deliberate research and hard work, sometimes through pure serendipity.* **serendipitous** (adjective).

servile (adjective)   like a slave or servant; submissive. *The tycoon demanded that his underlings behave in a servile manner, agreeing quickly with everything he said.* **servility** (noun).

simulated (adjective)   imitating something else; artificial. *High-quality simulated gems must be examined under a magnifying glass to be distinguished from real ones.* **simulate** (verb), **simulation** (noun).

solace (verb)   to comfort or console. *There was little the rabbi could say to solace the husband after his wife's death.* **solace** (noun).

spontaneous (adjective)   happening without plan or outside cause. *When the news of Kennedy's assassination broke, people everywhere gathered in a spontaneous effort to share their shock and grief.* **spontaneity** (noun).

spurious (adjective)   false, fake. *The so-called Piltdown Man, supposed to be the fossil of a primitive human, turned out to be spurious, although who created the hoax is still uncertain.*

squander (verb)   to use up carelessly, to waste. *Those who had made donations to the charity were outraged to learn that its director had squandered millions on fancy dinners and first-class travel.*

stagnate (verb)   to become stale through lack of movement or change. *Having had no contact with the outside world for generations, Japan's culture gradually stagnated.* **stagnant** (adjective), **stagnation** (noun).

staid (adjective)   sedate, serious, and grave. *This college is no "party school"; the students all work hard, and the campus has a reputation for being staid.*

stimulus (noun)   something that excites a response or provokes an action. *The arrival of merchants and missionaries from the West provided a stimulus for change in Japanese society.* **stimulate** (verb).

stoic (adjective)   showing little feeling, even in response to pain or sorrow. *A soldier must respond to the death of his comrades in stoic fashion, since the fighting will not stop for his grief.* **stoicism** (noun).

strenuous (adjective)   requiring energy and strength. *Hiking in the foothills of the Rockies is fairly easy, but climbing the higher peaks can be strenuous.*

submissive (adjective)   accepting the will of others; humble, compliant. *At the end of Ibsen's play* A Doll's House, *Nora leaves her husband and abandons the role of submissive housewife.*

substantiated (adjective)   verified or supported by evidence. *The charge that Nixon had helped to cover up crimes was substantiated by his comments about it on a series of audio tapes.* **substantiate** (verb), **substantiation** (noun).

sully (verb)   to soil, stain, or defile. *Nixon's misdeeds as president did much to sully the reputation of the American government.*

superficial (adjective)   on the surface only; without depth or substance. *Her wound was superficial and required only a light bandage. His superficial attractiveness hides the fact that his personality is lifeless and his mind is dull.* **superficiality** (noun).

superfluous (adjective)   more than is needed, excessive. *Once you've won the debate, don't keep talking; superfluous arguments will only bore and annoy the audience.*

suppress (verb)   to put down or restrain. *As soon as the unrest began, thousands of helmeted police were sent into the streets to suppress the riots.* **suppression** (noun).

surfeit (noun)   an excess. *Most American families have a surfeit of food and drink on Thanksgiving Day.* **surfeit** (verb).

surreptitious (adjective)   done in secret. *Because Iraq has avoided weapons inspections, many believe it has a surreptitious weapons development program.*

surrogate (noun)   a substitute. *When the congressman died in office, his wife was named to serve the rest of his term as a surrogate.* **surrogate** (adjective).

sustain (verb)   to keep up, to continue; to support. *Because of fatigue, he was unable to sustain the effort needed to finish the marathon.*

T

tactile (adjective)   relating to the sense of touch. *The thick brush strokes and gobs of color give the paintings of Van Gogh a strongly tactile quality.* **tactility** (noun).

talisman (noun)   an object supposed to have magical effects or qualities. *Superstitious people sometimes carry a rabbit's foot, a lucky coin, or some other talisman.*

tangential (adjective)   touching lightly; only slightly connected or related. *Having enrolled in a class on African-American history, the students found the teacher's stories about his travels in South America only of tangential interest.* **tangent** (noun).

tedium (noun)   boredom. *For most people, watching the Weather Channel for 24 hours would be sheer tedium.* **tedious** (adjective).

temerity (noun)   boldness, rashness, excessive daring. *Only someone who didn't understand the danger would have the temerity to try to climb Everest without a guide.* **temerarious** (adjective).

temperance (noun)   moderation or restraint in feelings and behavior. *Most professional athletes practice temperance in their personal habits; too much eating or drinking, they know, can harm their performance.* **temperate** (adjective).

tenacious (adjective)   clinging, sticky, or persistent. *Tenacious in pursuit of her goal, she applied for the grant unsuccessfully four times before it was finally approved.* **tenacity** (noun).

tentative (adjective)   subject to change; uncertain. *A firm schedule has not been established, but the Super Bowl in 2002 has been given the tentative date of January 20.*

terminate (verb)   to end, to close. *The Olympic Games terminate with a grand ceremony attended by athletes from every participating country.* **terminal** (noun), **termination** (noun).

terrestrial (adjective)   of the Earth. *The movie* Close Encounters of the Third Kind *tells the story of the first contact between beings from outer space and terrestrial humans.*

therapeutic (adjective)   curing or helping to cure. *Hot-water spas were popular in the nineteenth century among the sickly, who believed that soaking in the water had therapeutic effects.* **therapy** (noun).

timorous (adjective)   fearful, timid. *The cowardly lion approached the throne of the wizard with a timorous look on his face.*

toady (noun)   someone who flatters a superior in hopes of gaining favor; a sycophant. *"I can't stand a toady!" declared the movie mogul. "Give me someone who'll tell me the truth—even if it costs him his job!"* **toady** (verb).

tolerant (adjective)   accepting, enduring. *San Franciscans have a tolerant attitude about lifestyles: "Live and let live" seems to be their motto.* **tolerate** (verb), **toleration** (noun).

toxin (noun)   poison. *DDT is a powerful toxin once used to kill insects but now banned in the U.S. because of the risk it poses to human life.* **toxic** (adjective).

tranquillity (noun)   freedom from disturbance or turmoil; calm. *She moved from New York City to rural Vermont seeking the tranquillity of country life.* **tranquil** (adjective).

transgress (verb)   to go past limits; to violate. *If Iraq has developed biological weapons, then it has transgressed the United Nation's rules against weapons of mass destruction.* **transgression** (noun).

transient (adjective)   passing quickly. *Long-term visitors to this hotel pay at a different rate than transient guests who stay for just a day or two.* **transience** (noun).

transitory (adjective)   quickly passing. *Public moods tend to be transitory; people may be anxious and angry one month, but relatively content and optimistic the next.* **transition** (noun).

translucent (adjective)   letting some light pass through. *Blocks of translucent glass let daylight into the room while maintaining privacy.*

transmute (verb)   to change in form or substance. *In the Middle Ages, the alchemists tried to discover ways to transmute metals such as iron into gold.* **transmutation** (noun).

treacherous (adjective)   untrustworthy or disloyal; dangerous or unreliable. *Nazi Germany proved to be a treacherous ally, first signing a peace pact with the Soviet Union, then invading. Be careful crossing the rope bridge; parts are badly frayed and treacherous.* **treachery** (noun).

tremulous (adjective)   trembling or shaking; timid or fearful. *Never having spoken in public before, he began his speech in a tremulous, hesitant voice.*

trite (adjective)   boring because of over-familiarity; hackneyed. *Her letters were filled with trite expressions, like "All's well that ends well" and "So far so good."*

truculent (adjective)   aggressive, hostile, belligerent. *Hitler's truculent behavior in demanding more territory for Germany made it clear that war was inevitable.* **truculence** (noun).

truncate (verb)   to cut off. *The manuscript of the play appeared truncated; the last page ended in the middle of a scene, halfway through the first act.*

turbulent (adjective)   agitated or disturbed. *The night before the championship match, Martina was unable to sleep, her mind turbulent with fears and hopes.* **turbulence** (noun).

U

unheralded (adjective)   little known, unexpected. *In a year of big-budget, much-hyped mega-movies, this unheralded foreign film has surprised everyone with its popularity.*

unpalatable (adjective)   distasteful, unpleasant. *Although I agree with the candidate on many issues, I can't vote for her, because I find her position on capital punishment unpalatable.*

unparalleled (adjective)   with no equal; unique. *Tiger Woods's victory in the Masters golf tournament by a full twelve strokes was an unparalleled accomplishment.*

unstinting (adjective)   giving freely and generously. *Eleanor Roosevelt was much admired for her unstinting efforts on behalf of the poor.*

untenable (adjective)   impossible to defend. *The theory that this painting is a genuine Van Gogh became untenable when the artist who actually painted it came forth.*

untimely (adjective)   out of the natural or proper time. *The untimely death of a youthful Princess Diana seemed far more tragic than Mother Teresa's death of old age.*

unyielding (adjective)   firm, resolute, obdurate. *Despite criticism, Cuomo was unyielding in his opposition to capital punishment; he vetoed several death penalty bills as governor.*

usurper (noun)   someone who takes a place or possession without the right to do so. *Kennedy's most devoted followers tended to regard later presidents as usurpers, holding the office they felt he or his brothers should have held.* **usurp** (verb), **usurpation** (noun).

utilitarian (adjective)   purely of practical benefit. *The design of the Model T car was simple and utilitarian, lacking the luxuries found in later models.*

utopia (noun)   an imaginary, perfect society. *Those who founded the Oneida community dreamed that it could be a kind of utopia—a prosperous state with complete freedom and harmony.* **utopian** (adjective).

V

validate (verb)   to officially approve or confirm. *The election of the president is validated when the members of the Electoral College meet to confirm the choice of the voters.* **valid** (adjective), **validity** (noun).

variegated (adjective)   spotted with different colors. *The brilliant, variegated appearance of butterflies makes them popular among collectors.* **variegation** (noun).

venerate (verb)   to admire or honor. *In Communist China, Chairman Mao Zedong was venerated as an almost god-like figure.* **venerable** (adjective), **veneration** (noun).

verdant (adjective)   green with plant life. *Southern England is famous for its verdant countryside filled with gardens and small farms.* **verdancy** (noun).

vestige (noun)   a trace or remainder. *Today's tiny Sherwood Forest is the last vestige of a woodland that once covered most of England.* **vestigial** (adjective).

vex (verb)   to irritate, annoy, or trouble. *Unproven for generations, Fermat's last theorem was one of the most famous, and most vexing, of all mathematical puzzles.* **vexation** (noun).

vicarious (adjective)   experienced through someone else's actions by way of the imagination. *Great literature broadens our minds by giving us vicarious participation in the lives of other people.*

vindicate (verb)   to confirm, justify, or defend. *Lincoln's Gettysburg Address was intended to vindicate the objectives of the Union in the Civil War.*

virtuoso (noun)   someone very skilled, especially in an art. *Vladimir Horowitz was one of the great piano virtuosos of the twentieth century.* **virtuosity** (noun).

vivacious (adjective)   lively, sprightly. *The role of Maria in* The Sound of Music *is usually played by a charming, vivacious young actress.* **vivacity** (noun).

volatile (adjective)   quickly changing; fleeting, transitory; prone to violence. *Public opinion is notoriously volatile; a politician who is very popular one month may be voted out of office the next.* **volatility** (noun).

W

whimsical (adjective)   based on a capricious, carefree, or sudden impulse or idea; fanciful, playful. *Dave Barry's* Book of Bad Songs *is filled with the kind of goofy jokes that are typical of his whimsical sense of humor.* **whim** (noun).

Z

zealous (adjective)   filled with eagerness, fervor, or passion. *A crowd of the candidate's most zealous supporters greeted her at the airport with banners, signs, and a marching band.* **zeal** (noun), **zealot** (noun), **zealotry** (noun).

NOTES

NOTES

Need Help Paying for School? We'll Show You the Money!

Peterson's offers students like you a wide variety of comprehensive resources to help you meet all your financial planning needs.

Scholarships, Grants & Prizes 2002
ISBN 0-7689-0695-4, with CD,
$26.95 pb/$39.95 CAN/£18.99 UK,
August 2001

College Money Handbook 2002
ISBN 0-7689-0694-6,
$26.95 pb/$39.95 CAN/£18.99 UK,
August 2001

Scholarship Almanac 2002
ISBN 0-7689-0692-X
$12.95 pb/$18.95 CAN/£9.99 UK,
August 2001

The Insider's Guide to Paying for College
ISBN 0-7689-0230-4,
$9.95 pb/$14.95 CAN/£11.99 UK,
1999

Scholarships and Loans for Adult Students
ISBN 0-7689-0296-7,
$19.95 pb/$29.95 CAN/£16.99 UK,
1999

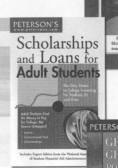

Grants for Graduate & Postdoctoral Study
ISBN 0-7689-0019-0,
$32.95 pb/$45.95 CAN/£25 UK,
1998

Scholarships for Study in the USA & Canada
ISBN 0-7689-0266-5,
$21.95 pb/$32.95 CAN/£16.99 UK,
1999

Visit your local bookstore or call to order: **800-338-3282.** To order online, go to **www.petersons.com** and head for the bookstore!

PETERSON'S
THOMSON LEARNING

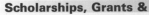

Petersons.com

—Your One-Stop Online Destination for All Your Educational and Career Needs

Visit Petersons.com today!

At **Petersons.com,** you can explore thousands of colleges, graduate programs, and distance learning programs, download online practice admission tests, and even see how you can upgrade your IT skills. You can even apply to college or graduate school online!

Whatever your goal, Petersons.com is your ticket to educational and professional success!

www.petersons.com
AOL Keyword: Peterson's

800.338.3282

PETERSON'S™
THOMSON LEARNING

College
Financial Aid
Executive Training
Grad School
Distance Learning
Career Exploration **Test Prep**
Study Abroad